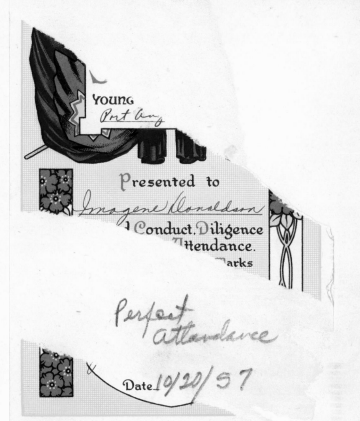

young
Port Ang

Presented to

Imogene Donaldson

Conduct, Diligence
Attendance.
Marks

Perfect
attendance

Date 10/20/57

Soldiers Without Swords

THE MACMILLAN COMPANY
NEW YORK • CHICAGO
DALLAS • ATLANTA • SAN FRANCISCO
LONDON • MANILA

**THE MACMILLAN COMPANY
OF CANADA, LIMITED**
TORONTO

SOLDIERS
WITHOUT
SWORDS

*A History of the Salvation Army
in the United States*

BY HERBERT A. WISBEY, JR.

New York · THE MACMILLAN COMPANY · *1955*

Preface

The Salvation Army is an organization familiar to most Americans. Seventy-five years of unselfish service in the United States have earned for it a reputation for "doing good." Beyond this general concept few people know very much about the basic objectives, the scope of activities, or the historical development of the organization.

The story of the Salvation Army in the United States forms a distinct and unique chapter in the history of the international organization. This book was written to provide a concise, accurate, objective history of the Salvation Army in the United States that would be of use both to Salvationists and to students of American social and religious history.

The research and writing that have gone into this work were spread over a period of eight years, and during that time the author received aid and encouragement from many quarters. Without the cooperation of the Salvation Army, this book could not have been written; and my greatest debt is to the many individual Salvation Army officers who furnished information not available from printed sources. The encouragement given by Professor Allan Nevins, of Columbia University, was invaluable. The late Don Pitt, former head of the Salvation Army National Research Bureau, read the entire manuscript and made numerous helpful suggestions.

I wish to acknowledge the friendly and courteous assistance of the staff members of the Columbia University Library, Union Theological Seminary Library, New York Public Library, Rose Memorial Library of Drew University, the Library of the Salvation Army Training College (Eastern Territory), and the editors and staff of the Eastern Territory *War Cry*.

Finally, I owe a special debt of gratitude to my wife, Adelia Wagner Wisbey, who offered encouragement at each step of the undertaking.

KEUKA PARK, N.Y.   H. A. W., JR.

Contents

Illustrations

Between pages 116 and 117

Soldiers Without Swords

I

The Invasion of America

A strange sight caught the attention of the small crowd that gathered to watch the ships dock at Castle Garden on March 10, 1880. Eight uniformed figures—a stocky, bearded man and seven women—came marching down the gangplank of the *Australia*. Over their heads a crimson, blue, and gold banner whipped in the raw March breeze, and they were singing hymns as they marched ashore and knelt in a circle to pray. Gilt letters on the red bands of their black derby-like hats spelled out the words "THE SALVATION ARMY."

The leader of the group, Commissioner George Scott Railton, was interviewed by newspaper reporters who pushed their way through the curious crowd that formed around the colorful detachment. The Salvation Army, they were told, was a movement for the reclamation of working-class people not connected with any church. This was the first group authorized to establish a branch of the Salvation Army outside the British Isles, where William and Catherine Booth had founded the organization fifteen years earlier, in 1865. The next day, detailed accounts of the arrival of the little band appeared in all of the New York daily newspapers.

These pioneer Salvationists came prepared to adapt themselves to American customs. Their first official service on American soil, held on the dock, began with hymns sung to the tunes of "The Old Folks at Home" and "My Old Kentucky Home." Their banner, a golden sun on a red background surrounded by a blue border, had in one corner a small American flag. Within the sun was the motto of the Salvation Army, "Blood and Fire," and "N.Y. No. 1." Railton's text for that first service was John 3:16, "For God so loved the world . . ."

The ocean trip had been a difficult one. After a rousing send-off from London on St. Valentine's Day, 1880, the passengers of the *Australia* did not see land again for twenty-three stormy days. The seven women were seasick for the entire voyage, and Railton himself had one attack, although he held services three times daily and did his best to keep up the morale of his seasick, homesick army. A cylinder burst in the engine room, and the *Australia* nearly foundered in the high seas. Some of the passengers were taken off by another ship, but the Salvationists refused to leave. Finally, on March 10th, the vessel docked safely in New York.

The pioneer party was met at the dock by some friends of the Salvation Army who had come to the United States earlier. The Reverend and Mrs. James E. Irvine, who had been associated with William Booth in England, took the group to their home in Jersey City for the night. The next day the group established "Temporary Head-Quarters" at the Pickwick Lodging House at 130 Liberty Street, New York City. Thirty-year-old George Scott Railton, the Army's first "commissioner," headed a detachment consisting of Captain Emma Westbrook, thirty-five years old and a veteran of ten and a half years' service in the Army; and Lieutenants Alice Coleman, Rachel Evans, Emma Elizabeth Florence Morris, Elizabeth Pearson, Clara Price, and Ann Shaw, ranging in age from eighteen to twenty-two. With the exception of Captain Westbrook, the girls had little experience and no formal training, except for classes on shipboard during the voyage.

American newspapermen made fun of their broad English accent, their pronunciation, and their practice of dropping the aspirate. They were described as "English peasant women of very limited intelligence," "very plain, unattractive in appearance," and "wholly without grace or ease on the stage." But these seven courageous young women with little education, inspired by a love of Christ and of their fellow men, ignored the jibes of their critics and marched into the slums of New York and other American cities to carry the message of salvation to the "unreached and un-churched." Before they had been in America a month a newspaper admitted, "None of them can aspirate the letter *h*, but they manage to get on the inside track with a good many hardened sinners, who would listen to some of our pulpit orators with deaf ears."

Despite some critical comments in the press, the Salvation Army was given a cordial reception in New York. The New York *Herald*, in an editorial welcome, expressed the hope that the Salvation Army would find "aid, comfort and allies," and declared:

Its method differs widely from that of any other body of men and women who have given battle to Satan in this city; but the plans of a commander are entitled to respect until some one who has gone successfully over the same ground can be found to criticise them. If by marching through the streets, with colors flying, stopping at corners to sing and exhort, the Salvation Army can persuade any considerable number of men to stop lying, stealing and cheating and to lead upright lives in the future, no one has the slightest right to complain of the way in which the work is done. Clergymen of various denominations complain frequently that there is a general lack of interest in religious affairs; perhaps if the Salvation Army gains some victories these gentlemen may gain a practical suggestion or two about the way of getting at the non-church-going class.

The newspaper publicity they received in the first few days after their arrival made the pioneer Salvationists minor celebrities. Mrs. Irvine took the group on a tour of the city, visiting the various missions; and wherever they went they received a friendly reception. So much interest was aroused that Railton knew that the opening meeting in New York would attract a sizable crowd. He tried unsuccessfully to get permission to use Union Square, and was unable to secure a hall of sufficient size to hold the first meeting indoors.

At this point a man named Harry Hill, attracted by the newspaper publicity, offered to let Railton and his lassies appear in his variety theater as a prelude to the regular performance. The commissioner seized this opportunity to reach a large number of the type of people the Army was dedicated to saving. When Railton went to inspect the establishment, a combination theater and saloon at

Houston and Crosby streets, a regular patron solemnly reassured him, much to his amusement, that this was "a respectable place and not like some." Here, he was informed, a person could drink until he passed out without having to worry that his watch and money would be gone in the morning. But a minister who learned of the arrangement exclaimed to Railton: "It is the most disreputable den in the country! In the worst slum in the city! Go there and your reputation will be lost at once and forever."

"Then that's the place for us!" replied the Salvationist.

New York was placarded with posters announcing the event:

> *The Salvation Army Will Attack*
> the Kingdom of the Devil at
> Harry Hill's Variety Theatre
> on Sunday, March 14, 1880,
> commencing at 6:30 P.M. sharp.
> After which the panorama of
> "Uncle Tom's Cabin."
> Admission 25 cents.

The day of the attack was "cold, damp and foggy and the slimy mud seemed to ooze up out of the sidewalks" as the small army left their headquarters on Liberty Street. All were in uniform. Railton, described as "a man of medium size with dark mustache and whiskers thinly distributed," wore a "dark blue suit trimmed with yellow cord about the collar upon which was embroidered the letter 'S.'" A patrol cloak and helmet-shaped hat with a crimson band bearing the words "Salvation Army" in gold completed the uniform. The women were dressed in plain black dresses with red cord on the collar, and wore black straw hats with crimson bands similar to that of the commissioner. Dividing his force into two parts, Railton sent one down each side of Greenwich Street, stopping at the barber-shops and barrooms that were open, and addressing the customers. In nearly every instance they were treated with courtesy and respect—a circumstance that caused Railton to compare the civility of everyone they met with the ruffianly conduct they had been used to in England.

After lunch in their lodgings, they walked more than three miles in the mud to hold a short service at the Hudson River Mission Hall at West Twenty-ninth Street and Ninth Avenue. It was against their principles to use the "trains" on Sunday. After this service they tramped back downtown to Harry Hill's variety theater.

The house was crowded, and people were standing three deep in the galleries when the meeting began. Out of deference to the Salvationists no liquor was sold during the service, but the usual mottoes lined the wall.[1] Harry Hill had offered to pay the Salvationists for their appearance, and when Railton refused payment Hill expressed his opinion that they were "a set of ——— fools." Railton, however, was very satisfied with the bargain. He had what he wanted: "as compact a crowd of thoroughly ungodly men and women as could have been hoped for, with perfect liberty to do as we liked whilst we were before them."

Railton led the service, following a familiar Salvation Army practice of singing a hymn and exhorting between the verses, taking a line or two for his text. He knelt for prayer, the "female lieutenants" kneeling in a semicircle behind him "in various and curious positions." Each of the women prayed in turn, while the commissioner, who remained on his knees, "his body swaying to and fro, first one arm working and then the other, continually ejaculated 'Amen!' and 'Hallelujah!'" One of the young women "intoned a hymn in a high tremulous voice, dropping her 'h's' and inserting 'ahs' with a rising inflection as she raised herself on her toes in a manner that made the irreverent audience laugh. The hymn as she read it invited the ''appy pilgrim' to go to Eden above, and the concluding refrain, 'We will go,' sung by the whole army was applauded with energy." The audience became restless as the meeting went on. No one answered the call to the penitent form, and when the Salvationists marched from the theater at nine o'clock and the "panorama of 'Uncle Tom's Cabin'" went on, the meeting might have been counted a failure.

But outside the theater a poor wretch who did not have a quarter for admission but who wanted to see the Salvation Army accosted the group. He was James Kemp, better known as "Ash-barrel

Jimmy." This nickname had been fastened to him since a policeman found his feet protruding from an ash barrel into which he had fallen while looking for his hat during one of his drunken sprees. The following day "Ash-barrel Jimmy" attended a meeting and was saved —the first official Salvation Army convert in the United States. The former down-and-outer reformed, joined the Salvation Army, and was a loyal soldier and officer until his death.[2]

After winning the first convert, the Salvationists were more successful. The meeting in Harry Hill's theater had dramatically publicized the class of people whom they hoped to save, and several missions opened their doors to them. At 44 Baxter Street, in the heart of the slums of the Five Points, a former brothel now converted into a mission was offered them. The Salvation Army conducted several meetings there with favorable results. One such meeting was described as follows:

A more motley, vice-smitten, pestilence-breeding congregation could seldom be found in a house of worship. There were negroes, dancing girls, prostitutes, and station house tramps sandwiched in between well dressed visitors who had sauntered in merely out of curiosity. There were young men with canes and eyeglasses; seedy old pensioners with faded hair and stovepipe hats (that looked as if they had done service when Jenny Lind sang at Castle Garden) walked in with catlike stillness and hid themselves in the corners, while glossy young negresses took prominent seats and stared at the modest English girls of the Salvation Army in an impudent way. . . . The floors were as clean as the deck of a man-of-war, but in a few minutes they were frescoed with tobacco juice, the stench became overpowering and a yellow fever pest house could not have been less attractive. It seemed as if the refuse of the Fourth ward dance cellars had been emptied for this occasion. Heads peered from the windows of tenements across the street, a hand organ wheezed on the sidewalk, while up in the upper rooms, where shoddy clothing is made for paupers, the clatter of a dozen sewing machines disturbed the peace of the day.

To hear the service with satisfaction the windows had to be closed, which nearly suffocated the inmates. But the Salvation Army did not seem to mind the air, and the ladies knelt on the floor and took turns in praying.

Wherever the Salvation Army held a service, the hall was crowded to overflowing. Two policemen had to be stationed in front of the Hudson River Mission to keep people from breaking in after the hall had been packed to suffocation and after the doors had been locked. Railton was greatly disturbed to have to turn people away because of the lack of a hall large enough to accommodate those who wanted to see and hear the Army.

The solution in England had been to hold outdoor meetings. The commissioner therefore went to Mayor Edward Cooper, son of Peter Cooper, the philanthropist, and asked permission to preach on the streets, particularly at the corner of Ninth Avenue and Twenty-ninth Street outside the Hudson River Mission. The mayor called his attention to an ordinance which provided that only ministers or licensed clergymen should be permitted to preach in the streets, and then only with the consent of the authorities. Railton was politely informed that because he was allegedly not an ordained clergyman, the mayor could not in compliance with the law grant him the permission he sought.

Railton's next move was to appeal over the mayor's head to the people of New York. The next day he appeared at City Hall and presented an announcement written and folded in the form of a legal notice. Unless permission to hold street meetings was granted within two days, the ultimatum read, Railton would move his headquarters from New York to some other city "where equal privileges are enjoyed by all citizens, ordained or not ordained, in the matter of serving the Lord and saving souls." The ingenuity of the appeal assured its publication in full in the city's leading newspapers.

When the mayor, after reexamining the ordinance on the subject, again decided that it was not within his power to give Railton the permission he asked because he was not a regular clergyman, the commissioner kept the issue in the newspapers by declaring the whole Salvation Army in America was going to pray for Mayor Cooper until he allowed street services. The idea of anyone praying for the mayor of New York City amused many New Yorkers. The *Daily Graphic* ran a cartoon of Mayor Cooper in a chair with the

Salvation Army lassies kneeling around him, under the caption "Past Praying For." The *Herald,* in an editorial, "Prayers for the Mayor," offered some suggestions:

Probably there are many people in this city, irrespective of creed, who would gladly give the prayerful some pointed hints on the petitions floating heavenward for the Mayor. For instance the Tammany General Committee would gladly give the supplicants points enough to keep them busy for the remainder of the season. The Aldermen, with memories of sundry vetoes and appointments still fresh in their minds, could do like wise.

While this was taking place, the Salvationists were filling mission halls at every service they held. Besides the Hudson River and Baxter Street missions, they were given the use of the Siloam Faith Mission at the corner of Dover and Water streets. At the end of five days from the time they began their work, they counted fourteen rescued sinners. These they classified as, "thoroughly saved, two; saved, ten; entering the King's highway and nearly saved, two." In addition to these they counted five persons who were "struggling to escape the bondage of Satan." Four days after this report, the number of converts was listed as forty-three.

As soon as it was clear that the authorities of New York were not going to permit open-air meetings in the streets, Railton made preparations to move his headquarters to Philadelphia. Captain Emma Westbrook and Lieutenant Alice Coleman were assigned to carry on the work in New York.

Before leaving New York, Railton wished to start a corps in nearby Newark, New Jersey. He called on Mayor William H. F. Fiedler of Newark for permission to hold meetings in the street. When the mayor refused, Railton hired the Odeon Theater on Market Street, a building of interesting ancestry. Originally a church, it had lately been used as a variety theater, and was known as a "notorious resort." For a year it had been closed following the indictment of its proprietor, and when Railton rented the structure its windows and doors were broken and it was "in the last degree of dirt and dilapidation." A newspaper commented: "There are sinners of the worst kind dwelling in the immediate neighborhood, so that the building would probably be filled at all the meetings."

The campaign in Newark began on Sunday, March 21st. Commissioner Railton, with Captains Emma Morris and Elizabeth Pearson and Lieutenant Ann Shaw, conducted the first service in the Odeon at 3:00 P.M., and the rickety structure was full. On the stage with the Salvationists were a number of Newark's "earnest Christian and temperance workers." The audience was attentive, and it was recorded that nearly everyone contributed when the collection tambourine was passed.

An even larger crowd turned out for the evening service. Every inch of standing room was occupied, and the galleries of the dilapidated old building were so packed it was feared they might collapse. Hundreds of persons were unable to get inside the doors, and policemen were stationed outside to keep the crowd back. The meeting was a thorough success. The audience joined in the singing and contributed to the collection for the purpose of renting the building. Sinners were saved on that first day, and the foundation was laid for a flourishing corps.

With the work in New York and Newark inaugurated, Railton turned to Philadelphia to pursue his dreams of a nation-wide Salvation Army.

II

Paving the Way

The United States in the last two decades of the nineteenth century offered a fertile field to the Church of the Poor, as the Salvation Army was sometimes called. American Protestantism had largely failed to meet the needs of the urban working class. Changes were taking place in American churches that reflected the vital economic and social changes of the times. It was a period of great material wealth. As a leading religious historian observed, "The most significant single influence in organized religion in the United States from about the year 1880, to the end of the century and beyond, was the tremendous increase in wealth in the nation." This increase in wealth helped a more easygoing intellectual religion to replace the hard, emotional religion which had characterized the American frontier. Poorly dressed workingmen felt out of place in the smaller, more costly churches where professional robed choirs and quartets substituted for simple music and congregational singing.

Not only the physical surroundings but the attitude both of the clergy and of the congregations of the Protestant churches discouraged poorer people from attending church. They found no sympathy or understanding for the problems of the poor or of laboring people. Many Protestants persisted in believing that human sufferings were "the penalties of idleness, disease or other similar causes, in a great measure the fault of the sufferers." Yet, others were observing that "the suffering poor had rejected this view and along with it the Christianity which championed it."

This was the Age of Big Business, characterized by the consolidation of industries and the growth of large corporations. Many of the men who were leaders in the creation of the large business organizations were at the same time stanch churchmen. The successful businessman became the symbol of modern America, and his ideals and methods began to permeate every phase of American life. Even the churches began to respond to this influence as successful businessmen began to assume positions of authority on church boards and as laymen exercised increasing influence in the operation of the church. Complaints were made that business meetings were taking the place of prayer meetings.

In their sermons ministers, increasingly influenced by contributions from the rich, ordinarily ignored or condoned the injustices suffered by the wage-earning masses. Henry Ward Beecher, one of the nation's leading clergymen, illustrates the popular attitude of the era toward the problems of labor. "Is the great working class oppressed?" he asked. "Yes, undoubtedly it is. . . . God had intended the great to be great and the little to be little. . . . I do not say that a dollar a day is enough to support a working man," he thundered. "But it is enough to support a man! . . . Not enough to support a man and five children if a man would insist on smoking and drinking beer. . . . But the man who cannot live on bread and water is not fit to live."

Had the masses of people that lived crowded together in city slums wanted to attend church, it would have been difficult to accommodate them. In the cities the building of churches lagged far behind the advance of population, while the shifting of residential districts left once prosperous houses of worship stranded and abandoned in factory and slum neighborhoods. It was generally true of large cities that those parts which needed the most religious attention got the least.

This situation was challenged by a family of English immigrants who had come in contact with the work of William Booth's Salvation Army. The Shirley family were plain working people, more deeply religious than average. In April, 1878, Amos Shirley, like thousands of other English workingmen, had emigrated to the

United States, land of opportunity. He left behind his wife, Annie, and their only daughter, Eliza. In that same year, 1878, sixteen-year-old Eliza was converted at a Salvation Army meeting and soon afterward was induced to enter full-time Army work. In America, Amos Shirley was successful in obtaining employment as a foreman in a silk factory in a suburb of Philadelphia. He at once sent for his wife and wrote to Eliza that Philadelphia was in great need of the kind of work General Booth was directing in England; if she would come with her mother they could all work together. "Come if the Lord wills," he wrote, "and we will start a work in America something like the Salvation Army." [1]

After prayer, Eliza Shirley decided to join her father, and wrote to General Booth of her decision. The seventeen-year-old lieutenant received in reply "a very solemn communication setting before her her call, her vows, her precious work, the souls she had led to the Cross, the possibilities before her. Dare she for the sake of the love of father and mother give up?" It closed with the statement: "We are not prepared to commence operations so far away. . . . But if your letter is the final decision, if you must go, and if you should start a work, start it on the principles of the Salvation Army, and if it is a success, we may see our way clear to take it over."

Lieutenant Eliza was allowed to farewell in the regulation way, and joined her mother in Coventry. Once again an attempt was made to persuade her to remain in England. General Booth's youngest son, Herbert, visited her. He bore the message: "Dissuade her if you can, but if she will go, tell her to be careful about the principles of the Army, to start right. She may call it the Salvation Army, and if it succeeds, report."

Mother and daughter were given a big farewell meeting in Coventry. Together they sailed for America, and in August, 1879, the Shirley family was reunited. Eliza Shirley, fresh from an active ministry as a Salvation Army officer in England, found a ready welcome at the camp and revival meetings in Philadelphia. The attractive and zealous young warrior was in constant demand to speak and sing at holiness and temperance meetings. Her sympathy, however, was with the "unloved, unreached masses." While Amos Shirley worked at the silk factory, daughter and mother walked around Philadelphia searching for a suitable place to initiate the Salvation Army in the United States.

It was September when they found a "one-story, flat-roofed, dilapidated, old chair factory. The unplastered walls were black, there was no floor, old chairs were piled in one corner and an old horse solemnly looked out of another, while patches of blue sky showed plainly through the roof."

"Oh, Mother," exclaimed Eliza, "what a wonderful place for the birthplace of the Salvation Army! Our Jesus was born in a stable, and cradled in a manger; this is all right for us." The owner of the building was willing to rent it for $300 a year, but was shocked at the prospect of letting it to two female preachers. Amos Shirley and a month's rent in advance, drawn from his wages, were required to convince the landlord that his building would come to no harm. The family set about to clean up the place, often working far into the night. They whitewashed the walls and built a platform of rough unplaned lumber. With a $50 contribution from a gentleman whose interest was aroused, they had a patch of flooring laid and secured benches to seat about fifty or sixty people.

At last everything was ready, and October 5, 1879, was chosen as the opening date. Scarlet posters were obtained bearing the inscription: "Blood and Fire. The Salvation Army. Two Hallelujah Females Will Speak and Sing for Jesus in the Old Chair Factory at Sixth and Oxford Streets October 5, at 11 A.M., 3 P.M., and 8 o'clock. All are invited." After dark, Mr. Shirley set out with a bundle of these posters and a bucket of paste, and posted them on conspicuous billboards and wherever else he could find space. The next morning crowds of puzzled people were noticed where the bills had been posted. The title "Hallelujah Females" was used because Mr. Shirley objected to calling his wife a "lassie" and could not bring himself to consider his seventeen-year-old daughter a woman.

Sunday, October 5th, was a beautiful fair day in Philadelphia. Suppressing their excitement, the army of three set out. At a street corner a couple of blocks from their "Salvation Factory" they sang: "Will you go? Will you go? Oh, say, will you go to the Eden above?" At that time the Salvation Army had not yet adopted uniforms, but Eliza Shirley wore a severely plain dress and the "little close-fitting bonnet with strings, of Christian Mission days." The tiny band attracted little attention, and when they reached the factory for their first meeting only twelve persons made up the congregation.

Later that day, as they held an open-air meeting before marching to the factory, they were pelted with mud, sticks, stones, rotten eggs, vegetables, and refuse. This was the beginning of persecution that grew fiercer as time went on—persecution which had its counterpart in England at the same time, and which the Salvation Army had to face in the next few years in nearly every American city in which it operated. When the two women mustered up their courage and appealed to the mayor of Philadelphia for protection, that august personage told them that they were the cause of the disorder, and ordered them off the streets.

Four weeks passed without any success. Regularly the faithful trio held open-air meetings in a dark vacant lot some six or eight blocks from their factory, and conducted services in the building. One evening a crowd of mischievous boys rolled a tar barrel onto the vacant lot and set fire to it. Flames shot up; the fire department was called out and a crowd gathered. When the source of the fire was discovered to be nothing important, many of the people turned in curiosity to the embryonic Salvation Army.

Amos Shirley spoke. From out of the crowd "a poor besotted, blear-eyed man, with ragged clothes, tousled hair, and unsteady gait" approached the speaker. "Is it true what you say? Will your God take the devil's leavings and make something of them? I'll give him a chance." No one could have looked better to these earnest seekers of souls. With their first captive securely in tow, they marched proudly to their factory. The crowd followed and entered, curious to see the outcome. For the first time the benches of the old factory were filled.

After the meeting began, the man was allowed to sleep off some of the effects of his drink for about an hour. Then he was awakened and told that it was time to get on his knees and pray. "It was a real battle for a soul; nearly an hour it lasted, but the man was in earnest. He had got to the end of himself, and must be saved that night. At last victory came, and he arose and told his story." Thus "Reddie" became the first convert of the unofficial Salvation Army in the United States.

When the news that "Reddie" had joined the Salvation Army reached his old cronies, many of them came around to see for themselves, and the Salvation Factory was filled night after night and the penitent form lined with seekers. Money poured in, and the old building was made comfortable for the winter. A reporter from the Philadelphia *News* was sent to look up "the two Hallelujah Females" who were the object of so much commotion. He attended one of the meetings, interviewed Amos Shirley, and wrote a long account of the work of the Shirleys for his paper. The Shirleys' Salvation Army was a success. Eliza Shirley was able to write to General Booth, telling of their work and enclosing a clipping from the newspaper.

Amos Shirley, in the meantime, had been paying the rent on the Salvation Factory from his wages and leading the meetings on Sundays and after work in the silk factory. One day after the article in the newspaper he was called into the office and told that while his work was satisfactory he must either give up this Salvation Army nonsense or lose his job. The courageous Englishman made his decision without hesitating, and came home to tell his family that now he would devote his full time to leading the mission.

In January, 1880, two months after the opening of the Salvation Factory, a second corps was established in a hall at Forty-second and Market streets in West Philadelphia. It was an immediate success, and the meetings conducted by Eliza Shirley and a girl convert were crowded each night. It was not long before Eliza received word from General Booth that she was promoted to the rank of captain. Amos and Annie Shirley continued to lead the original corps at Sixth and Oxford streets.

When the Shirleys' letters and newspaper clippings reached England, William Booth was faced with a dilemma. With the Shirleys' inauguration of the Salvation Army in Philadelphia an assured success, he was forced to decide whether to lead his forces into foreign fields or to lose control over this movement in the United States. Because the need for the work of the Salvation Army in England was so great, Booth hesitated to weaken his forces by expansion abroad. In its short fifteen-year history the Salvation Army had grown with amazing rapidity.

The organization was founded in 1865, when William Booth, appalled by the misery of the East London slums, established a mission known as the East London Christian Mission, later renamed the Christian Mission. It seemed to him that the orthodox religious denominations were failing to reach the multitudes that a growing industrial economy forced into the cities, where misery and want nurtured all forms of vice.

William Booth himself was a victim of England's Industrial Revolution. Born in Nottingham in 1829, the son of an unsuccessful speculative builder, he experienced want and privation throughout his youth. As a pawnbroker's apprentice he came to know well the misery of the city's poor. Even in his old age, when many of the experiences of his early youth had been forgotten, he recalled memories of children crying for bread on the streets of Nottingham.

At fifteen, William Booth became a communicant of the Wesleyan Methodist Church, and by the time he was seventeen he was preaching on the streets in his spare time. The tall gaunt youth with piercing dark eyes and Hebraic features was singularly successful as a lay preacher. Following a schism among the Wesleyan Methodists, Booth joined the Reform branch of that church and in 1852 began to devote his full time to lay preaching. Troubled by a lack of education and status in the Reform group, Booth entered training for a regular ministry in another Wesleyan sect, the Methodist New Connexion. After a few unhappy months as a theological student, and several spectacularly successful years on evangelical tours, he was ordained in 1858.

One of the most fortunate events of William Booth's life was the discovery of the woman who became his wife. Catherine Mumford Booth was her husband's equal in Christian zeal, originality of ideas, compassion for the distressed, and capacity for hard work and sacrifice. From the time they were married in 1855, she served both as a stimulant and as a stabilizer to her talented husband. An inspiring evangelical preacher in her own right, Catherine Booth worked unsparingly at her husband's side as they ministered to the poor and wretched. The Mother of the Salvation Army, as she came to be called, was more than a partner to William Booth; she was a tender, affectionate wife who made a home for him under the most difficult circumstances and who bore him eight children in the thirteen years which encompassed the Army's formative era.

William Booth served as a minister in the Methodist New Connexion until 1861, when he withdrew from that sect. For four years he and Mrs. Booth toured western England and Wales as independent evangelists, until in the slums of East London they found the challenge that led to the founding of the Salvation Army.

Booth rejected the Calvinist doctrine of predestination and salvation of the elect. "The Lord Jesus Christ has by his suffering and death made an atonement for the whole world so that whosoever will may be saved," he proclaimed. To carry his message to "the unreached and unchurched," William Booth preached wherever he could find an unoccupied place that would hold a crowd—in tents, sheds, stables, theaters, saloons, and even in a Quaker cemetery. An integral part of his service was a call for those who were truly penitent to come forward to seek forgiveness of sin and to signify publicly their desire to serve God. From this practice developed the penitent form of the Salvation Army. Converts were urged to testify as soon after their conversion as possible. It was discovered that the testimony of these crude and uneducated yet sincere Christians made a far more effective appeal to their own class than did the polished sermons of educated clergymen.

From its earliest beginning as the Christian Mission, the Salvation Army was nonsectarian, and disclaimed any intention of becoming a competitor of the regular churches. It ministered to all, regardless of sect, race or color, or depth of depravity. Converted outcasts who desired to return to their original church or to join an established denomination were returned to the faith of their choice with the Army's blessing. William Booth was quick to see,

however, that some organization must be developed for those converts who had no church or who felt out of place in the regular
churches. His success attracted many able evangelists who desired
to work with him, and among his converts were many who desired
to join him in serving others of their own class. Christian Missions
like the original one in East London were soon opened in other cities
in England, Wales, and Scotland.

A good illustration of the character of William Booth was the
form of government he established for his rapidly expanding organization. Conscious of having a divine mission, and convinced that he
was under the direct command of his Lord and Master, William
Booth was impatient of any human restraint and resentful of any
criticism or opposition. He demanded implicit, unquestioning obedience of his subordinates. It was his boast that with a telegram he
could send any of his officers to the uttermost parts of the earth.

The basis of the present polity of the Salvation Army is a deed
poll filed in Chancery in 1878. This document invested the "over-
sight, direction and control" of the Christian Mission in one person,
the General Superintendent. It secured William Booth in that office
for life, gave him the power to appoint his successor, and complete
control of all the property and money of the Mission. In effect William Booth became absolute head of the Salvation Army, endowed
with dictatorial powers.

The Christian Mission developed gradually and almost imper-
ceptibly into the Salvation Army. When the name was first used in
May, 1878, the organization already had many of the characteristics
of an army. William Booth, George S. Railton, and Bramwell Booth
were reading proofs of the yearly report of the Christian Mission,
in which Railton had described the Mission as a "Volunteer Army."
William Booth objected to the use of the term "Volunteer" on the
grounds that the members of the Mission were "regulars"; then,
leaning over Railton's shoulder, he wrote in the word "Salvation,"
and the Salvation Army had its name. The two names were used in-
terchangeably for some time, until gradually the older name
ceased to be used.

As early as 1876, Elijah Cadman had begun to dramatize the

struggle against Satan as "war," and referred to himself and his companions as "troops" and as an "army." He was the first Salvationist to call himself "captain" and the first to advertise Booth as the "General." As the Christian Mission became the Salvation Army, the branch missions in various cities were called "corps," uniforms were designed, ranks and titles were made standard, and a whole vocabulary of military terms came into use. General Superintendent William Booth became the General of the Salvation Army.

The Salvation Army was an aggressive army seeking out sinners and battling with Satan in his own strongholds. Any means was justifiable, decided General Booth, if it would attract sinners to listen to the message of salvation, and many special techniques were inaugurated to enable the evangelists to reach the hopeless, the debased, and the neglected elements of the community. Brass bands and street parades attracted crowds of persons who scorned the regular churches. Many to whom the toll of church bells meant nothing followed the sound of the big brass drum and the tambourine into Salvation Army meetings. William Booth believed that men and women should be happy in the worship of their God, and Salvation Army music reflected this belief. The brass bands played catchy tunes that set the foot tapping and the hands clapping. "Why should the Devil have all the best tunes?" replied Booth when chided for appropriating the music of popular songs for his hymns. Sacred lyrics were sung to the tunes of familiar sentimental "song hits," spirituals, and even well known drinking songs while tambourines beat out the rhythm.

To reach those who would not come to the meetings, William Booth followed the command, "Go out quickly into the streets and lanes of the city, and bring in hither the poor, and the maimed. . . ." The Christless were sought out on the streets, in dives and saloons, and even in the hovels that were their homes. Sweet-faced "hallelujah lassies" went into saloons to sing, to pray, and to distribute tracts. Slum sisters visited the homes of the poor, cared for children, nursed the sick and dying, then left after a short prayer, letting their lives and deeds rather than their words tell Christ's message.

The theology of the Salvation Army was simple enough for the least of its converts. It included the basic principles common to most Protestant evangelical denominations, and ignored the controversial issues that have caused factionalism and interdenominational strife. The doctrines held and taught by the Salvation Army were recorded in the deed poll of 1878, and included belief in a divinely inspired Bible, the Trinity, original sin, salvation for all who will it, and immortality of the soul. After observing baptism and communion for a short time, these, as well as the other sacraments, were abandoned by the Army as causes of dissension.

When the Booths began their work in the slums, they found drunkenness a close ally of poverty and vice. From this they deduced that liquor was a fundamental cause of poverty, vice, and sin. Total abstinence was made, and remains, a primary condition of membership in the Salvation Army. The use of tobacco was always discouraged, and finally prohibited for officers. Catherine Booth proved by her work that women could preach and win souls for Christ as well as men. Thus, from the beginning, men and women served as equals in the Salvation Army.

A magazine to acquaint the general public and the mission workers with the progress of the organization began publication in 1868. This periodical evolved with the Salvation Army until in December, 1879, a weekly newspaper named the *War Cry* made its first appearance. The news columns of the *War Cry*, a name that became famous in many different languages in the various countries where the Salvation Army was carried, helped to keep each officer and soldier acquainted with Army activity and helped to build morale. The sale of the paper also provided a source of income, and served to introduce the Army and its work to the general public.

The increased militancy of the Salvation Army brought it greater publicity and consequently intensified opposition. Queen Victoria was greatly disturbed at the temerity of a clergyman who dared assume the title of General and found an army within her realm. The sensibilities of many respectable and well bred people were offended by some of the actions of the Army's exhorters. These people, including many clergymen, without bothering to look into the Army's work, ridiculed it or denounced it, according to their disposition, and wrote letters of ill will to *The Times*. Because the brewer, the distiller, and the tavern keeper had real reason to curse the Salvation Army as they watched some of their most profitable customers leave them, they hired ruffians to beat Salvationists and to break up their meetings. But the Salvation Army throve on persecution, as had Christianity itself eighteen centuries before. New recruits were gathered; new corps were opened; and prominent friends were made as the value of the work became evident.

Within a century the Salvation Army was to grow into a great international organization, but in 1879, when the Shirleys' request for official recognition and support reached General Booth, it seemed that the rapidly expanding work in Britain was taxing the resources of the Army to the utmost. Only a few years earlier the vitality of William Booth's movement had resulted in the establishment of a branch of the Christian Mission in Cleveland, Ohio. From 1872 to 1876, James Jermy, a Christian Mission worker who had emigrated to America, carried on mission work similar to that in England. Although William Booth sent encouragement, the Cleveland Christian Mission was not under his direct leadership and the Salvation Army had not yet evolved a strong organizational framework into which it could be drawn. Thus, this premature beginning of Salvation Army work in America collapsed soon after Jermy returned to England.[2]

Other men influenced by contact with William Booth found their way to America. In July, 1875, the Reverend James E. Irvine, described as "a revival minister," came to New Jersey to engage in evangelical work. During the previous year he had conducted meetings at the Whitechapel and Chatham stations of the Christian Mission, and early in 1875 he married Miss Mary C. Billups, a member of the Booth household. Mrs. Irvine wrote from Jersey City in December, 1876, expressing her eagerness to have the Christian Mission extended to the United States.

In England one of the most enthusiastic advocates of expansion abroad was George Scott Railton. If the Salvation Army recognized sainthood, Railton would be assured of canonization. In an organization where dedication, loyalty, self-sacrifice, and hard work are accepted as commonplace, Railton stands out above his comrades. More than anyone outside the immediate Booth family, he was responsible for the early success of the Salvation Army. He had joined the Christian Mission in 1873 as William Booth's secretary, and he continued to serve the General and the Salvation Army until his death in 1913. Possessed of a simple and steadfast faith in God, by temperament impulsive, ingenious, and impatient of restraint, he frequently required the steadying hand of his leader. But no man was a more loyal or devoted follower and friend than Railton was to William Booth.

While the General sought to reach a decision, Railton presented the arguments for sending the Salvation Army to America, and begged to be allowed to lead it. In a letter to Mrs. Booth he pleaded: "I feel sure that our own affair in Philadelphia will go with such a sweep that unless we get hold of it, and lead, and go in at full speed at once, I doubt if we should ever be able to get the reins at all. Then it will be a wild affair with no competent direction, and there will be after a while as complete a lull as follows almost all such things. . . . I do not see why they should not let me go."

Somewhat reluctantly, General Booth announced his decision to send a detachment to the United States. "We were anxious to avoid this a little longer, seeing how much remains to be done for the millions who remain in utter darkness even in this land of light," he stated. "We refused to allow the Shirleys formally to inaugurate our work in the States; but we cannot blame the love and zeal which has driven them without waiting for us, to open the attack." When General Booth made up his mind to act, he moved quickly. The first account of the meetings held by the Shirleys appeared in the *War Cry* on January 31, 1880. Two weeks later Railton and the pioneer band of seven women sailed from England. In less than a month after his arrival in the United States, there were flourishing corps in New York and Newark, and Railton had established his headquarters in Philadelphia.

III

Laying the Foundation

In the period of less than a year during which George S. Railton directed the Salvation Army in the United States, he laid the foundation for an organization which steadily prospered and grew despite adversity and temporary setbacks. His strength of character inspired those with whom he came in contact, and his influence was felt long after he left America for a life of travel all over the world in the service of the Salvation Army. As Eliza Shirley wrote, "His influence was precious and fruitful, and while the fight was necessarily slow for some time, the work was of a solid character—a sort of foundation-laying for the coming years."

The Salvationists in Philadelphia prepared a real hallelujah welcome for their new commander when he arrived to establish his headquarters on March 24, 1880. Thanks to the Shirley family, the Salvation Army was firmly established there, and during Railton's command in the United States, and for more than a year after, the City of Brotherly Love was the center of the Salvation Army in America.

Amos Shirley had met Railton and the pioneer party at the ship in New York and had been commissioned captain, the first Salvation Army officer commissioned in the United States. He had then returned to Philadelphia with two of the lieutenants, Rachel Evans and Clara Price, while Railton and the five remaining lassies had stayed behind to "open fire" in New York City.

Railton's first official act on the evening of his arrival in Philadelphia was to present the Shirleys with the flag brought from Eng-

land. Large crowds were attracted by this ceremony. A detachment of police had difficulty in clearing a way for the procession of
Salvationists that marched from the old chair factory to Athletic
Hall on Thirteenth Street above Master. About two hundred Salvationists, nearly all wearing red hatbands with "The Salvation
Army" lettered in gilt, escorted the commissioner to the hall.
There was standing room only as fifteen hundred people filled the
auditorium. The service consisted of singing, short prayers by some
fifteen or twenty persons, and exhortations by Railton, Shirley,
and others. Many of those who testified were recent converts described as "apparently thrifty young artisans."

Newspapermen who attended the meeting recognized Railton
as "a man of some education and considerable general knowledge.
. . . Mr. Railton is a youngish man of rather slight build, very bald
in front, with black hair, black whiskers and moustache and rather
sharp features. He is a ready and fluent talker, prompt, earnest
and to the point, seldom speaking over two or three minutes at a
time and not permitting the singing to go beyond a verse or two."

The Army's first National Headquarters was opened at 45 South
Third Street, Philadelphia. A sign reading "The Headquarters of
The Salvation Army for America" was painted across the full length
of the building, but the quarters in which the commissioner worked
and lived were in the basement. Railton, who endured privation and
discomfort cheerfully, remarked, "It was a delightfully cool place
that summer."

With headquarters established in Philadelphia, new corps were
opened in and around that city. The rank-and-file of the two original
corps established by the Shirleys served as a source from which new
officers were recruited. Lieutenant Jennie Dickinson, the first American officer commissioned in the United States, assisted Captain
Emma Morris in opening a corps in Frankford known as the 3rd
Pennsylvania. Germantown was "invaded" before the end of March,
1880, and another corps established there. In May, 1880, Railton
cabled to General Booth that the American forces consisted of eight
batteries, sixteen officers, forty cadets, and 412 privates, with stations in Philadelphia, New York, and Newark.

In New York, Captain Emma Westbrook faced a real battle before a corps was established. Rowdies disturbed her meetings with coughs and catcalls and mimicked the broad English accents of the officers. When the sturdy captain marched to police headquarters and brought charges against some of the leading culprits, the meetings were more orderly and more successful. In April a new hall, with a porch that could be used for open-air meetings, was secured on Seventh Avenue. By the end of summer Railton was able to report to London that the 1st New York Corps was out of debt.

Across the river in Newark, the 1st New Jersey Corps, in the Odeon Theater, made rapid progress. Three weeks after the initial meeting, Captain Pearson reported nearly seventy converts, seven of them young women and the rest young men, "mostly of the rougher classes." In addition to the regular schedule of meetings, a direct appeal was made to workingmen at their place of employment. On March 30, 1880, three women officers visited Bannister's slipper factory in Newark and held a short service on the third floor of the building where about twenty men were at work.

Meanwhile, Railton was setting a pace that his small army was not always able to match. This dynamo of energy wrote in April: "I am all the time fretting and fuming because I cannot go at the same speed and be in every way as big as a first-class concern. But it's no use, a few weeks are not enough. Still, what am I here for but to 'fret and fume' if things do not go fast enough? It is surely not my duty to set my affections on things beneath."

He visited many cities alone to investigate possibilities for starting the work, and on these occasions he was "Captain, Lieutenant, Sergeant-Major, Hall-Keeper, and Chucker-out!" Often he would leave the platform in the middle of an address, put out some hopelessly unruly man, usually the worse for drink, and then go calmly back to take up the thread of his discourse.

The spring of 1880 was unusually hot. In New York, on May 27th, the mercury reached a record 96 degrees, while in upstate New Jersey the temperature was 103 degrees in the shade. "Nothing like such weather has been known at this season for twenty-five years," declared a metropolitan newspaper. The oppressive heat was particularly severe on the overworked women officers of the pioneer party, who were used to the cooler, damper climate of England. In October three of them returned to England with broken health. Of these, two came back to the United States as soon as they recovered.[1]

Finance was Railton's greatest problem in America. He was never able to collect enough money to make the work in the United States self-supporting. His financial straits could be understood by every Salvation Army officer who pioneered in the United States. Men and women whose spirits soared to the heavens found that physical necessities kept their feet firmly on the ground. The early Salvation Army officers understood the problems of those to whom they ministered because they too were plagued by the problems of meeting the minimum requirements of shelter, food, and clothing. Constant privation that struck hardest at the children in their family drove some officers to leave the Army. For the majority, however, no physical comforts could have compensated for the feeling of spiritual satisfaction they received from their ministry. A soul saved was adequate recompense for many a supper lost.

The first officers' councils held in the United States convened in Philadelphia and in New York at the end of May, 1880, and were very successful, according to Railton's account. In October the Salvation Army in the United States celebrated its first anniversary, twelve months after the Shirleys began holding services in Philadelphia. At that time, only seven months after Railton's arrival, the Army consisted of twelve corps holding 172 services a week. Over fifteen hundred persons professed conversion at Salvation Army meetings that first year.

During the summer Railton went West, traveling 4,200 miles in forty-nine days. In this time he delivered eighty addresses and numerous shorter talks. He wrote, "For fifteen days I was at it almost without ceasing from 6 A.M. to 10 P.M.," yet returned to Philadelphia "not a particle worse in health. . . . I slept on straw, or on railroad seats, or chairs, thirty-one nights out of forty-nine, and lived altogether a real soldier life, and enjoyed it."[2]

One result of Railton's Western tour was his decision that the young Salvation Army must "go West and grow up with the country." Filled with enthusiasm, the impetuous and often impractical crusader resolved that he would carry the Army flag singlehanded across the Mississippi. He chose St. Louis, Missouri, "the place where I learnt most to fight alone," as headquarters for the Western campaign. Much smaller than Chicago, St. Louis, with a population of about 350,000, seemed large enough to support a Salvation Army corps and was a central location for further operations. Although all active forces of the Salvation Army were still confined to the Philadelphia and New York area, Railton left the East in November, 1880, and, all alone, carried his headquarters farther west.

I shall never forget the cool November morning when the train slowly pulled into my headquarters city. As I looked into the long line of streets, while the cars were creeping over the Mississippi bridge, I involuntarily asked myself, 'Who shall bring the light to this big city?' and I had a glorious realization that through God we shall do valiantly.

But I had no idea how long it would take to do it.

The difficulties Railton faced in St. Louis were a real test of the stalwart commissioner's faith. He lost the use of a hall placed at his disposal when the audience at his first meeting spat on the floor and caused a disturbance. A rumor spread around town "that the men who spat on the floor also broke up the seats" made it impossible for him to hire any other building. He was prohibited from preaching on the streets by the city authorities. "Surely if ever Providence did its level best against anybody and anything it's against me and this expedition," he wrote in despair. "If I am to be crushed," he continued, "you may be sure I'll make the machinery pretty hot before it gets through!"

Railton was not crushed. With characteristic ingenuity he solved the problem of reaching the citizens of a city apparently reluctant to receive the message of salvation. "It struck me that the authorities could have no power over the iced Mississippi, especially on the Illinois side, so after distributing handbills to most of the men hard at work breaking Sunday, cutting and hauling ice, I went over to the part where the skaters were and began to sing. It was quite a novelty to have a congregation come skating around me at a speed that made it seem certain some would overturn others, but they all seemed too much at home for that, and I spoke plainly to them, urging them to seek pleasures from the Giver of all good and perfect gifts." Ervine adds to this account, "Is not the picture of this indomitable, ill-clad, impoverished man, who probably had not had a proper meal that day, singing for the salvation of plump and well-clothed people on the frozen Mississippi, immensely moving? There is no saint in the Calendar of the Roman Catholic Church, neither Francis of Assisi nor Ignatius Loyola, to both of whom he was spiritually related, more worthy of a halo than this singular Scot who thought it no hardship to starve for Christ."

Not until January 1, 1881, was Railton able to begin meetings in a hall. He secured a market hall with a balcony overlooking Broadway and North Market streets. The invitation to the first meeting, distributed at saloons, groceries, and from the street corners of St. Louis, was in the form of a railroad handbill:

$0.00 TO HEAVEN
(Limited)
BY THE OLD RELIABLE
REPENTANCE, FAITH
and
HOLINESS LINE
N.B. This is the real fighting line
that never gives up or breaks down.

No sleeping car or reclining chair
coaches on this line. For terms and
all particulars, apply to the Commissioner
of The Salvation Army at Headquarters:

STURGEON MARKET HALL

Sunday 7 A.M.; 3 and 7 P.M. Week nights,
every night, 8 P.M. Holiness meeting,
Friday, 3 and 8 P.M.

G. S. RAILTON

Railton seemed on the defensive as he wrote, "Everybody [who] read the message, and who got it folded it up and put it in their pocket. Let that be sufficient reply to any who might ask why we have opened up in the West. The wisdom of the move was demonstrated by the good number of the ungodly who attended our first meeting." Subsequent events proved the overambitious commissioner wrong. The small post established at the Sturgeon Market, isolated as it was from other Salvation Army corps, disappeared within a year after Railton left St. Louis. Railton's time and energy might have been more profitably employed in the larger Eastern cities and in working his way westward gradually. When the Salvation Army reentered St. Louis in 1889, no trace of the earlier effort remained.

Yet it was from St. Louis that Railton published the first American edition of the *War Cry* on January 15, 1881. The first issues of the *War Cry* distributed in the United States were brought from England by the pioneer party, and additional shipments of the English edition were made when this supply was exhausted. This arrangement did not satisfy Railton, who began to publish a paper, the *Salvation News*, on July 3, 1880, from Philadelphia. This periodical suspended publication after a few issues when Railton left that city for St. Louis. The first issue of the *War Cry* referred to its predecessor with the statement, "The War Cry will be supplied to subscribers like the News. $4 for 52 numbers." The new publication had no regular schedule. "War Cry No. 2 will be issued on the 15th of February or sooner if possible, but the trouble is, the Commissioner's hands are full with St. Louis at present."

In St. Louis, Railton stayed in the home of a George Parker, "who took me in," he wrote, "housed and fed me a whole winter, simply because I was trying to get people saved." With Spartan simplicity the commissioner cut his personal expenditures to an absolute minimum. On one occasion he was tramping through the snow so nearly barefoot that the owner of a shoe store whom he approached for a donation to the Army insisted that he accept a pair of overshoes instead.

While working alone and against heavy odds in St. Louis, Railton received word from General Booth that he was needed in London. This soldier who never complained about the hardships he endured was sorely tried at the thought of leaving his work just when success seemed within reach. He wrote eloquent protests against his recall, arguing that his departure from America would have disastrous effects on a young and weak organization.

General Booth cabled, "Must have you here."

With visions of all of his hard-won accomplishments being lost, Railton wrote again:

We are all, no doubt, outrageously overtaxed. . . . But the simple truth is we cannot gain the apostolic results we desire without the apostolic price. We are paying the price in full, I firmly believe, and if so, God cannot fail to supply all our need. He satisfied me yesterday that no matter what floods of anguish and shame we might have to go through, He would keep us up, and give us according to our faith after it all. It is not according to our strength or our wisdom or our ability, or even our efforts, but according to our faith.

I hope you will not fancy I am preaching this to you, for you have always been much more patient than I was. I am just telling you the lesson I got here all alone yesterday morning so that you may understand how I can be so hardhearted as to grasp in your letter an assurance that I may dismiss all calculations of return and plan accordingly.

General Booth cabled, "Come alone."

The cablegram arrived on New Year's Day, 1881, the day he began services in Sturgeon Market Hall, St. Louis. Argue and plead with his General, Railton could do, but he never thought of disobedience. When his arguments and appeals failed to move the General, Railton left for England, sailing from Boston in March, 1881.

It was part of the genius of William Booth that he could remain unmoved by the piteous appeals of a man he dearly loved. Booth knew the needs of his Army better than anyone else, and put its needs before all things. Railton's recall was not an arbitrary and capricious act. The General shared Railton's belief that God would provide for His own, and felt that if the United States was to be saved the United States must do the saving. The Salvation Army was rapidly becoming an international force, and Booth desperately required Railton's help at home. The Army had begun operations in France and Australia, and other nations were calling to be invaded. Catherine Booth was failing in health. The Salvation Army was still persecuted in England. Never before had the General needed Railton's unique assistance so much.

Once Railton reached England, he threw himself heart and soul into the work there. His feelings found expression in a song he wrote while crossing the Mississippi on his way back East. It was characteristic of this man that in spite of his deep disappointment, he should set the words to the rollicking tune "A Life on the Ocean Wave":

> No home on earth have I,
>   No nation owns my soul;
> My dwelling-place is the Most High,
>   I'm under His control;
> O'er all the earth alike
>   My Father's grand domain,
> Each land and sea with Him I like;
>   O'er all He yet shall reign.
>
> No spot on earth I own,
>   No field, no house be mine;
> Myself, my all, I still disown,
>   My God, let all be Thine!
> Into Thy gracious hands
>   My life is ever placed:
> To die fulfilling Thy commands
>   I march with bounding haste.
>
> With Thee, my God, is home;
>   With Thee is endless joy;
> With Thee in ceaseless rest I roam,
>   With Thee, can death destroy?
> With Thee, the east, the west,
>   The north, the south, are one;
> The battle's front I love the best,
>   And yet—'Thy will be done!'

IV

The Brickbat Era

The Salvation Army had no more than a precarious foothold in the
United States when Commissioner Railton was recalled to London
in 1881. To succeed Railton, General Booth appointed Major
Thomas E. Moore commander of the forces in America. The three
and a half years of Moore's administration were difficult ones for
the Army in the United States. Writing of the Salvation Army in
this period, the New York *Tribune* declared, "The first few years
of its existence have been happily named the brickbat era of its
history. Few had a good word to say for it, and its members suffered
all kinds of personal violence from the vicious and depraved elements of society."

The years from 1881 to 1884 have been slighted or omitted in
many Salvation Army historical sketches because Major Moore re-
volted against the authority of General Booth at the end of his
term as head of the Salvation Army in America. A fair evaluation
of this important formative period in Salvation Army history can
be made only if this event is not allowed to overshadow Moore's
years of constructive work.

Major Thomas E. Moore was about forty-two years old when
he assumed command in America. He had been in charge of the
London and Southern divisions in England. Observers were impressed with a soldierly bearing which enhanced his height of five
feet, eight inches. Penetrating eyes dominated a face whose fine
features were set off by dark curly hair and a large beard, tinged

with gray. Possessed of seemingly boundless energy, he habitually emphasized his points with dramatic gestures. When addressing an audience his hands and arms were constantly in motion. His voice was clear but marked by a strong cockney accent. He demolished his *h*s as well as various "wicked" things, commented one observer.

Major Moore was a better spiritual than temporal leader. He preferred the field—the active struggle to save souls—to the tedious duties of headquarters, and most of his time was spent in active campaigning, traveling from Canada to West Virginia, speaking night after night. Although hampered by a lack of funds and indifferent or hostile public opinion, he led his small Army forward, opening new stations, winning converts, and enrolling new officers.

The Salvation Army in the United States was confined to four cities—Philadelphia, New York, Newark, and St. Louis—when Major Moore arrived at National Headquarters in Philadelphia in June, 1881. The American edition of the *War Cry*, an irregular monthly, had appeared only five times since its inception in January, 1881. Moore's first project was to begin to publish the *War Cry* as a weekly with issue No. 6 in June, 1881. In that same month, new corps were opened in Jersey City and Baltimore. To assist him in his new command, Major Moore appointed Captain Amos Shirley as his aide-de-camp. Shirley, who commanded the 1st Pennsylvania Corps, had been given the general supervision of the Army when Railton returned to England. He was unable to get along with Moore, however, and after a month as his aide he left the Army. His wife, Annie, and daughter, Eliza, continued to serve as corps officers.[1]

The Army grew slowly in 1881. At the end of the year only three corps operated in Philadelphia; a strong corps under Captain Annie Shirley won converts in Baltimore; and a desultory work was carried on in New York. Three posts, listed in St. Louis, Newark, and Jersey City, were abandoned early the following year. But the year 1882 saw successes which more than offset these losses.

The Philadelphia corps were consolidated and new posts were opened in Franklin, Allegheny City, and Easton, Pennsylvania. New Jersey saw Salvation Army corps established at Paterson,

Trenton, and New Brunswick. The Baltimore, Maryland, corps continued to flourish. The New York "Invincibles" were strengthened and supported by four new corps in nearby Brooklyn. So important did Brooklyn become that National Headquarters was moved from Philadelphia to Brooklyn in July, 1882.

In addition to the fourteen corps active in the United States, the Salvation Army entered Canada in 1882, when corps were established in Toronto, London, Hamilton, and Chatham. These Canadian corps were administered from the Brooklyn headquarters, with Major Moore assuming the title of "Commissioner of the Salvation Army in the United States and Canada."

The growth during 1883 and 1884 was even more rapid. In March, 1882, the Army had only five stations and eleven full-time officers in the United States. In July, 1883, it operated forty-three stations and employed seventy-nine full-time officers. By March, 1884, seventy stations were in operation, and two hundred officers followed the flag. Salvation Army corps were active in most of the larger cities of New England, New York, New Jersey, Pennsylvania, Ohio, Michigan, and West Virginia.

The Salvation Army's rapid growth in America was the result of hard work by the officers in charge of the local corps. Each corps held at least one meeting every evening in the week and three or four meetings on Sunday. The schedule of meetings of the Baltimore Corps is a study in human fortitude: Open-air meetings and hallelujah marches every evening at 7:25 P.M., followed by indoor meetings at eight o'clock; Wednesday was Soldier's roll call, Friday a holiness meeting, and Saturday a "Hallelujah Free-and-Easy." Services on Sunday included knee drill at 7 A.M., open-air meeting at 10:30 A.M., and consecration service at 11:00 A.M. In the afternoon another open-air meeting at 2:15 P.M. preceded an experience meeting at three o'clock. Finally, a grand open-air march at seven o'clock introduced a great salvation meeting at eight in the evening.

Conducting public services by no means concluded the Salvation Army officer's duty. He was expected also to devote several hours a day in house-to-house visitation, to spend an hour a day drill marching, to train the corps' soldiers to play band instruments and the lassies to beat tambourines, to visit all soldiers absent from roll call, and to instruct young converts. Detailed weekly reports, including the number of issues of the *War Cry* sold and the number of hours spent in visitation were required by Headquarters. In addition, each officer was asked to send a weekly report on "the State of the War" to the *War Cry* for publication.

Officers' incomes were modest: single officers received a weekly allowance of five dollars, and married officers ten dollars a week with an extra dollar for each child. Even this small amount was not assured, but depended on the officer's collections, from which current expenses had first to be met.

The rapid expansion of the Salvation Army would not have been possible had not an increasing number of young American men and women dedicated their lives to work as officers in the Salvation Army. Although as many English officers were sent to America as could be spared from the work there, recruiting in the United States was so successful that Major Moore was able to announce in February, 1882, "There are just now equal numbers of American and English officers in the Army with three more Americans awaiting orders."

The Army in America was in some respects a youth movement, for many of the officers responsible for its amazing growth were young people in their teens, holding positions of responsibility beyond their years. Officers were usually assigned in pairs to open new stations. With only a few dollars in pocket, they would visit a strange city and hire a hall, part of which might serve as their living quarters. Their first meeting might be announced by a "bombardment" of posters proclaiming the opening of "Fort Salvation." To attract a crowd to their service, the officers in their colorful uniforms of blue and crimson would parade through the streets with whatever musical instruments they could play. When they enrolled enough of their converts as soldiers, the group was officially recognized as a corps with the presentation of colors by the national commander.

"Fort Salvation" was usually a small building in the poorest section of the city. The well-to-do were welcomed at the meetings if they chose to come, but their salvation was considered the responsibility of the established churches. It was to aid the people who had no one at all to turn to for help and guidance that the Salvation Army was founded. "Don't Despair!!" it advertised. "However POOR you may be, However WRETCHED you may be, However BAD you may be, You have Two Friends! One is Jesus Christ, and the other is the Salvation Army." Major Moore in his orders to his officers cautioned, "Keep to the army plan of putting the poorest, roughest looking in the best seats and nearest the Penitent form, and while you treat everyone with respect avoid showing preference for people richly dressed."

Salvation Army meetings drew large crowds in most cities. Undoubtedly many people were first attracted by the novelty and came to satisfy their curiosity. That many of these people were spiritually touched, joined, and remained with the Salvation Army may be attributed to its multiple appeal. Because its leadership was young, a large number of the recruits and officer candidates of the Salvation Army were young people. The Army seemed able to touch a chord of idealism that is inherent in youth. The use of uniforms, military titles, and brass bands to "free souls from Satan and sin" appealed to a generation a bit too young to have served in the Civil War, but who had grown up in the atmosphere of that semireligious crusade to free an unfortunate group of people from physical bondage.

To many of the older people nearly crushed by the burdens of life, the Salvation Army meetings of the 1880's offered release from despairing reality—from the stark, dull, dreary, monotonous everyday world of the slums in which they eked out a miserable existence. At the evening hallelujah meetings they could lose themselves in the glory of a new world that was theirs if they but confessed their sins and sought forgiveness through Christ. The meetings offered entertainment, escape, security, fellowship, and absolution from sin—all wrapped in the one package "salvation." And what must have seemed most miraculous, this salvation was for those who were poorest in the world's goods and who were the worst of sinners.

Not all Americans welcomed the Salvation Army's tactics, however. It is difficult today to comprehend the bitterness the Salvation Army generated in the hearts of some people in the first few years following its introduction in the United States. It was no surprise that saloon keepers and their habitual customers hated the Army and used all means in their power to combat its work. Such opposition was expected and even welcomed by the Salvationists. They were, after all, soldiers of Christ, and did not expect Satan to succumb without a fight. But the attacks that must have perplexed them came from a quarter where they had a right to expect to find allies or at the least a benevolent neutrality.

Many of the Salvation Army's severest tribulations were caused by people who considered themselves respectable Christians. The mobs who attacked Salvation Army lads and lassies were not always ragged hoodlums and roughs. At times well dressed men led or joined the attackers. Christian ministers as well as tavern orators inveighed against the Army and its methods. Policemen "looked the other way" while angry crowds broke up street parades and meetings and beat up the Salvationists themselves. When the Salvationists turned to the police for protection, they found themselves arrested for inciting a riot or disturbing the peace. Respectable judges fined and imprisoned members of the Army for such offenses, and mayors and members of city councils passed ordinances designed to prevent or handicap Salvation Army work and to drive out its workers.

Salvation soldiers everywhere—here, as in England—made close acquaintanceships with mud, bricks, stones, tomatoes, rotten eggs, dead cats and rats, and buckets of water. Yet the greater the barrage and the louder the jeers and curses, the stronger became their songs and prayers. Each evening before the regular meeting it was the customay practice for the corps members to parade with drum and songs to the barracks or hall. On one such march by the 1st Pennsylvania Corps of Philadelphia, a young fellow sent an old washboiler, then came a brick or two, then came a few large boulders, old tomatoes, cans, etc., and they kept coming too, until we got into the barracks. The saloon keepers find that by placing bath tubs out in front of their rum holes and keeping them overflowing, (wasting the city water) teams will stop. . . . Well there's a grog shop at almost every corner, so as we came up to the tubs we found them surrounded by gamins their hats dipped in full of water and didn't they give us poor warm soldiers a decidedly cool, cooling off. . . . Then we had the lassoe gang to contend with. . . . Then the trip rope squad was on hand . . . but Hallelujah, we came through it all and soon were safely housed in our barracks with joyous hearts, wet, tired, sore, and pretty well mussed up, but went right in for a Hallelujah praise meeting.

The patient endurance of the Salvationists in the face of such treatment could not fail to impress the general public and even the tormenters themselves. Repeated time and again were cases like that of Andrew Mohrant who, after accepting fifty cents from a saloon keeper to go to a Salvation Army meeting while drunk and break it up, was converted and became a corporal in the Army. As long as "fools, who came to scoff, remain'd to pray," the Salvation soldiers could not be daunted by physical attacks.

Even persons unsympathetic with the Army's methods found themselves supporting the victims of such persecution. A Philadelphia newspaper noted that "the calm courageous bearing of the 'Army' under very trying circumstances when brutally attacked by organized bands of ruffians has . . . compelled admiration and respect even from those ready to accuse them of fanaticism," and went on to say that "in spite of all its outlandish eccentricities which shock not a little good, quiet, easy-going, orthodox people, there can be no question but that the Salvation Army is doing a wonderful amount of good among the class of society which ordinary preachers and preaching entirely fail to reach."

But more than moral support was needed: the police were not only lax in protecting the Salvationists from attacks by hoodlums, but they often did their best to discourage the Army from operating in their bailiwick. Incidents of police persecution of the Salvation Army occurred in many cities in which the Army operated.

In June, 1882, the "Blood-washed Warriors" of the 3rd New Jersey Corps of Paterson were arrested for "making improper noises on the street." The Salvation Army had been allowed to sing and to exhort from the Brooklyn City Hall steps for a year when the "City of Churches" began a series of retaliatory moves in June, 1883, by arresting a group of eight men and three women. Arrests for parading, beating the drum, or singing in the streets were made in Syracuse, Buffalo, Bridgeport, New Haven, Cleveland, Wheeling, and other cities at about the same time. In each case the procedure was similar. The Salvationists pleaded not guilty to the charges of disturbing the peace. If fined they chose prison rather than pay the fine, and appealed for a court trial.

The Salvation Army was not seeking a cheap martyrdom in its fight for the freedom to call men to Christ in the streets of the American cities. It asked no more than the traditional American freedom of worship and speech provided. Actually, street parades such as the Army staged were a common form of entertainment in American cities and towns in the 1880's. Various fraternal societies, the local militia, and labor organizations regularly had parades, while the annual circus parade was a major event in all sections of the country. In addition to these large processions, organ grinders and occasional medicine men were also allowed to give their performances on the streets. The Salvation Army felt with justification that its marches prior to meetings were in accord with American tradition. The bass drum and tambourine served them as church bells to call their congregation to worship. As one newspaper noticed:

That which many citizens, in their dislike for the Salvation Army fail to perceive, is that the revivalists, in parading the streets, avail themselves of a common American privilege and that to arrest these missionaries is to exercise discrimination in the treatment of religious bodies. In fact, circus troups are permitted to march around, playing musical instruments, but a company of evangelists is placed under arrest for walking and singing religious songs.

In its court fights the Salvation Army never lacked competent defense attorneys who volunteered their services because they recognized the police persecution of the Army as an infringement of the basic concept of freedom of worship. The defense lawyer of a group of Salvationists arrested in New Haven in December, 1883, for "making a disturbance in violation of the city ordinance," pointed out that the city soldiers marched through the streets on Sundays with a brass band, that the police chief himself had marched and sung with the Knights Templar organization, and that a Temperance Society had used the State House steps for singing. The Salvationists explained the purpose of the Army and demonstrated their singing and regulation handclapping to the court. With the courtroom crowded with a curious throng made up of "men, Yale students, loungers, and women," the judge dismissed the case, declaring that the Army's object was a good one and that the Salvationists had not broken any law.

The liquor interests who had sponsored many of the attacks by ruffians also initiated some of the attempts to drive out the Salvationists by frequent arrests. A saloon keeper of Bridgeport, Connecticut, complained that when the Army came along with its drums his customers left the bar, went out to see them, and that many did not come back. Because he paid for his license, he thought he should be protected from such competition. In Bridgeport, as in other cities, the liquor interests were well organized and had plenty of money with which to exert political influence. The Marshalltown, Iowa, *Electric Light* declared:

Take all the kicking against the Salvation Army and eliminate the saloon element's part of the kicking, and you have none left. . . . The saloon-keepers are the only ones who are making the grand kick against the Salvation Army, because it keeps their customers away and keeps the crowd where they remain sober. . . . What this city needs is a few less saloons, a little less hell in general, and more Salvationists.

Meanwhile, the arrests of Salvation Army officers and soldiers not only failed to discredit the organization but actually increased its prestige and widened its influence. When arrested officers were acquitted or served their terms and returned to lead meetings, they attracted far larger crowds than before. Captain Stillwell, arrested in Booklyn, was introduced after his release as the "Hallelujah Jail Bird," and told of his prison experiences to large crowds. The *War Cry* ran a picture on the front page of the group arrested in Brooklyn entitled "Salvation Jail Birds."

The sporadic mob attacks and arrests on trumped-up charges that characterized the "brickbat era" continued with decreasing frequency into the twentieth century. But despite the persecution, or perhaps because of it, the Salvation Army's progress was rapid and continuous.

An important strategic advance was the acquisition of the first real Headquarters building—the old Lyceum on Washington Street in Brooklyn. During the early part of 1882, there was a lull in Salvation Army activity in Philadelphia. Not until March did the Philadelphia *Press* report, without great enthusiasm, that "the recently allayed Salvation Army fever was again breaking out in the city." By that time Major Moore was already planning to move his headquarters to Brooklyn—third largest city in the country, with a population of over half a million, and aptly called the "City of Churches." Each Saturday its leading newspaper listed as many as ninety items in the Religious Notices column. The offerings were varied. At Plymouth Church, Henry Ward Beecher preached to a huge congregation. One of his sermons was described in a newspaper headline as "An Argument that Poverty is Not a Divine Blessing but Simply the Fault of Those Whose Curse it Is—Possession of Riches Commended." At the Roosevelt Street Ferry, "weather permitting," Dr. John W. Kennion preached " 'Christ crucified,' not 'Isms,' " and distributed coffee, bread, and soap to "drunkards, tramps, outcasts, harlots, and criminals." Thomas De Witt Talmage filled the Tabernacle each Sunday, and Charles Cuthbert Hall, later president of Union Theological Seminary, served at the First Presbyterian Church. Thus Brooklyn, as the home of some of the nation's most influential clergymen and of several bizarre sects, was inclined to pay little attention to the Salvation Army.

Nevertheless, in April, 1882, the following announcement appeared in a Brooklyn newspaper:

THE SALVATION ARMY HAVING leased the Lyceum on Washington st, Major Moore, commissioner, would be glad to meet Christians of all denominations there on Saturday evening at 8 o'clock, to lay before them the objects of the Army.

Major Moore himself led the attack. As his "chief executive officer" he had Captain Emma Westbrook of the pioneer band. Lieutenant "Hallelujah Abbie" Thompson, a recently converted vivacious nineteen-year-old brunette, and Captain Frederick Schaff, a middle-aged German, completed the force. On Tuesday, May 2nd, they held their first open-air meeting in Brooklyn on the City Hall steps. Their song, "Stop, poor sinner, stop and think, Before you further go—Can you sport upon the brink of everlasting woe?" attracted a large crowd, a portion of which followed the Salvationists down Washington Street to the Lyceum for an indoor meeting. On Sunday the Army began its regular sabbath schedule with meetings at seven, eleven, three, and eight o'clock.

The Brooklyn campaign was an immediate success. By the end of 1882, nearly 1,200 converts were reported, and four corps were operating in various sections of the city. The *War Cry* office was moved from Philadelphia, and publication began in Brooklyn in October, 1882.

Brooklyn got its first full-scale view of the Salvation Army when about eight hundred Salvationists from the United States and Canada "invaded" the city in March, 1883, for the third anniversary celebration of Railton's arrival in America. This, the Army's first real convocation in America, was such a success that for many years after, the annual anniversary celebration was the biggest event on every Salvationist's calendar.

Four thousand people paid an admission charge to the meeting in the Brooklyn Rink that followed a two-mile parade. Major Moore led the services assisted by such pioneers as Captain Annie Shirley and Captain Emma Westbrook, who was introduced as "the Stonewall Jackson of the Army." The national commander was able to report that the Salvation Army in America had increased its stations from five to twenty-eight in the past year and that the number of officers had grown from eleven to sixty-four. During the same period the circulation of the *War Cry* had risen from 3,000 to 20,000 copies a week.

A memorable event was the presentation of a flag to the first Salvation Army missionaries sent abroad from the United States— Lieutenant Annie Hartelius, her sister Mary, and Anna Gabriel, all bound for Sweden to aid in the evangelizing of that country, where Salvation Army work had been begun by Hanna Ouchterlony less than three months before. The three young women who comprised the "Swedish Detachment" were accompanied to the boat on the morning following the celebration, and sailed from the United States on March 13, 1883.[2] This early example of missionary interest is significant in view of the fact that twice within the next two decades the concept of internationalism on which the Salvation Army was based was challenged by a nationalistic type of organization. In both cases internationalism triumphed, and today a noticeable characteristic of American Salvationists is their interest in missionary activities and their appreciation of their membership in an international organization.

The Salvation Army Auxiliary League was an interesting innovation of this period. Formulated to combat the active forces who opposed the Army in the "brickbat era," the League's express purpose was "to link our friends in one united body to defend us and assist us in supplying an increase of funds to carry forward the precious work of saving souls. . . ." The first public announcement of the organization appeared in the *War Cry* of July 26, 1883. To become a member a person had to pledge himself to pray for the Army, to speak in its favor whenever possible, and to subscribe five dollars a year. In return he received a year's subscription to the *War Cry*, a badge, a special pass to all meetings, and "a share in the joy of helping men and women out of sin."

The Salvation Army Auxiliary League eventually became an important means of organizing the support—personal and financial —of many important Americans. However, its success came after 1887, and its initial progress was slow. A balance sheet for the period of March 8, 1883, to June 23, 1884, listed only $343 under "Subscriptions to Auxiliary League."

Running apace with all these advances and innovations was the rigorous schedule of Major Moore. Frequently he traveled all day to address a meeting in the evening that might last well into the night. Within a six-day period in November, 1883, he traveled two thousand miles through Kentucky and Indiana and had nine speaking engagements. In addition to his tours, which helped him to know personally the officers of every corps, the commander wrote an article or two for nearly every issue of the *War Cry*. Unfortunately, the major's success as a field commander was marred by certain inadequacies as an administrative leader which came to light in the last year of his term of office.

V

Secession—The Moore Split

In October, 1884, the world-wide unity of the Salvation Army was endangered when Major Thomas E. Moore, in violation of orders, sought to establish the incorporation of the Salvation Army in the United States independent of General William Booth. Although it took International Headquarters by surprise, Moore's action was not hasty or precipitous but came as the logical culmination of a long series of events. The storm clouds that broke in October had been slowly gathering throughout the year of 1884.

The fourth anniversary celebration is an example of the strained relations between the United States and London. The anniversary program was planned for the usual date—in March. Announcements were made that General William Booth or Bramwell Booth, the Chief of Staff, might visit America to attend the festivities. When a cablegram announced "The General or Chief of Staff cannot come in the Month of March," the celebration was postponed in the hope that one of them would make the trip at a later date. Not until two months later, on May 13th, was the celebration finally held—without the General or the Chief of Staff.

American Salvationists were disappointed at what seemed to them to be a lack of appreciation on the part of their international leaders. They were proud of the progress they had made in the last year—progress which was to be illustrated by events in the fourth anniversary celebration. The Salvation Army in America had grown to a force of about three hundred officers, with some five thousand converts in the ranks, and more than a hundred stations. Salvationists from as far as West Virginia, Kentucky, Indiana, Ohio, and Michigan joined with others from New England, New York, and New Jersey to attend the exercises. An excursion boat was chartered to carry Salvation Army "troops" from Canada, upper New York State and points west, down the Hudson River from Albany to Brooklyn. No less than two thousand Salvationists, accompanied by several brass bands, marched in the big parade prior to the evening meeting on May 13, 1884.

The *War Cry* account of the meeting declared:

The Army colors, the intense enthusiasm, the brass instruments, the waving banners and handkerchiefs, and the large audience reminded us of scenes we had witnessed in Exeter and Congress Halls, London, and proved how thoroughly the Army there and here is pervaded and moulded by one Spirit.

General William Booth was personally unknown to all but the few Salvationists who had come from England. Had he visited America in 1884 and seen for himself the spirit of the American Salvationists, and had they been given the opportunity to feel the influence of his unique personality, it is probable that the course of events would have been very different.

This convocation was also the last attended by Canadian Salvationists as part of a combined United States and Canadian Salvation Army. In a dispatch dated May 3, 1884, General Booth announced, "I have heartily concurred in the suggestion that Canada should have a Major and Headquarters of its own, seeing that no one man could possibly overtake the boundless opportunity, or endure the enormous responsibility that must be involved in the development and direction of our operations in two of the largest countries in the world." Major Thomas B. Coombs was appointed commissioner of the newly formed Territory of Canada. He was given a gala welcome when he arrived in New York, and was accompanied to Canada by Major Moore, who installed him in his new position.

In the first years, as long as the American branch of the Salvation Army owned no property, the problem of internal government was not acute. Though Major Moore, acting as General Booth's agent, carried out his general policies, he was allowed considerable autonomy in making decisions regarding local conditions with which he was most familiar: he commissioned officers, assigned and reassigned them, and determined where new posts could be established. Money collected or secured through the sale of the *War Cry* or booklets was held by the major and disbursed according to his direction.

When property such as barracks, halls, and the land on which they were erected was acquired, however, questions of title in property deeds became acute. In England, General Booth held all of the real and personal property of the Salvation Army in his own name, and he wished to have any property acquired in America similarly deeded to him. This would have been very difficult, and in some states impossible, because of the difference of the laws of the various states regarding the rights of aliens to purchase and to hold property.

Major Moore, having declared his intention of becoming a naturalized citizen, was able to own real estate, and all of the property of the Salvation Army in the United States was deeded in his name —as General Booth's representative. In the eyes of the law, however, the buildings and land of the Salvation Army in America were the personal property of Thomas E. Moore. This situation was embarrassing, both to the officers of the Army, who were sometimes taunted with the charge that they were making money for Major Moore and General Booth in England, and to Major Moore, who as the owner of all Salvation Army property might be held personally liable for any debt or suit for damages brought against the organization.

The difficulty of Moore's legal position is illustrated by an incident in New Brunswick, New Jersey. Leaders of the corps established there became dissatisfied with the arrangements for holding property, and incorporated under the state laws as "The 5th

New Jersey Corps of the Salvation Army," a corporate body entirely independent of the regular Salvation Army. Major Moore became a subject for abuse when he refused to turn over to the new corporation the funds held by National Headquarters in the account of the former Salvation Army corps. In December, 1883, one of the trustees of the New Brunswick corporation had Major Moore arrested while the major was in New Jersey conducting a meeting at Rahway. This unhappy experience, and a similar one at Newburgh, New York, convinced the major that the only real solution to the problem of holding the Army's property was to incorporate the Salvation Army as a religious and charitable organization under the laws of the various states.

This was not a new idea. Major Moore first proposed it to General Booth in the latter part of 1882 or early 1883. For nearly two years before he secured the incorporation of the Salvation Amy in the United States, the American commander not only openly advocated and planned the action, but also did everything in his power to obtain General Booth's consent to the step.

At the third anniversary celebration in March, 1883, a newspaper reported that just before the collection was taken, "Major Moore stated that the property was deeded to the society, which would be incorporated within the next few days." Application papers for incorporation had already been filed in July, 1883, when Major Moore and two veterans of the American field, Captains Jonas Inman and Emma Westbrook, went to England to present the case for incorporation. These American officers failed to convince the General that incorporation would not limit the authority of International Headquarters, and on September 13, 1883, they returned to the United States unsuccessful.

In the summer of 1884, two officers were sent from International Headquarters to study the situation in the United States. After a careful investigation they recommended to keep the property in the name of Major Moore but to mortgage it for more than its real value to General Booth. To help explain the situation a notarized statement entitled "How the Army Property is Held, as Sworn by the General," was printed in the *War Cry* of July 24, 1884. In the statement General William Booth quoted from the deed poll of 1878:

(1). That the Salvation Army was always to be under the control and direction of one person—myself this deponent.

(2). That all the properties of the Salvation Army were to be conveyed to, and held by the General of the Salvation Army for the time being, who was to have absolute liberty to deal with such properties as he might think fit, provided only that he should use and dispose of them only for the benefit of the Salvation Army, as defined by the said Deed Poll. . . .

Major Moore was confronted with a double predicament. On one hand he was held responsible to General Booth for all the property acquired in the name of the Salvation Army. On the other hand, because the property was held in his name, he was also legally responsible for any claims against the property of the Army. The fact that General Booth asserted his claim to the property in a notarized declaration meant nothing in the eyes of the law. Nor did the fact that the property was mortgaged to General Booth relieve Major Moore from his personal legal responsibility.

The representatives from International Headquarters, in addition to rejecting the idea of incorporation, reported unfavorably on other aspects of Major Moore's administration. After examining his books at National Headquarters, they informed London that the accounts were in great confusion. Eight divisions had been created in the summer of 1884, to facilitate the administration of the rapidly expanding Army. The divisional officers (DO's) included several who were dissatisfied with Major Moore's leadership and who added their criticisms of him to those of the London examiners.

These reports convinced General Booth that Moore should be replaced as national commander. Farewell orders were issued, and Major Moore was ordered to take command of the Salvation Army forces in South Africa, where the work had only recently been inaugurated. Moore may have believed that if he went ahead with the incorporation, and could show the General that he had the support and confidence of the great majority of American Salvationists, the General would modify his decision. On the other hand, he may have recognized that incorporation would mean secession, and decided to go ahead despite the consequences. Whatever his motives, Major Moore took the preliminary steps toward incorporation.

News of his plans reached International Headquarters, and Major Thomas B. Coombs, recently appointed commissioner of Canada, was ordered by cable to hasten to Brooklyn to relieve Moore of his command. When Major Coombs appeared at Moore's headquarters and demanded that all of the property and money of the Salvation Army in the United States be turned over to him, he was met with a flat refusal. Coombs then wired each of the field officers that Moore had been removed by the General, and instructed them to "hold all moneys." A few hours later the bewildered officers received another telegram—from Major Moore—with the instructions: "Disregard Coombs' message. Go on with your work as usual."

When a summons to attend an important council at National Headquarters arrived a few days later, about 125 corps officers hastened to Brooklyn with aroused curiosity. Major Coombs and some of the DO's were not admitted. Moore, always an eloquent and convincing speaker, told the group of his proposal for incorporation, of his efforts to secure General Booth's approval, and of his recent order to farewell. So firmly convinced was he that incorporation was in the best interests of the Salvation Army in the United States, he declared, that if the council approved of his plans to incorporate, and the General accepted the decision, he would acquiesce in his farewell and go wherever the General wished to send him. In no case, he insisted, would incorporation mean breaking away from the spiritual leadership of General Booth.

Most of the officers present were Americans, and few had ever known General Booth personally. It is significant that the only opposition to Moore came from those officers who had served with the General in England. One of these, Captain William Thompson, made a plea to accept the orders of International Headquarters. A rising vote was taken, and of the 125 present all but four voted to support Major Moore.

Notice of the council's action was sent to General Booth, and

Major Moore continued the incorporation proceedings. Articles of incorporation were signed on October 21, 1884, by Thomas E. Moore and five other men. Three days later a certificate of the incorporation of "The Salvation Army" was filed and recorded in the office of the Secretary of State of the State of New York. According to the certificate, the objectives of the organization were "the evangelization of the masses, mutual improvement in religious knowledge and the furtherance of religious opinion and benevolent and missionary purposes."

Major Moore turned over to the new corporation the title to land, barracks, musical instruments, books, hymnals, and uniforms —which had previously been held in his name alone. Even the familiar insignia of the Salvation Army and the *War Cry*, which had been copyrighted, became the property of the newly incorporated Salvation Army. Moore continued to publish the *War Cry* from the Brooklyn headquarters, and used its columns to explain his actions regarding incorporation.

His position seemed unassailable. His actions were entirely in accord with the law. In fact, his incorporated Salvation Army could, if it chose, obtain an injunction to prevent any other group from operating under that name or from using the copyrighted title the *War Cry* for a newspaper. As Major Coombs ruefully confessed in an interview shortly after the incorporation, "Hat present Moore 'as rather the best of the fight."

Although Major Moore must have realized that his action in direct violation of orders constituted insubordination, he stoutly maintained his respect for General Booth's leadership. "In our present attitude there is no spirit of self-seeking, no wish to separate from the spiritual advice of General Booth, and no desire to create a spiritual gulf between England and the United States. We were incorporated in order the better to carry out the desires of General Booth for the Salvation of sinners, in order also to adapt ourselves to the customs of the people, and also for the better protection of the property, and to prevent wicked men from assailing us by slander and imprisonment on false charges," he declared.

But General Booth was firmly convinced that the Army's unity and highest usefulness could be preserved only through the centralization of authority, with the final and supreme direction vested in its ruling head. His opposition to incorporation appeared to be from the fear that it would remove the individual corps from the authority of International Headquarters. As he explained:

It having been represented to us that much of the persecution and difficulty we encountered might be overcome if the Army were to become incorporated as all religious denominations are under the laws of the States, we sent out the heads of our foreign and property departments to consult with Major Moore and the best legal advisers they could find on the subject, and to try to arrive at some settlement of the property held for the Army there, which would in every way be satisfactory and would, if possible, put us on a better footing before the law, and also to see whether there were not other causes for the general dissatisfaction.

We found, however, that incorporation, under the denominational laws existing, would of necessity destroy the Army's very existence as such, and would change it in fact into a sect, whose every congregation would have power to determine more or less what would be the character of their services.

Of course we could not for a moment consent to anything of the kind, no matter what difficulties might still have to be faced. . . .

The difficulties still to be faced were many. Any possibility that the situation could be settled by a compromise vanished soon after Major Frank Smith arrived from London to take command of the American forces. His first action was to visit Major Moore's headquarters in Brooklyn and to demand immediate and unconditional surrender of the command of the troops and of all the money, property, and supplies of the Salvation Army in the United States. He was met with a firm refusal.

Major Smith made it evident that in his eyes Moore and all those who followed his leadership were rebels unworthy of any further trust or consideration. His arrogance and total lack of understanding or tact alienated many Salvationists who were ready to return to the parental body as soon as they saw that incorporation was, in effect, secession. Many officers, among them Richard E. Holz, who supported Moore in the incorporation but who had no desire to leave the leadership of General Booth, approached Smith for information only to be denounced without an opportunity to explain their position.

The situation confronting Major Smith seemed hopeless, yet he faced the future with that confidence born of the strong conviction that he was right and his enemies without virtue. Six of the eight divisional officers supported him, but only seventeen corps accepted his leadership. A few weeks after Smith arrived, a group of fifty or sixty officers recruited from the English field personnel was sent to reinforce him. Frank Smith was typically and thoroughly British, and so were nearly all his followers, a condition not calculated to win the support of the American public in the late nineteenth century.

John Bull and Brother Jonathan were not on the best of terms in the 1880's. England was represented in Washington by the obtuse Sackville-West whose thoughtless letter in 1888 aroused the country and brought about his dismissal—too late to undo the damage to Cleveland's campaign for reelection. Canadian seizures of New England fishing boats added fuel to the flames tended by a well organized group of Irish-Americans whose undying hatred of all things English was fully exploited by the newspapers and politicians of both parties.

Major Moore was quick to seize the advantage of being "American." While General Booth's system might be all right for England, he explained in the columns of the *War Cry*, incorporation was necessary in the United States to bring the Army's government "into harmony with the laws, usages and Constitution of this country, and to enable it to hold funds as provided for by law." "To the Americans we have become Americans," he exclaimed, and he promised that no longer would the Salvationists be looked upon as "nomads, gypsies, wanderers, or foreign emissaries." Later he announced that of the two hundred officers in his organization, he and one other were the only two that had come from England, the rest having been recruited in America.

When it became obvious that no compromise could be worked out with General Booth, Major Moore determined to fight to the finish. In January, 1885, he assumed the title of General, and in March, 1885, he reincorporated his organization as "The Salvation Army of America," a name designed to strengthen his appeal to the American people. His "Incorporated" Salvation Army of America and Smith's "World-Wide" or English Salvation Army competed in a race to invade new territory—a struggle that must have seemed bewildering to an already confused public.

Although incorporation was the basic cause of the break between Moore and General Booth, other issues were injected to give the dispute a bitterness that only intimate family quarrels can engender. "We are not fighting him [Major Moore] so much as incorporation," Major Coombs admitted to the press in October, 1884. But Major Smith had a different interpretation. In a *War Cry* article published on November 22nd, he declared, "The Cause of Estrangement Between Major Moore and The General was not Incorporation, but Mismanagement and Insubordination." He charged that the books had been found in "a hopeless state of confusion," a condition which Major Moore had not been able to explain. When about to be relieved of his command, the charge continued, Major Moore "at the last moment" brought up the incorporation "to cover his mismanagement." In an attempt to infer that General Booth had not objected to incorporation, Smith added, "The General is not opposed to any scheme that will promote the glory of God and open the way for this movement on the lines it has been working so successfully for the past nineteen years."

Such statements set the pattern for official writing on the subject ever since. In his report for the year 1885, Major Smith, in a summary of the history of the Army, wrote that Major Moore had been appointed in 1881 because he was "the only man available at the time." With no mention of Moore's three and a half years of successful labor, he declared, "Unfortunately he fell into financial fogs, and after a time . . . was requested to resign, he at once founded what is now known as the Incorporated Army." Implied in the account of Moore's break with General Booth, not by forthright accusation but by insinuation, was that Major Moore was dishonest, had embezzled funds, and that incorporation was something he undertook on the spur of the moment just as his financial discrepancies were about to be revealed.

Major Smith was a better soldier than a historian. Either he did not know or chose to ignore the events preceding the incorporation. A more judicious evaluation of Major Thomas E. Moore seems to be that he was a good spiritual leader but an inadequate administrator. Many people who knew him personally have testified to his splendid Christian character. His honesty seems to be unquestionable, although he was mistaken in his judgment that incorporation would in itself mean success for the Salvation Army in the United States. Deprived of the inspired leadership of General William Booth and the Army's international kinship, Moore's "Incorporated Army" gradually declined, while the "World-Wide" Salvation Army under Major Smith prospered and grew.[1]

VI

Rebuilding from the Foundations

Jehovah is our strength, And He shall be our song;
We shall overcome at length, Although our foes be strong.

Salvation Army history has justified the ring of confidence in this popular Army hymn. No episode better supports the true Salvationist's faith in the destiny of his Army than the events that followed the break between Major Moore and General Booth.

To the few American Salvationists still loyal to General Booth and the international Army in 1884, the future looked dark indeed. Major Moore, fortified with the support of more than 80 per cent of the American officers and soldiers, and with all the property, supplies, and equipment of the Salvation Army, seemed assured of victory; the *War Cry*, the uniforms, battle flags, insignia, and even the very name Salvation Army were his by law. Familiar with conditions in the United States, and aided by a liberal form of government, Moore's Army could hopefully appeal to the American people, confident of success. As General Booth's representative in the United States, Major Moore had been amazingly successful for three and a half years. But from the time he broke with General Booth, both his personal influence and the organization he led went into a steady decline.

As soon as news of the incorporation reached International Headquarters, Major Frank Smith, then commander of the London Division, had been ordered to the United States to replace

Moore. He had little more than his title, General Booth's blessing, and a few faithful followers when he arrived in New York on November 3, 1884. But with confidence born of a conviction of absolute righteousness, the newly appointed commissioner rallied his forces and rebuilt the Salvation Army in America from its very foundations to a position stronger than ever before.

The thirty-year-old commissioner was a man of striking appearance. His picture shows a man with narrow face, bushy hair, a mustache and goatee, and nose topped by pince-nez glasses. He was described by a newspaper reporter as having "a long pinched nose, looking as though it had been caught in the jam of a door, [and] hair that stands straight on end." To another reporter, who complimented his rich baritone voice, he appeared to be "tall, wiry, nervous; with a face like a stage Mephistopheles, he moved about waving his long arms and looking as if he were uttering an incantation."

This was the man, "capable but fanatical, aggressive and headstrong," who rallied and rebuilt the Salvation Army in America. He established headquarters in a few rooms of a small building in New York City and took stock of his forces. No more than fifty officers, out of nearly three hundred, and only seventeen corps remained loyal to the international Army, and these were without meeting places or supplies—in fact, with literally nothing but their faith.[1]

Among the loyal officers were Staff Captain Annie Shirley, who as divisional officer of the Massachusetts and Maine Division added another to her long line of "firsts" by becoming the first woman DO. Other divisional officers who achieved prominence in Army circles were Staff Captains Jonas Inman, Charles Wass, and William Evans. Another pioneer who followed Smith was "Ash-barrel Jimmy," Railton's first convert in the United States, now Captain James Kemp.

The "World-Wide" Salvation Army, as it was called to distinguish it from Moore's "Incorporated" Salvation Army, was an extralegal organization plagued by various legal restrictions affecting ownership of property, liability to suit, and nonrecognition in the eyes of the law—ironically, the same issues that had hampered Moore and led to the incorporation. Even the familiar crest of the Salva-

tion Army—the sun containing the motto "Blood and Fire" around
an "S" intertwined with a cross and crossed swords and topped by a
crown symbolizing the Crown of Life—was copyrighted by Moore.
Smith had to design another, different enough to escape infringement of copyright, yet similar enough to represent the insignia that
had already become traditional. He omitted the crown and placed an
eagle over the crest. This crest is official in the United States today,
although in the rest of the Salvation Army world the crest is
topped with a crown.

The new emblem appeared on Commissioner Smith's *War Cry*,
published for the first time from New York on November 22, 1884.
In size and format, the four-page paper resembled the *War Cry*
that Major Moore continued to publish from Brooklyn.

A major problem was the lack of suitable meeting places. Commissioner Smith advertised in the *War Cry*, "We are still in want of
more Barrack accommodation all over the country . . . keep a
sharp look out for buildings likely to suit such as empty churches,
skating rinks, music halls, theatres, circuses, markets, or ware-
houses."

The year 1885 saw the international Salvation Army regain lost
ground and forge ahead under the leadership of loyal native officers,
others sent from England, and new recruits from the United States.
On May 19th the one hundredth corps was opened in Newark,
New Jersey. Only fourteen months after Smith reorganized the Salvation Army, it was stronger than ever before, with 143 corps and
290 officers.

Statistics cannot tell the full story of that reestablishment of
the Salvation Army in the United States. They can illustrate but
not explain why Moore's superior legal position and appeal to patriotism was defeated by William Booth's dream of a world-wide Salvation Army in which men of all nations would be equal before God.
Perhaps the loftier ideals and harsher disciplines of the international
Salvation Army served to cull out all but the most zealous and
sincere. Certainly the more democratic government of the American Salvation Army, and the observation of the sacraments of baptism and holy communion, did not hold the loyalty of the best

officers, and many of these left Moore's Army to reenter the original Salvation Army as soon as they were able.

The story of the first difficult year is told in a small book, *The Salvation War in America for 1885*, written by Commissioner Smith. Recorded in the thin volume are chronicles of progress and of persecution. Between the lines is the spirit of its author, later to become one of the pioneers of Britain's Labor party. Commissioner Smith's concept of the Army's mission was somewhat revolutionary. "The Army after all," he wrote, "is but another phase of that great advance of the people on to new ground, out of the restraints which have been put upon them for thousands of years, and which would continue upon them if they did not begin to think, and preach and pray out their own deliverance."

The Salvation Army's advance in this period of rebuilding was contested by the same forces that led the earlier opposition. Influenced by saloon keepers and their customers, the police and public officials continued their persecution. Not only did such persecution fail to stop the Army's spread, but it probably contributed to the spectacular growth of the organization. This was the conclusion reached by the New York *Tribune* after a lengthy speculation on the reasons for the persecution of the Salvation Army:

Nothing that is persecuted perishes during the persecution. This is the rule as regards all organizations, and therefore this craze . . . may be kept from dying, and given a foothold at last, through the stupidity of those who cannot restrain their inclination to make targets of the hallelujah lads and lassies.

The press sometimes condemned but more frequently supported the Army. When nine Salvationists, including four lassies, were arrested in Dayton, Ohio, the Dayton *Syndicate* came to their defense. After describing the Army's good work in Dayton, the paper declared, "The authorities should no more think of arresting these people, than they would think of entering a church during service, and landing the minister behind the bars." Plymouth and Sharpsburg, Pennsylvania, were scenes of bitter persecution, as were Buf-

falo, Schenectady, and Utica, New York. When Captain Emma Jane
Bown was arrested in Taunton, Massachusetts, a distinguished
judge volunteered to act as her defense lawyer. The jury declared
her not guilty of the charge against her—that of "committing a
nuisance by beating a bass drum." Another trial in Boston vindi-
cated the Salvationists there and confirmed their right to preach
on historic Boston Common.

Well might the Salvationists sing:

> Serene 'mid angry, howling mob I stand,
> Or lies and slander silently endure;
> Contempt and scorn I meet on ev'ry hand.
> But nought can touch my peace, in God secure.
>
> Behind the bars for Jesus' sake I stand,
> But though my body's chained, my soul is free;
> And in God's time once more I'll walk the land,
> To warn the heedless world from wrath to flee.

Although the initial objective of Smith's administration was to
win back the ground lost by the Moore secession, the Salvation
Army was not content with this achievement alone. A characteristic of the organization has always been the tendency to expand
into new fields. Not always has this expansion been undertaken
cautiously. The early Salvationists never pondered the questions:
"Can we afford it? Do we have the funds and trained personnel?"
The main question they put to themselves was, "Is there a need?"
If a need was evident the Salvation Army did its best to meet it,
and trusted in the Lord for the means, on the premise that He
never failed to provide for His Army.

Having figured in one of the major social problems of American
life in the 1880's—poverty and spiritual neglect of thousands of its
victims—it seems natural to expect that Salvationists would catch
the flame of related problems of racial distress and discrimination.
Dedicated to the downtrodden and unfortunate, the Salvation
Army could not overlook the plight of the six and a half million
Negroes in the United States.

The Salvation Army's first American commissioner, George S.

Railton, was greatly interested and deeply concerned about the salvation of the "Africans," as he called them. In the northern cities of New York and Philadelphia everyone was admitted to Salvation Army meetings, regardless of race or color, as a matter of course. Negroes who were converted were enrolled in the corps along with whites. Brother Robinson, a Negro recruit, was reported taking an active part in the campaigns in Philadelphia in March, 1880. On October 5th, 1884, just before the Moore split, a Negro corps was opened in Baltimore, but disappeared in the subsequent controversy.

In the early summer of 1885, an all-out campaign was launched "to save the colored people, and to make that a living, practical reality, which the grand deeds of twenty years ago [had] so far only succeeded in making a *written* right." This was no easy task; popular prejudices were strong. As Commissioner Smith stated: "We found much antipathy remaining, even between Christians and people of color, and we determined, by the help of God to be among the first white Christian communities of America, who would faithfully and wholly break down this wall of partition, separating the white from the colored, whom the Lord has brought from a common captivity and bondage. We desire, above all things, to exemplify this true spirit of Christian republicanism on our own platform, by looking only to the gift and grace within, and not at the externals of any soldier, and we appealed to every Salvation soldier and every lover of Christ to set their faces against any such discrimination. Real Christianity demanding that circumstances outside the control of any individual should not be permitted to weigh against his interest."

Salvation Army corps for Negroes were established in Washington, D.C., Fredericksburg, Alexandria, and Richmond, Virginia. At Fredericksburg the officer in charge reported, "white and colored are all on one level—sitting together in our meetings, and testifying of God's power to save." Among the Negroes who believed that the Salvation Army offered the greatest opportunity to serve their God and their race was Captain W. S. Braithwaite. This outstanding officer, born and converted in British Guiana, had studied medicine in England and in Boston, where he was aided by Wendell Phillips and William Lloyd Garrison. He was an ordained minister of the African Methodist Episcopal Zion Church when he became acquainted with the Salvation Army in Asbury Park, New Jersey, and accepted a Salvation Army commission.

White officers as well as Negroes dedicated themselves to work with the Negroes of the slums. One of these, Aide-de-Camp Joseph Pugmire, cut himself off from the white community to make his home in the colored districts, eating and sleeping with the Negro families whose souls he sought to save. His sincerity and Christian example won the affection of his chosen people, who called him "the curly-headed white man," and flocked to his meetings.

This campaign illustrates how the Salvation Army, ridiculed and scorned by the general public, could afford to treat with just contempt un-Christian prejudices however popular they were. The principle of racial equality, so well expressed by Commissioner Smith in 1885, has been a basic ideal of the Salvation Army throughout its history. Unfortunately, the pursuit of this ideal has wavered in the face of "regional prejudices." As the Salvation Army spread into the South, and as it became accepted by the public, it hesitated to offend public opinion by emphasizing an ideal which could be easily kept in the background. In the North, and wherever the mores of the public permitted, the Salvation Army opened its corps and social institutions without regard to race or color. In the South, however, it accepted the prevailing social system and segregated its work with the Negro. This is not accepted by the Army with an easy conscience. While some officers would wait for the passing of time to solve today's social problems, others constantly challenge the Army with the difference between practice and principle.[2] In November, 1954, the Salvation Army Commissioners' Conference endorsed the United States Supreme Court's historic decision outlawing segregation in the schools and stated: "A ruling so soundly based on Christian principle cannot but receive understanding and cooperation from all Salvationists dedicated to the ideal that in Christ all are one. We accept our full Christian responsibility to work earnestly and sympathetically to the end that a practical implementation of the decision may be successfully effected." Thus, the Salvation Army and the United States are both meeting the challenge.

The Salvation Army was from the beginning, as it is today, an urban organization. As early as 1885, however, the spiritual needs of rural and village dwellers were recognized, and an attempt was made to meet them. Meetings were held in some of the small villages of New York State which resulted in a religious revival in that region.

The Salvation Army's program of social work in America grew from a modest beginning in the administration of Commissioner Frank Smith. Prison work was begun in 1885, and women's social work in 1886. The details of their beginning and growth belong to a later chapter.

In comparison to the anniversary celebration in 1886, that of the previous year seemed very modest. Only three hundred loyal soldiers and officers gathered in New York to commemorate the Army's fifth year in the United States on March 19, 1885. By the following March the Army had expanded to the point where it was necessary to observe the sixth anniversary in three different cities in different parts of the country. Celebrations were held in Boston, Washington, D.C., and Chicago.

The Salvation Army had grown in prestige as well as in numbers. In Washington, President Grover Cleveland received Commissioner Smith and a group of Salvationists at the White House on March 23, 1886. Only six years after Railton explained the principles of the Salvation Army at the Battery in New York, a group of Salvationists marched up to the White House to be presented to the President of the United States. Cleveland was the first American President to recognize the Salvation Army, but every President who followed him has endorsed the Army and its work.

The high point of a year that saw a huge tri-city celebration and that brought official recognition from the President of the United States came in September when General William Booth made his first visit to America. His trip to inspect his overseas forces in the United States and Canada was the first time the Salvation Army's Founder had traveled outside the British Isles.

To hail his arrival a group of Salvationists waited all day Sunday, September 26, 1886, at the Cunard pier in New York for the steamship *Aurania*. Impatiently they watched the vessel dock and a stream of passengers flow down the gangplank until they spied the tall gaunt figure of their leader. William Booth wore the regulation Salvation Army uniform topped by a tall black silk hat. He was greeted by shouts of "Hallelujah!" from the Salvationists and by a barrage of questions from curious reporters. The next day every major New York newspaper carried a story about the General's arrival and plans.

After a night in Brooklyn, General Booth left for Toronto to spend four weeks in Canada before beginning his six-week tour of the United States. The itinerary was a strenuous one for the fifty-seven-year-old evangelist, and he was constantly troubled by ill health. He went to Prince Edward Island, and traveled through New Brunswick, Nova Scotia, and Quebec before concluding his Canadian campaign in Hamilton, Ontario.

Chicago, where he arrived on Saturday, October 30, 1886, was the scene of his first important appearance in the United States. The conditions which William T. Stead were to expose eight years later made Chicago second only to San Francisco for organized vice and corruption. Stead, an English journalist and friend of the Salvation Army, listed in his book *If Christ Came to Chicago* the names and addresses of the gambling dens and houses of prostitution and their owners. He attacked the apathy of the majority of Chicago's churches, which had "succumbed largely to the temptation of 'being at ease in Zion.'" In the midst of conditions dreadful to describe, he observed, "the various churches are wealthy, comfortable, served by able and zealous ministers and sung to by choirs of ecclesiastical nightingales." [3]

Such complacency came under attack when General Booth spoke in Chicago. At his disposal was the Princess Rink, one of the best known Salvation Army buildings in the country, secured by Major

William Evans in May, 1886. Even this former skating rink, with a capacity of two thousand people, was not sufficient for the General's major meetings, which were held in Central Music Hall. The General was described as "an excellent speaker—as earnest as Mr. Moody and as entertaining as Sam Jones, without the heaviness of the one or the flippancy of the other." He spent three full days in Chicago before continuing his tour.

An indication of the General's strenuous schedule may be seen in a letter he wrote to his son Bramwell from Chicago:

Do remember the whirl I am in. Today I had Officers two hours and a half to plan the building of our Temple with architects . . . This afternoon I had to speak to a great crowd on the laying [of the cornerstone] in the open air. To-night, Tuesday, I have been interviewing people; then big meeting; and at 10:30 same night go off for 500 miles to Kansas City. Meeting there to-morrow, and come out next morning 675 miles, again travelling till Friday to Dayton, and Columbus Saturday, Sunday, and Monday.

The most difficult part of the journey for William Booth was not the strain of innumerable meetings; not the hardship of continuous and uncomfortable rail travel over long distances nor the inconvenience of strange lodgings in various cities. It was the separation from his beloved wife, Catherine. She had been ill when he left, and was in fact, although it was not known at the time, dying of cancer and had but four years to live. His letters reflect his concern, loneliness, and tender affection for the brave woman who was the Salvation Army's Mother, his wife, and the love of his life.

General Booth was well received wherever he went. He liked America and was greatly impressed by the vastness of the country. "Oh what a future there is for us in this country, and oh what a country it is!" he wrote to Bramwell. "The possibilities of this immense Country are practically limitless!" From Washington he wrote, "I like the 'South' so far better than the North. They told me I should, and the farther South I go the warmer-hearted they say the people are. Anyway, I like these Washington people. Oh what a splendid City this is and is going to be. I have no doubt but they will make it the finest City in the world."

The last week of the General's tour was spent in New York, with a gigantic send-off meeting on the evening before he sailed for England. Meetings were held in the morning and afternoon at the West Twenty-fifth Street Presbyterian Church. After a "banquet" of sandwiches and coffee was served at five o'clock, the Salvationists marched to Steinway Hall, which was packed for the General's farewell address. General Booth spoke about the Army and its work and his visit to America. During his eleven-week trip, he declared, he had spoken for a total of 198 hours and addressed 180,000 people. At the end of his talk he introduced the collection with the remark: "You say we are always after money. Well, we are sorry; but we have to come after it. You don't come after us with it, do you?" About $200 was contributed.

After the Steinway Hall meeting the Salvationists marched back to the Presbyterian Church for an all-night of prayer which lasted until 3:40 A.M., when the General was finally escorted to the pier. The *Servia*, carrying General Booth, pulled out at 6:00 A.M. on Saturday, December 11, 1886. As it proceeded down the harbor it passed the Statue of Liberty, whose unveiling had taken place during the General's visit in the United States.

General Booth's visit to America was an important stimulus to the Salvation Army in the United States. His unique personality, his vision, and his ideals inspired his American soldiers and officers. Many Salvationists who had followed Major Moore realized their mistake for the first time when they heard the General speak. America influenced the General as well. America had seen General Booth, and, more important for the Salvation Army, General Booth had seen America—and liked it.

One immediate effect of the General's visit was his decision to replace Commissioner Smith. A logical choice to replace the ailing leader was the General's twenty-seven-year-old son Ballington, who had made a tour of the United States and Canada in the spring of 1886. He made such a favorable impression that newspapermen spoke about him when they interviewed his father, and others approached the General to inquire about him.

A cablegram from International Headquarters dated April 7,

1887, announced, "The General Salutes the American forces and has consented in view of Commissioner Smith's physical condition and call for relief to appoint Marshal Ballington Booth to command in the States." The new commander and his wife arrived in America soon after the cablegram, and began a tour of the country. Commissioner Smith relinquished his command with evident relief. In his farewell message he declared, "It has doubtless been apparent to you for some time past that I have been working under the disadvantage of a severe physical strain." The commissioner looked "excessively haggard," according to the *War Cry*, when he sailed for England.[4]

Frank Smith, serving in an arduous crisis, had illustrated a Salvation Army belief that God will provide the right type of man at the right time for the job to be done. He had come to the United States faced with a difficult job. When he left, the mission was accomplished, and a stronger Army was his monument.

"Two and a half years ago . . . we had a shattered remnant left to us of twenty-one corps, sixteen of them in financial difficulties, some of them so irretrievably shattered that they had soon to be closed." Some fifty officers were loyal to the old flag. When Smith left the United States, he turned over to his successor a Salvation Army of 654 officers operating in 312 cities and towns. It was an Army made wise by its experience with the Moore secession. Although it was nearly to yield to an even greater temptation to split asunder, never again were any large numbers to leave the "World-Wide" Salvation Army.

VII

Carrying the War to the Far West

The American West has a unique place in the history of the United States. Spanish conquistadors, Anglo-American mountain men, savage Indians, humble pioneers, cowboys and Forty-niners of gold-rush days are but a few of the characters in the great drama of its history. All of these elements helped to make up the character of the West. Wherever the Salvation Army has gone, it has adapted its program to peculiar regional or national characteristics of the people. Nowhere in the annals of the Salvation Army is there a more dramatic story than that of the impact of the Salvation Army and the American West.

"I would shake the dust off my feet as a witness against them! I would not stay here if I were you! I never saw such a wicked place!" So a shocked Australian exclaimed on his first visit to San Francisco's Barbary Coast in the mid-1880's. He was speaking to a Salvation Army officer he had buttonholed on the streets when it seemed that he could no longer keep to himself his horror at the sights he had seen.

"Shaking the dust off his feet as a witness against them" was an easy way to get out of a disagreeable job, but it did not give promise of rescuing the lost, or making a bad mess better, thought the officer. He explained that the Salvation Army did not flee from sin but sought it out to battle and defeat it. But he must have thought that God had indeed set him on a difficult battlefield. Was there a place in the country—perhaps in the world—where Satan reigned with less restraint than in San Francisco's Barbary Coast?

The whole West Coast was still under the influence of the gold rush of three decades ago. San Francisco was the metropolis of the West, and its Barbary Coast was the moral cesspool of San Francisco. In 1890, 3,117 establishments, or one for every 96 inhabitants, were licensed to sell intoxicating beverages, and an estimated 2,000 speakeasies operated without a license.

Escaped or paroled convicts from Australia, known as Sydney Ducks, first brought notoriety to the Barbary Coast. The word "hoodlum" originated in San Francisco, and gangs of them terrorized the Chinese and anyone else who crossed their path. Prostitution was the Barbary Coast's largest vested interest. With it were the inevitable by-products of pimps, white-slave traffic, and disease. With the connivance of corrupt public officials, the worst forms of vice were openly flaunted, to the despair of the few honest and God-fearing people of San Francisco. No missionary going to a heathen land faced a greater challenge than that which confronted the Salvation Army as it launched its attack in San Francisco in 1883.

As the Shirley family paved the way for Railton to begin the Salvation Army on the East Coast of the United States, so was the trail broken for the official Salvation Army on the West Coast. A small group of Christians living in Oakland, San Jose, and San Francisco, California, was striving under the rather pretentious name of the Pacific Coast Holiness Association to combat the general immorality and godlessness that characterized California in the 1880's. The band was led by the Reverend George Newton. In 1881, one of the group received a copy of the Salvation Army *War Cry* in the mail from England. The paper was passed around to the other members of the Holiness Association, and all agreed that the methods of William Booth, if applied to their own group, would enable them to become more effective in their work. They proceeded to collect uniforms, give themselves titles, and organize processions. "Corps" were established in Oakland, San Jose, and San Francisco.

Then they wrote to General Booth for recognition and for officers to lead them.

The Holiness Association "Salvation Army" struggled along until 1883, until William Booth found the officer he wanted to send to California. The young man he chose was twenty-four-year-old Alfred Wells, then an aide-de-camp in Northern Ireland. Wells was one of the first thirty "Training Home lads" to complete training at the London Training Home, and he had spent most of his active service as an officer in Northern Ireland. The request to go abroad came to him without warning, but his answer was an unhesitating "Yes." He had a few days to farewell in Ireland and to say goodbye in England. Chosen to accompany Wells, who was promoted to the rank of major, was Captain Henry Stillwell, twenty-two years old. The two young men arrived in New York from Liverpool on the steamship *Wisconsin* on May 16, 1883. Here they were met and entertained by Major Thomas E. Moore, then commander of the Salvation Army forces in the United States and Canada.

For six weeks the two pioneers waited in Brooklyn for word from the Holiness Association, and when the desired information did not arrive Major Wells decided to go to California alone. The "California Expedition" was given an official send-off from the Brooklyn Lyceum by Major Moore and the full staff of officers on Thursday, June 7, 1883. After a nine-day train trip with stop-offs to present colors to newly established corps at Louisville, Kentucky, and New Albany, Indiana, Major Wells arrived in San Francisco on July 21, 1883. On the following evening, July 22, 1883, he began the official operations of the Salvation Army on the West Coast in a little hall at 815 Montgomery Street. The Holiness band's "Salvation Army" had about thirty members when Major Wells arrived in California and accepted them into the real Salvation Army. The Army yoke proved to be too galling to some of the unruly spirits of the group, and by the end of the first month about half of the Association had dropped out.

Major Wells was the only officer in California until October 6th, when Captain Stillwell joined him. During this period he set up headquarters near the docks at 142-1/2 Fourth Street, and supervised three corps, in San Francisco, Oakland, and San Jose. After Stillwell arrived and took charge of the corps at San Jose, the two friends saw each other only three times during the next year. Wells, dividing his time between Oakland and San Francisco, conducted a Salvation Army meeting every night for twelve months.

California was treated to a hallelujah double wedding a year after operations began on the West Coast, when the first Salvation Army lassies sent to California, Captain Polly Medforth and Captain Mary Matthews, became Mrs. Major Wells and Mrs. Captain Stillwell. The two girls had made the long trip across the ocean alone and crossed the continent in an emigrant train that moved so slowly and stopped so frequently they were able to get out and pick flowers along the way. Captain Matthews had lived in Canada, and felt a bit more at home in America than did Captain Medforth, who was an English lassie and who had known Major Wells, her intended bridegroom, only a few days before he left England. Mary Matthews had known Captain Stillwell before she entered the Army, and the two had been engaged for five years. At last they reached San Francisco on Sunday, July 6, 1884, and found no one to meet them. They inquired directions to the boardinghouse where Wells lived from a policeman who told them the trolley car to take. Hot and tired as they were after the nine-day train ride, the two lassies would not ride on Sunday, so they walked until they found the boardinghouse. The two men got a tongue lashing for not meeting them, until Major Wells explained how he had taken a boat to Oakland and there waited until midnight to meet the overland train on Friday night, when he expected the girls to arrive.

Finally romance prevailed, and the two couples were married on the 9th of July, three days after the girls had arrived. On the 10th, Captain and Mrs. Stillwell took charge of the Oakland corps. Mrs. Major Wells and two girl cadets left San Francisco three months after her marriage to open Sacramento, a city that had been too tough for the men officers. The three lassies were adored by the rough miners, pioneers, and gamblers who crowded the hall at every meeting. Women were so scarce in California at that time that it was said a man would walk five miles to see a petticoat on a clothesline. The moral code of the men of the West demanded respect for "good women," and every man of their congregation was a self-appointed protector for the three lassies. Many converts were won, and the whole moral tone of the community improved through their efforts.

The work was advancing in the rest of the state. Major Wells had purchased instruments for a brass band, and after only seven lessons the band was leading the regular processions, making up in enthusiasm what it lacked in harmony. Major Wells's 2nd California Corps, in San Francisco, was a veritable Tower of Babel. Among the members, in addition to Americans, English, and Scotch, were Germans, Swedes, Danes, a Norwegian, a Turk, and an Armenian. The 1st California Corps, in Oakland, led by Captain Stillwell, included a Russian and a Greek among its members; and the 4th California Corps, in Stockton, under the leadership of California-trained Captain Milsaps and Lieutenant Bird, reported two Chinese converts.

The Moore schism found the California forces loyal to "The Salvation Army of the World." "We are grieved and shocked," wrote Major Wells, "at the idea of a part of the Eastern work seceding from the 'parent Body.' " At the beginning of 1885, after seventeen months of action, the Salvation Army colors flew in five different towns and one outpost village in California. Nine officers had been enlisted. One of the greatest problems that faced the Army was the "transient state of the inhabitants." It was considered fortunate when a third of the converts settled down to become "Blood and Fire Soldiers."

The first officer recruited and commissioned in California was Captain John Milsaps—a Texan whose grandfather had died in defense of the Alamo and whose father had served in the Confederate Army. As a young man he had wandered through the West working as wagon-train cook, prospector, mule herder, railroad grader, teamster, locomotive fireman, and miner. He was converted in Texas at the age of twenty-two, and when he met a procession of the Holiness Association "Salvation Army" in San Francisco he joined the group on January 15, 1883. When Major Wells accepted the band as members of the Salvation Army, John Milsaps was in the group, and after a year and eight days as a soldier he accepted a commission as captain, the first officer commissioned on the West Coast. He was sent to open a corps in Stockton and later was in charge of corps in San Francisco, Sacramento, Oakland, and Napa City. His contributions to the Western *War Cry* were so notable that he was appointed its editor in December, 1886.

The Pacific Coast edition of the *War Cry* began publication in November, 1883, on a monthly schedule. At first Major Wells had to use his pocket money to pay its way, but by 1887 it was well established, being published twice a month in issues of 9,000 copies. Two years later, in November, 1889, it became a weekly.

One of Captain Milsaps' converts from the depths of the Barbary Coast became one of the Salvation Army's stanchest members and most colorful officer. Joseph Garabed, or Joe the Turk, as he was better known, stood six feet two inches, and had the build of a prizefighter. He was a fighter, too, but for most of his long life he fought for the Lord in the ranks of the Salvation Army.

The Turk was actually an Armenian, but he accepted the nickname and capitalized on it by wearing a uniform of crimson pantaloons and jacket and a Turkish fez. The eccentricities of Joe the Turk are still topics of conversation wherever older Salvationists gather. He carried an ink pad and a stamp with the words "Jesus Saves," and wherever he stayed—in private home or hotel—he stamped the motto on walls, furniture, and linen. Each week he sent copies of the *War Cry* to prominent people with his compliments. Included on his mailing list was Pope Leo XIII, at the Vatican.

It was this original, self-educated man who broke the police persecution of the Salvation Army. "Arrested fifty-seven times for Jesus" was his boast. Joe the Turk traveled on the West Coast and across the country wherever Salvationists were arrested for holding open-air meetings or parading. When arrested he would demand a trial, and if convicted he appealed until he won his case. He always won, and with each victory he obtained a judicial decision that protected the Salvationists that remained behind.

By the turn of the century there was no more famous Salvation
Army officer in the United States than Captain Joseph Garabed. Joe
the Turk, with his colorful uniform, his umbrella, and his bugle, was
already a legend in his own lifetime—a dramatic contribution of
San Francisco's Barbary Coast to the Army and to the country.

Major Alfred Wells was the commanding officer of the Salvation
Army operations on the West Coast until May, 1886, when he was
relieved and with Mrs. Wells visited England to participate in the
celebration of an International Congress. Captain Stillwell was temporarily in charge of headquarters until Major Britton arrived on
November 28, 1886, to assume command.

Meanwhile, Mrs. Captain Stillwell was sent to Oregon to begin
work in that territory. She left in August, 1886, to open a corps in
Portland. Haste was believed necessary because it was rumored that
Moore's American Salvation Army was planning to begin operations
in Portland ahead of the international Army. It was Christmas,
1886, before Stillwell, promoted to adjutant, was sent to join his
wife as the commander of the district consisting of Oregon and
Washington Territory.

Britton was recalled to the East early in 1887, and Brigadier
Edward Fielding arrived to assume the command of the Pacific
Coast on April 8, 1887. The Pacific Coast lost its position as a separate command when Ballington Booth became the national commander of all of the Salvation Army forces in the United States.
Shortly after coming under the direct jurisdiction of National
Headquarters, the Pacific Coast celebrated its fourth anniversary.
At that time it was at work in twenty-five cities and had sixty-three
officers and cadets. A year later, in April, 1888, there were five districts, thirty-two corps, thirteen outposts, and over one hundred officers in the West. In addition, a Rescue Home and Training Garrison were in operation.

Although officially under the direction of New York since 1887,
the Salvation Army in the Far West never lost its unique identity. It
continued to publish its own edition of the *War Cry*. From California and the Coast, the Army spread across the Rockies to Utah

and Idaho, then to Montana, Wyoming, Colorado, and Arizona. It jumped the Pacific to Hawaii, and in the 1940's to Alaska and the Philippine Islands, whose Salvation Army corps were administered from the Pacific Coast.

VIII

Personalities and Progress

The appointment of Ballington and Maud Booth as commanders of the Salvation Army in America began a new era in Salvation Army history. For nearly fifty years thereafter the command of the American branch of the Army was held by one of the children of William Booth, the Founder. The period of nine years of Ballington Booth's leadership was one of unchecked progress marred only by the circumstances of his estrangement from his father and his resignation in 1896.

Ballington Booth, the second eldest child of William and Catherine Booth, inherited from his parents a full share of that touch of genius that was present to a greater or lesser degree in all of the Booth children. Of the eight children, three boys and five girls, all but one became evangelical preachers.[1] Ballington Booth was born July 28, 1857, in Brighouse, England, while his father was still a poor Methodist preacher. His mother, Catherine Booth, did not believe in exposing her children to the evils of the world by sending them away to school, and directed their early education at home.

Because William Booth's dominating interest was his ministry, and because his wife was as active as he in preaching and testifying, the children were nurtured on a strong diet of evangelism. It is not strange that their games often consisted of preaching and that their talk was of the penitent form, backsliders, and sinners. Ballington and his older brother, Bramwell, would preach to a congregation consisting of their younger brother and sisters and their dolls.

As a small boy, Ballington with great enthusiasm would coax, drag, and bang a poor reluctant penitent (usually a pillow) up to the mercy seat, exclaiming, "Ah, this is a good case, bless him! Give up the drink, brother!"

The Booth children were taught to shun tobacco and liquor as the Devil himself. A Puritan simplicity in dress and appearance was strictly enforced. On one occasion Ballington came in to tea with a ring he had purchased for a shilling adorning his finger. His horrified brothers and sisters began to chant, "Ballington's a backslider!" "Silence," commanded the father. "His mother will deal with him later." The meal proceeded with great solemnity. When it was over, Ballington and his mother were closeted for about ten minutes. He came out with red eyes and without the ring.

Ballington was eight years old when his father began the work of the Christian Mission. Like the other Booth children he grew up with the Salvation Army. His entire education was aimed at making an evangelist for the Army. At seventeen he was giving out hymns and speaking a few words. Soon after he began to lead meetings by himself. The youth was endowed with an extraordinary voice and his father's powers of touching oratory. By his early twenties Ballington was an evangelist of note with the ability to melt audiences. "He could play with an audience as a Paderewski can with his instrument," commented an observer.

In 1880, at the age of twenty-three, Ballington Booth was placed in charge of the first Training Home for men officers at Clapton. One of the highest officials of the Army described Ballington as the most human of the members of his family. Certainly he both inspired and won the affection of the trainees under his charge. He worked with them in the field, where his powers as an orator and a soloist won him great success. After three years in charge of the Training Home, the young evangelist was sent to Australia as joint commander of the work there. He served with Commissioner T. H. Howard, later the international Chief of Staff. There his popularity knew no bounds. He was the idol of Salvationists, and was well received by the general public as well.

In the spring of 1886, Ballington returned from Australia to England. On the way he made an evangelical tour through Canada and the United States, and showed that there too he had the faculty of winning the public's favor. On the eve of General Booth's departure for his first visit to the United States, on September 16, 1886, Ballington Booth was married to Maud Elizabeth Charlesworth in Congress Hall, Clapton. His father conducted the service.

The bride was as outstanding as Ballington himself. Born on September 13, 1865, the year the Salvation Army itself was conceived, Maud Charlesworth was the daughter of a well-to-do Anglican clergyman, the Reverend Samuel Charlesworth. After the usual education for a Victorian "gentlewoman," she showed her independence and strength of character at the age of sixteen by going to France in the company of Catherine Booth, the third of the Booth children, known as "La Maréchale." Maud was a member of the group of Salvationists who braved severe persecution to bring the Salvation Army to Switzerland. There, to the horror of her very respectable father, she was arrested and expelled from the country.

The Reverend Charlesworth's strongest protests failed to prevent his daughter from entering Salvation Army officership, and at eighteen she held a roving commission. Her attractive personality and resourcefulness contributed to her popularity and success. When in England the young woman stayed at the Booth home. The General's handsome son Ballington courted and won her affection, and their engagement was announced. The two were an unusually attractive couple. Ballington Booth—his rank was that of marshal—was a handsome man with flashing brown eyes and dark black hair and mustache. He was six feet four inches tall, and wore his uniform with the air of a military commander. His ever present sense of humor endeared him both to his followers and to the audiences that he addressed. Maud was as sweet and feminine as Ballington was manly. Only a bit over five feet tall, she was a woman of unusual physical beauty, with an accompanying sense of spiritual goodness.

The new commanders arrived in the United States on April 21, 1887, and spent the first four weeks in continuous travel. They covered 4,540 miles, addressed seven councils, most of which lasted from five to seven hours, and thirty-three public meetings. On this tour they made the acquaintanceship of many of the officers and soldiers in their command and gained a personal knowledge of the problems—both local and national—they faced. When they finally settled down at National Headquarters in New York, it was not to rest but to begin work.

One problem to which Ballington Booth turned his attention was the healing of old wounds. Moore's Salvation Army of America, although steadily declining in importance, was a constant source of irritation to the international Army. Funds intended by donors for the Booth organization were sometimes received by Moore's Army. Within Moore's Army an increasing number of persons became dissatisfied with his administration, and on January 10, 1889, three of the trustees voted to annul his appointment. Colonel Richard E. Holz was chosen as "Spiritual Director and Commander" pending a general election.

Colonel Holz had long realized the mistake of dividing the Salvation forces. On one occasion soon after the split he went to see Commissioner Smith at his headquarters to seek information and guidance and was brusquely told he could attend Smith's meetings at the New York corps for information. In 1885, while on furlough to Germany, Holz made a trip to London at his own expense to visit International Headquarters. There he explained the attitude of many of the officers of Moore's Army and indicated his desire to see it reunited with the parent organization, but Holz had no position of authority in the Salvation Army of America and nothing came of his visit. When Holz finally became the leader of a portion of Moore's Army, Ballington Booth was the national commander in the United States. In contrast to Smith, Ballington was cordial and conciliatory when approached by Holz. He treated Holz and his staff with friendliness and courtesy even to the point of inviting them to attend his meetings and giving them a place on the platform.

In the meantime other officers who had followed Moore found that Ballington Booth had opened the gate for them to return to the fold. The *War Cry* for April 6, 1889, announced, "Staff-Capt. Emma Westbrook having expressed her sincere regret for having severed herself from the Salvation Army has made arrangements with the Marshal to take command of a corps." Thus a pioneer of the original party returned to the ranks of the original Salvation Army. Other officers applied for readmission, were forgiven and assigned to positions in the Army commensurate with their ability.

Together Ballington and Holz worked out a reconciliation re-uniting the officers of Holz's group with the parent organization. The ceremony took place at the Town Hall in Saratoga, New York, on October 16, 1889. Over a thousand people watched as Marshal Ballington Booth publicly welcomed Colonel Holz, who was read-mitted with the rank of major and given command of the New York division. Some thirty-one officers followed Holz's lead and were re-accepted into the world-wide Salvation Army.

The place and time were perhaps ironic: October 17th was the anniversary of Burgoyne's surrender at Saratoga to the Americans during the Revolutionary War, and signs appeared in the town call-ing attention to the surrender of an American Army to the British. Although the commander pointed out that six-eighths of the offi-cers in the Army were American by birth or naturalization, anti-English feeling was not difficult to arouse in the 1880's, and the Salvation Army was primarily "English" to many Americans. In vain could the *War Cry* exclaim, "Nobody knows *Why* certain par-ties call our Army an English one when out of nearly 1,000 officers in the States, over 800 have either been born here or became officers after having been converted at some of our American stations."

Still, many Americans found it difficult to appreciate the inter-national scope of the Salvation Army, even though reflections of this internationalism could be easily found in its work in the United States during this period. From 1887 to 1896 nearly four million im-migrants from all over the world poured into the United States. Many of these were attracted to the large cities, where they swelled the slum areas. "The Poor Man's Church" was quick to see the need of these people, and began to work among these new Americans in whose homeland the Salvation Army was in many cases already at work.

The most important Salvation Army work among non-English-speaking people in the United States was the Scandinavian work. While not the first foreign-language work to be begun, the Scandinavian branch of the Salvation Army was long the largest and most successful of the non-English-speaking groups in the United States. Much of its stimulus came from Scandinavia itself, where the Salvation Army was strongly established.

Scandinavian work in the United States began through the efforts of Swedish immigrants who were Salvationists. In 1884 three Salvationists from Stockholm—Amalia Ljunggren, Mina Eklund, and Anna Larsson—emigrated to Brooklyn, where they were joined the following year by Anna's sister, Mathilda. The four women attended a Swedish Baptist church, but found it lacking in that sort of lively, demonstrative quality of the Salvation Army with which they were familiar. At last, in the winter of 1886-1887, they discovered the Brooklyn No. 1 Corps of the Army and began to attend meetings there. They had difficulty understanding what was said, and noticed that there were many other Scandinavian people there who understood even less English than they did. After the regular service, they arranged to conduct a meeting in Swedish as nearly like those in the old country as they could remember.

Larger and larger crowds were attracted to these Swedish-language meetings, and several converts were made. Later, with the proceeds from the collections taken at these after-hour meetings, the four women rented a little store on Atlantic Avenue and began to hold meetings in Swedish conducted along Salvation Army lines. In the meantime Captain Annie and her sister, Lieutenant Mary Hartelius, who had left the United States in March, 1883, to help open Salvation Army work in Sweden, returned to America to see their widowed mother. Though they were without assignment during the summer of 1887, they conducted meetings in Brooklyn, gaining the nickname of the "Singing Pilgrims." They met the four women who were holding meetings in the Atlantic Avenue store, and after obtaining authorization from Commander Ballington Booth at National Headquarters, the first Scandinavian Corps (known as Brooklyn No. 3) was officially opened on December 23, 1887, with Mary Hartelius as its first captain, assisted by her sister, Annie.

Thus the Hartelius sisters became not only the first Salvation Army missionaries to leave America, but the first officially to open the Scandinavian work in the United States.

The first such corps was an immediate success. Scandinavians so crowded the small hall that non-Swedish-speaking visitors often had to be turned away for lack of room. In the first twelve days Annie Hartelius reported "the capture of thirteen souls." By March, 1888, the corps had moved to a larger hall and was filling this as it had the former building. Other Scandinavian corps were soon opened in Minneapolis, Chicago, Providence, and New York.

Copies of the *Stridsropet* (War Cry), published in Sweden, were sold at the meetings of the Scandinavian corps in America and to the Swedish-speaking public. The New York *War Cry* published a Scandinavian column and an occasional hymn in Swedish, but by 1891 there was sufficient demand to make necessary the publication of a Swedish-language paper in the United States, and the first issue of the New York *Stridsropet* appeared on February 7, 1891. By May of the same year, twenty-five copies or more were sold each week by forty-three corps. Today, in the sixty-fourth year of publication, the New York edition of *Stridsropet* has a weekly circulation of about 8,000 copies throughout the country.

The Scandinavian work in America was given an impetus in 1892 by the visit of Commissioner Hanna Ouchterlony, the pioneer who began Salvation Army work in Sweden and Norway. About eighty corps compose the Scandinavian branch of the Salvation Army in the United States today. Most of these are Swedish, but there are also Norwegian, Danish, and even one Finnish corps.

The large number of German-speaking immigrants were not overlooked by the Salvation Army in the United States. In 1880, when Railton arrived, there were nearly 2,000,000 Germans in the foreign-born population, and by 1890 there were over 2,780,000. Indeed, the first work in America with non-English-speaking people was among the German-Americans. The first issue of the *Salvation News*, published July 30, 1880, carried a notice of "Our First German Corps," the 2nd New York, and described meetings held at a hall on west Fifty-third Street. This first German corps did not even survive until Railton left America, and no extensive appeal was made to the German-speaking population until 1887. By that time Railton, again the pioneer, was in Germany leading the *Heilsarmee* in that country. His reports in the American *War Cry* were a challenge to the Salvation Army in the United States. "What are we doing for German America?" Ballington Booth asked himself and his followers. The answer came quickly. On November 6, 1887, the first German meeting since Railton's time was held in New York City. The meeting was a success, and German-speaking officers were recruited to form German corps.

On October 29, 1892, *Der Kriegsruf*, a German *War Cry*, was first published in New York. Even with the aid of the newspaper, organization of German corps was slow. By the middle of 1895 only nine corps were in operation. Even these did not flourish, and eventually the German work was given up. The New York edition of *Der Kriegsruf* was published as a monthly until February, 1897, when it came out twice a month until it was discontinued in January, 1903. There are no separate German-language corps in the United States today.

Special appeals were made to other national groups. The slum sisters, officers who substituted simple clothes for uniforms and who lived in the slums, found that they had to learn Italian to help effectively a large group of the slum dwellers. Evangelical work among the Italian-Americans was not begun until 1894. Three soldiers of New York No. 4 Corps—Louis and Erme Natino and Frank Raggo—held open-air meetings in Italian for about six months before they were arrested at Mulberry Bend on November 19, 1894. The Italian-American campaign continued, but no large numbers of Italian-Americans have been weaned from the church of their ancestors.

The largest foreign groups on the West Coast, the Chinese and Japanese, lacked the background to understand the Occidental and Christian culture from which the Salvation Army came. Yet the Army made surprising progress. In 1889 a twenty-year-old Chinese boy, Fong Foo Sec, who had been seven years in America, was converted at a Salvation Army meeting and entered a Training Garrison as a cadet. On June 1, 1889, he was promoted, and Lieutenant Fong Foo Sec became the first Chinese officer in America. The first Chinese corps was established at 25 Turk Street, in San Francisco's Chinatown, in 1886. Captain Nellie Keefe was the first corps commander. Today this Chinese corps (at Sacramento Street and Waverly Place) owns its own property and carries on an active program.

In addition to the Army work with various national groups within the country, the Salvation Army in the United States aided the world-wide missionary efforts of the international Army. Interest in the Army's work in India was aroused by a visit from Frederick de Lautour Booth-Tucker, son-in-law of William Booth and Commissioner for India. This man, known to the Indians as Fakir Singh, gave up a comfortable position in the civil service to live the primitive life of an Indian in order to reach the masses with Christ's message. Booth-Tucker arrived in New York on May 30, 1890, to tour the United States seeking financial support for the work in India. He was accompanied by Cadet Lord Ratna Pala, a converted Buddhist priest; Captain Kantahella, a Hindu from Ceylon; Lieutenant Abdul Aziz, a Persian "Mohammedan sheik"; and Staff Captain Jai Singh and wife.

In the following year "La Maréchale" Catherine Booth, the General's oldest daughter, made a similar tour on behalf of France and collected $10,000. Between October, 1891, and January, 1892, she appeared in most of the major cities in the East and Midwest.

Among the distinguished Salvationists who visited the United States during this period was Herbert Booth, third son of the General, who was known as the "Commandant." He arrived at San Francisco while on a tour around the world, and was met there by Maud Booth, who accompanied her brother-in-law across the country to New York. Commissioner Frank Smith returned to the United States at the same time and was present at the reception for Herbert Booth on December 31, 1888. The beloved pioneer, Commissioner George Scott Railton, visited New York in November, 1893, for the celebration of the Columbian Congress.

These outstanding personalities gave an impetus to Salvation

Army work in the United States. It was a period in which personalities, particularly those of Ballington and Maud Booth, were far more important than policy in the administration of the Salvation Army. The physical growth during this era of personalities was rapid. In March, 1887, the Army had 654 officers in action and its flag flew in 312 cities and towns. By June, 1890, the number of officers and cadets had passed the one-thousand mark. In January, 1896, just before Ballington's resignation, 1,778 officers and cadets were active in 668 corps and outposts. During the nine years of Ballington's leadership in the United States, the number of corps more than doubled and the officers increased two and one half times. These figures show the advance primarily in the evangelical work, and do not indicate the amazing increase in training garrisons, slum posts, rescue homes, food and shelter depots, and other aspects of the social work.

Winning National Recognition

The Salvation Army in the United States steadily assumed a position within the international Army second only to the work in Great Britain itself. In America the Army was gradually being accepted by the general public. Its sincere concern for the welfare of the slum dwellers slowly won the grudging respect of the poorest workers of the cities. Its success with the poor, its social work, and the personalities of its leaders brought the approval and support of the established churches, the press, and many of the wealthiest people.

When General William Booth made his second visit to the United States in the winter of 1894-1895, he could not fail to notice the changes that had occurred since his first visit. "The spirit is very different from that displayed when I was here eight years ago," he told reporters as he expressed his appreciation for the cordial reception he received from the American people and the friendly reception from the press.

This tour of America began in Canada, where the General landed at Halifax, Nova Scotia, on September 20, 1894. He was welcomed by the Prime Minister of Nova Scotia, William S. Fielding, whose guest he was during his stay in Halifax. For a month the General traveled through eastern Canada before entering the United States.

A grand Jubilee Congress opened in New York on October 22, 1894, to mark the commencement of General Booth's coast-to-coast tour of the United States. The sixty-five-year-old patriarch had arrived in the city on Friday evening, three days earlier. On Saturday he held a press conference and on Sunday he rested at his son's home in Montclair, New Jersey. With him on this trip were Colonel John Lawley and Colonel Alex Nicol.

Carnegie Hall was filled for the General's first public appearance at the opening of the Jubilee Congress. It was filled again on the following night, when Chauncey M. Depew introduced the General to a crowd of 4,500, including a number of wealthy men and women. General Booth spoke of his "In Darkest England" scheme.

"It isn't wicked to be reduced to rags," he said. "It is not a sin to starve, to pawn the few sticks of furniture to buy food and pay the rent. It is a misfortune that comes to people, honest and good people, in hard times or when work is hard to get. It is such people that the social scheme means to help."

The tall gaunt man rocked on his heels and his fingers toyed restlessly with the rack as he spoke. The prominent hooked nose and long gray beard gave him the appearance of an Old Testament prophet. His voice showed the strain of overuse. It was throaty, but at times it rose clear and strong, with a timbre that sent chills down the backs of his audience.

From New York to California, wherever the General spoke, his meetings were crowded. Paupers and millionaires, the ignorant and the educated, clergymen and sinners listened to his plea for the unfortunate. After an address by the General in Cambridge, Professor Charles Eliot Norton, of Harvard, compared him to St. Bernard at the time of the first crusade.

His itinerary included Washington, Pittsburgh, Cleveland, Detroit, Chicago, St. Louis, Denver, San Francisco, and Vancouver, whence he returned east by the Canadian Pacific. In all, he traveled 18,453 miles, held meetings in 86 cities, and addressed 340 meetings attended by 437,000 people. About 2,200 persons came to the penitent's bench. During his tour of twenty-four weeks he spent 847 hours on trains. These statistics the General held on the tip of his tongue and rattled off with obvious satisfaction at his last press conference in New York.

Of his visit to America, the General declared: "I have been de-lighted, more than delighted, with my whole experience. I do not think that any plain Britisher was ever so cordially received; that is, no man who has nothing but his social and religious character and doings to commend him to the people. The American people re-ceived me in a most hearty manner—more than hearty—sympathetic, I may say. The press has been more than fair; it has been friendly.

"I found the Army here far beyond my expectations. I am more than satisfied with the spirit of the officers and the soldiers," Gen-eral Booth told reporters just before he sailed for England on the *Paris* on February 27, 1895.

Well might General William Booth be proud of his American officers and soldiers. Much of the early progress of the Army may be credited to individual officers who noticed a need and did some-thing about it. Such initiative among officers was encouraged, as an editorial in the *War Cry* explained:

The Salvation Army is adaptive, and therein lies one of the secrets of its success. Rules for the conducting of its operations remain only hard and fast as long as they are successful; when a change is thought bene-ficial, said change is tested and tried. No officer will exceed his authority in indulging in an occasional change of tactics; in fact every intelligent man and woman is cognizant of the fact that there is a great power in fresh and attractive features, in the Salvation Army or out of it, and it should be imperative to every officer that he endeavor to stir up life and interest in this manner, without, of course, going in for anything gro-tesque or unseemly.

Illustrative of this spirit is the action taken by some officers to aid the destitute families of striking workmen. The Salvation Army's position in the struggle between capital and labor that was particu-larly bitter during this period was what would be expected from an organization that recruited its members from the working classes, from the downtrodden and poor. Officially the organization took no stand in the great strikes, but quietly its officers worked to re-lieve the suffering of the strikers and their families.

When Captain Alexander Lamb arrived in Fall River to take

command of the corps there, he found that a strike against the textile mills then in its seventh week was causing great suffering to the children of the workers. When a merchant of the town offered through the local paper to supply meat and vegetables up to $25 a day if someone would prepare and serve dinners for the hungry children, Captain Lamb was quick to act. He offered the Salvation Army barracks as a dining room and secured a kitchen. He laid the plan before the corps soldiers at roll call; since most of them were out of work because of the strike he was able to obtain a full contingent of cooks, dishwashers, waiters, doormen, and other workers. On the first day about 500 children were fed, and by the end of the first week 1,050 showed up for the meal.

In Chicago on the day Staff Captain Wallace W. Winchell read Governor Peter Altgeld's exposé of the suffering and destitution in Pullman's model town caused by the Pullman strike, he went to the governor and the newspapers with a plan to aid the workers. Handbills calling on Chicagoans to donate food, clothing, fuel, or money to aid the starving inhabitants at Pullman were distributed. The Princess Rink was opened as a collection point for the donations. A mass meeting was held to raise funds. Horses and wagons filled Haymarket Square as the Salvation Army transported the materials collected to Pullman, where Captain Winchell went from house to house distributing supplies.

The same Captain Winchell, later to gain fame as the "Bishop of the Bowery," was a man of great ingenuity. When he had handbills printed in the form of subpoenas, he not only secured a crowd; the Chicago newspapers also gave the story a big play. The "subpoena" read as follows:

You ARE WANTED to Appear at the court room (Princess Rink, 558 West Madison Street,) on THURSDAY, FEBRUARY 8, A.D. 1894, at 8 P.M. sharp, in the case of the Salvation Army, plaintiff, vs. Satan; alias the "Devil;" alias the "Serpent;" alias the "Angel of Light," who has been indicted in one thousand crimes for murder to petty larceny.

Robert Ingersoll is also subpoenaed.

W. W. WINCHELL, *Sheriff.*

Colonel Robert Ingersoll, the famous lecturer and agnostic, was also sent a separate subpoena, a challenge he did not accept. A prominent clergyman acted as judge; and, as one newspaper remarked, there was some talk that the jury was packed. The judgment was for the plaintiff.

It has been the official policy of the Salvation Army to avoid entering any public controversy—political, social, or economic. The most notable exception to this general rule occurred in London when Bramwell Booth, then Chief of Staff, joined by W. T. Stead, the journalist, exposed the white-slave traffic in England and the Salvation Army secured signatures on a petition two miles long which, when presented to Parliament, stirred that legislative body into raising the legal age of consent for girls from thirteen to sixteen. In the United States the Salvation Army has not as an organization officially concerned itself with the great political battles of the country, even those such as woman's suffrage and prohibition, which the Army might be expected to favor strongly. This rule or tradition, of course, does not prevent officers from expressing themselves on the political or social issues of the day as individuals.

Sometimes the line between a moral issue, on which the Salvation Army feels compelled to express itself, and a political one is difficult to draw. In 1892 the *War Cry*, official organ of the Salvation Army in the United States, expressed itself editorially against opening the World's Fair on Sunday and in opposition to the presentation of the Oberammergau Passion Play at the fair on the grounds that it might create a desire in its observers to see other "less moral stage performances." It refused to back the candidates of the Prohibition party, however, but made clear its position on the "moral issue" of prohibition. "We have frequently been asked The Army's attitude to the Prohibition question. . . . While eschewing party politics, we must confess we look forward to the time when every drop of rum, whiskey and lager in the Union shall have been emptied into the right place—the gutter." Public misunderstanding of the Army's position on this question continued, and forty years later Evangeline Booth's fight against the repeal of prohibition brought a charge of political interference. The Army has a good record of avoiding partisan arguments, although it has been quick to take a stand on social and moral issues.

The Salvation Army not only took a stand against lynching in the editorial columns of the *War Cry*, but the personal courage of two of its officers made an even more effective protest against this barbaric crime. In 1895 a frightened Negro named Jim Bowens lay huddled in the jail at Frederick, Maryland, accused of the attempted assault of a white woman. Outside, a sullen mob was forcing its way in to lynch him. No voice was raised in his defense until Captain Eugene Mott and Lieutenant William Antrim of the Salvation Army pushed their way through the crowd and began to plead with the people to save the Negro's life. They were thrust aside, and Jim Bowens was seized. The Salvationists followed the mob to the scene of the lynching, and when it was evident they could do nothing to stop it they wormed their way to the Negro's side and asked to be allowed to pray with him. There in the eerie light they prayed for God's mercy on Jim Bowens's soul. As they repeated the familiar words of the Lord's Prayer, Jim Bowens repeated the words. In the crowd of three hundred lynchers and spectators standing with uncovered heads, others also joined in. The prayers over, the Negro, vowing his innocence, was strung up in a tree, and the officers returned to their barracks to pray for the souls of the lynchers as well as for that of their victim.

The social problems of a rapidly growing nation were also the problems of the Salvation Army, an American institution that was growing with the country. The physical aspect of that growth may be symbolized by the construction of the National Headquarters Memorial Building. The idea of a memorial to his mother was conceived by Ballington Booth after her death on October 4, 1890. Detailed reports of Catherine Booth's courageous fight with cancer had appeared in the *War Cry* throughout the year,[1] and when death finally came Salvationists all over the world felt a keen personal loss. The plan to honor the memory of the beloved Mother of the Salvation Army with a splendid new building seemed appropriate. The Headquarters Building at 111 Reade Street had proved to be too small within two years after it was first occupied in April, 1888, and more space was necessary for the growing departments of the Army.

Nearly five years of hard work elapsed before the Memorial Headquarters Building materialized. First, fund-raising committees were organized, and contributions began to come in. In May, 1893, the site for the building was secured. The property had a frontage of 75 feet on west Fourteenth Street some 200 feet west of Sixth Avenue—in all, about 12,000 square feet. The land was valued at $200,000, and the estimated cost of the building to be built was $80,000. An architect's drawing of the building appeared in the *War Cry* in June, 1894. After an older structure on the site was torn down, a cornerstone-laying ceremony was held on August 14, 1894. Work was being pushed on the interior construction of the building during General Booth's second visit to the United States, and the various departments began to move in from the old headquarters in May, 1895. On April 27th the last issue of the *War Cry* was printed at the old building, and the next week's issue came out—on time—from the new headquarters.

The dedication of the new National Headquarters Building as a memorial to Catherine Booth took place on June 3, 1895. The eight-story building at 120-124 west Fourteenth Street was gaily decked with bunting—red, white, and blue, mixed with the crimson and yellow representing the "Blood and Fire" of the Salvation Army. Some two thousand Salvationists paraded to the ceremony. The new building's final cost exceeded $350,000, including land. It resembled a castle in style, and was quite similar to the Armory across the street, which is still standing.[2] In the front of the building were two stores which could be rented for income, and in back of these was a meeting hall on the first floor that could seat 500 and an auditorium on the second floor with a capacity of 2,500. The remainder of the eight-floor building was used to house the printing plant and offices.

Although the construction of the new building coincided with a depression that had begun with the financial panic of 1893, funds continued to be contributed. The substantial financial support of the organization was an indication of the increasing prestige of the

Salvation Army in the United States. Commander Ballington Booth was aware of the dangers of popularity. "The Salvation Army in no sense desires to become respectable," he emphasized as he laid the cornerstone of the Headquarters Building. "We are not going to give up the ungloved hand for the kid glove; the drum for the church bell; the cornet for the piano or organ." But, despite the disavowal, the commander must have realized even as he spoke that the Salvation Army in the United States was becoming more respectable and less sensational. The most bitter persecutions had ceased, and occasional attacks by roughs were the unusual rather than the commonplace. In almost all places where the Army operated, the police protected it and the public officials were sympathetic. Even the newspapers were coming to the Army's support. As the *War Cry* observed in 1889, "A great change is noticeable in the attitude of American newspapers towards the Army. All the 'funny men' who used to write us up have apparently been dismissed. Serve 'em right. Anyway we get somewhat of a fair show in the columns of the dailies and weeklies now, for which we are thankful."

A New York *Tribune* of 1892 observed that public reaction to the Salvation Army had first been violent persecution, then a period of "contemptuous toleration." "The Army has lived through, or rather lived down, that era of contempt, almost worse than the former era of abuse, and today nearly all the people in and out of the churches whose opinion is worth anything frankly acknowledge the good it has done and is doing."

Two important factors in winning public support for the Army were Maud Booth's drawing-room meetings and the activities of the Auxiliary League. The Auxiliary League was begun by Major Moore in 1883, but not until Maud and Ballington Booth began to direct its operation did it become an effective means of winning friends and financial assistance for the Army. Subscribers to the League contributed $5 a year and were entitled to a year's subscription to the *War Cry*, a small badge to wear, and a ticket to all Salvation Army functions. They were asked to pray for the Army (at twelve-thirty each day if possible), defend the Army when they had an opportunity, and support it with gifts. Many ministers who were sympathetic with the work of the Army joined as Auxiliaries, and many socially prominent people were included in its ranks. The 2,000th Auxiliary was enrolled on November 14, 1893, and by 1896 the Auxiliaries numbered 6,000. Some of the prominent members were the Reverend Josiah Strong, the Reverend Lyman Abbott, Dr. Charles A. Briggs, Frances E. Willard, Edward Everett Hale, Mrs. Cleveland Dodge, Mrs. W. K. Vanderbilt, and Chauncey M. Depew.

Many of the recruits for Auxiliaries were drawn from Mrs. Booth's famous drawing-room meetings, remembered to this day by many of the older Army officers. The meetings, begun in 1888, were held in the homes of socially prominent people. The *War Cry*, in January, 1889, commented, "Mrs. Booth has been conducting some important drawing-room meetings in and around New York, and has more important engagements in Boston to fulfill of the same character." By February, 1889, the meetings were attracting the attention of the major New York daily newspapers. Three thousand invitations were printed for a meeting at Y.M.C.A. Hall in New York conducted by Mrs. Booth. "As the meeting is strictly for the class Mrs. Booth has lately been reaching in her drawing-room meetings," the *War Cry* warned, "the invitations will be restricted to them alone."

One of the most outstanding drawing-room meetings was held in Washington in the home of John Wanamaker, Postmaster General of the United States. It was attended by Mrs. Benjamin Harrison, the wives of several Cabinet members, and some Senators and Congressmen. At the meetings Maud Booth, dressed in her uniform, quietly explained the aims and objectives of the Salvation Army, and described its work in the slums. "Help us to lift them up!" was her plea. From such meetings and from the Auxiliaries much of the money for the Memorial Building was obtained. Mrs. Booth became a celebrity and perhaps something of a fad among the society of the East. She was invited to Wellesley College and given a warm welcome there. Frances E. Willard, president of the Women's Christian Temperance Union, invited her to address the national conference of that organization at Atlanta, Georgia, in 1890. Even more remarkable, while Maud Booth was raising money and winning friends through her drawing-room meetings she was at the same time directing the Army's slum work and visiting prisons.

Coinciding with the increase of popularity of the Salvation Army in the United States were the introduction and development of the Army's social welfare program. Public interest in this branch of the Army's program ran high, and the slum work brought with it more favorable newspaper publicity and increased public support. The social work in the slums was the major topic of the drawing-room lecture; nevertheless, while this aspect of the Army's work was emphasized to the general public, the officers and soldiers were never permitted to forget the primary mission of the Army—saving souls.

X

"In His Steps"

In 1897 the Reverend Charles M. Sheldon, of Topeka, Kansas, published *In His Steps: "What Would Jesus Do?"*—a book that became one of the best sellers of the next generation and that is still popular today. For seventeen years before Sheldon wrote his novel, the Salvation Army had been working in the slums of American cities. Although their first efforts were devoted mainly to the spiritual welfare of the poor, it soon became obvious that preaching was not enough. Salvationists discovered many years before Sheldon's book that if they were to follow "in His steps" they must minister to the physical as well as to the spiritual welfare of their congregations.

In March, 1880, when "Ash-barrel Jimmy"—a homeless tramp —became the Army's first convert in the United States, he was permitted to sleep in the hall after meetings, in return for which he kept the place swept out and clean. It was not just charity that the Salvation Army dispensed. There were already many charity organizations in America. The Salvation Army offered its helping hand to anyone who wanted to rehabilitate himself; but, more than this, Salvationists worked to give those who had no hope the desire to help themselves. This belief that only a person who wants help can be benefited is the basis of all Salvation Army social activities and a principle of modern scientific social work. Salvationists believe that to give a destitute man assistance without trying to reach

96

and cure the cause of his poverty may result in more harm than good.

Even then, the Salvation Army refused to make the distinction commonly accepted at the time between the so-called "deserving" and the "undeserving" poor. In their eyes all men were deserving of help. Had not Jesus Christ died for the Salvation of all men? This was the message that these soldiers of Christ dispensed along with soup and soap, shelter and clothing. To be sure, if a man did not wish to help himself, there was little of lasting value that could be done for him. But as long as there were life and hope in a man, he might be convinced to let Christ guide his life and then he would help himself. And who was qualified to judge whether a man was "deserving" or "undeserving" of help? Not the Salvation Army.

The Army's social service had a dramatic beginning. General Booth was crossing London late one night in 1888, when something he saw cost him a night's sleep and ultimately set in motion the Salvation Army's program of social work. When his son Bramwell came to see him the next morning, the General was half dressed and pacing the room. "Bramwell, did you know that men slept out all night on the bridges?" Bramwell knew but what could be done? "Go and do something!" was the command. "We *must* do something! Get them a shelter. Get hold of a warehouse and warm it, and find something to cover them." That such a project would cost money did not trouble the General. Men were sleeping outdoors —in the cold—on stone bridges. Something must be done! This was the beginning of Salvation Army Shelters.

In 1888 a cheap Food Depot was established in Limehouse where thousands of hungry people went for meals, and within two and a half years three more depots were in operation in other parts of London.

A Rescue Home for "fallen women"—predecessor to America's present Homes and Hospitals for Unwed Mothers—was opened in 1884 under the direction of Mrs. Bramwell Booth. In the same year a Woman's Rescue Home was opened and Prison Gate Rescue Work was commenced in Australia. Wherever a need was discovered, the Salvation Army set out to "do something." Slowly the tradition developed that wherever there was human suffering it was the duty of the Salvation Army to help alleviate it. No elaborate theory preceded the development of Salvation Army social work. Like Topsy, the structure of social institutions and services "just grew."

Salvation Army social work was brought forcibly to the attention of the general public when General Booth's book *In Darkest England and the Way Out* appeared in 1890. Capitalizing on the interest aroused by Stanley's famous *In Darkest Africa*, which was popular at the time, the book contained dramatic descriptions of the poverty, misery, and vice of *Englishmen* living in the slums of England's largest cities. According to Booth's figures, three million people—"the submerged tenth"—of Britain's population were homeless, starving, criminals, or inmates of state institutions, as ignorant, superstitious, hopeless, and hungry as any savage in "Darkest Africa!"

How long would Englishmen ignore these conditions? How long would they look away from the homeless wretches who slept on the bridges across the Thames, the growing number of prostitutes, the poverty of the unemployed? When would the churches learn, as William Booth and the Salvation Army had learned, that a hungry man will instinctively think about his stomach more than about his soul? "What a satire it is upon our Christianity and our civilization, that the existence of these colonies of heathens and savages in the heart of our capital should attract so little attention. . . . Why all this apparatus of temples and meeting-houses to save men from perdition in a world which is to come, while never a helping hand is stretched out to save them from the inferno of their present life?" challenged General Booth.

The book was written by journalist William T. Stead, who put the General's detailed notes and ideas into a vigorous prose. The title was arresting, the style clear and direct and, most of all, the timing of the book was perfect. The plight of the English working classes had been troubling serious minds, and now *In Darkest*

England described in dreadful detail the social evils of the day. One of its prime achievements was to shock the respectable middle class out of its complacency.

In addition to this, William Booth had a solution—he offered to point *the way out*. William Booth's plan was not Utopian. "I leave to others the formulation of ambitious programmes for the reconstruction of our entire social system," he stated. His "scheme," as it was called, was to begin at once; in fact it was already under way on a small scale. The minimum standard he proposed to achieve was dramatized by the illustration of a London cab horse. When the horse fell down it was helped up, given shelter for the night, food for its stomach, and, finally, work was allotted by which it could earn its grain. This was the essence of William Booth's plan for men—help them to their feet and supply shelter, food, and work. To carry out this objective three communities or colonies were planned: a City Colony to gather the destitute and give them temporary aid; a Farm Colony to train colonists in agriculture; and Overseas Colonies in South Africa, Canada, Australia, or other places where land was plentiful and cheap. The Salvation Army, Booth pointed out, had the machinery for carrying out such a plan and in fact was already at work on it. The scale on which it could operate depended only on public support. Booth called for £100,000 to begin the scheme. Four months later—February, 1891 —he had received £108,000, and by September, 1892, the sum had increased to £129,288 12s. 6d.

After 1890 and the publication of *In Darkest England*, social work was begun on a large scale by the Salvation Army—in the United States as in Great Britain. Social work here had begun on a modest scale several years earlier, when the first of a vast network of social institutions operated by the Salvation Army in the United States was begun in New York City in a frame building three floors high, known as Morris Cottage. The "Cottage" was open in October, 1886, when a notice of its opening, together with an appeal for contributions in money or of parcels of clothing appeared in the *War Cry*. The October 23rd issue carried a story of "Our

First Rescue Home in America," and a picture of Morris Cottage appeared on November 6, 1886, together with the following notice:

The Rescue Home for the fallen and the falling is now opened for young women who desire and are earnestly seeking the salvation of their bodies and souls. All Christians and friends desiring further information or willing to help on this important undertaking in these earliest days of its need are invited to communicate with the Commissioner.

The work with "fallen women" was directed by Maud Booth after she and Ballington Booth assumed the command of the Salvation Army in the United States in April, 1887. Week after week the *War Cry* contained an appeal "For the Rescue Home." A sewing machine was requested, and the receipt of one was acknowledged in the column. "Officers having any of these dear girls saved at their meeting, or being appealed to by any such to save them from their lives of sin, should (if satisfied of their reality and anxiety to be good) beg their fare from friends and send them to us. . . . A loving welcome and happy home awaits them."

Every effort was made to maintain a home-like atmosphere. Rules were kept to a minimum, and the girls were always free to leave. Training in cooking, sewing, and other household tasks was offered, and girls who were deemed reformed were found positions as domestic helpers or maids in Christian homes. Constant effort was expended to help the girls experience conversion, for it was believed that only this would ensure their permanent reformation.

Rescue work on the West Coast began in April, 1887, under the supervision of Mrs. Brigadier Fielding. A year later two homes, one in Oakland and one in San Francisco, were in operation. About sixteen nights in a month, Salvation Army lassies went out into the depths of the Barbary Coast to rescue any of its inhabitants if they could. Periodic visits were made to the county jail in San Francisco where women inmates were offered the sanctuary of the rescue home when their sentences expired. In 1888 a Michigan Rescue Home was opened in Grand Rapids.

Meanwhile, work in the slums was moving forward in New

York City, where a "Garret, Dive and Tenement Brigade" was in operation as early as March, 1889. Salvation Army slum work in the United States is closely associated with the name of Emma Jane Bown. The captain (later the first woman brigadier in the United States) was a lassie from Liverpool who joined the Salvation Army, went through the Training Home in England, and was sent to America to reinforce Commissioner Frank Smith after the "Moore split." At Taunton, Massachusetts, she was arrested for beating the drum during a wave of persecution. In the trial that followed, the plucky English lass, defended by an able volunteer lawyer, won the respect and admiration of the town. The "not guilty" verdict was an important victory for the Army. By 1889, with five years of service in the United States, Captain Bown had served in Boston, Shenandoah and Plymouth, Pennsylvania, and had directed the "Lyceum Training Garrison for female cadets" in Brooklyn. After that year, her whole life during a long career in the Salvation Army was devoted to social work.

In August, 1889, Emma Jane Bown and another girl traded their blue and crimson uniforms and bonnets for patched rough gowns, gingham aprons, shawls, and ancient hats and took a room in the heart of Manhattan's notorious Cherry Hill district. Never identifying themselves with the Salvation Army for fear of alienating those they sought to serve, these women lived a truly Spartan existence. Their room was as void of luxuries as the rooms of their neighbors, with cleanliness its only distinguishing characteristic. Each day the two "Slum Sisters" or "Slum Saviours" or "Angels of the Slums" (they were called by various names in the press, although the official designation was Slum Officers) went out to visit the tenement families in the neighborhood. In simple ways they won the confidence of the wretched victims of the slums. They bathed and cared for children, nursed the sick and the aged, and spoke words of cheer and hope to all.

Thus slum work, while never conducted on a large scale, became an important phase of the Salvation Army's activities. Slum Officers without uniforms or brass bands were able to aid people that even corps officers could not reach. The slum problem was so critical that none but the most calloused could ignore it. Jacob Riis, in a series of books beginning with *How the Other Half Lives* (1890) and *The Children of the Poor* (1892), hammered at the public conscience; journalists "exposed" the conditions of the slums; government officials "investigated" them—but the Salvation Army went into the slums and really worked to make them better. The work was well publicized by the press, and helped to bring about the public approval and increase in financial support that characterized the 1890's.

In March, 1890, a Day Nursery or "Salvation Army Crèche" was established in connection with the slum work in New York City. At the end of a year of slum work in Manhattan, six Slum Sisters were active. During the year they had visited 5,500 families, assisted 613 families with food, and supplied 942 persons with clothing; 777 babies were cared for in the nursery from 7:00 A.M. to 6:30 P.M. Sixteen conversions were reported.

Salvation Army social work in the United States was given a real impetus by the publication of General Booth's *In Darkest England and the Way Out*. The first Food and Shelter Depot was established in an old church building at Bedford and Downing streets in New York in December, 1891. A second depot was founded in 1893 in Buffalo, where Auxiliaries furnished funds for the institution. The first cheap lodginghouse or Salvation Army Hotel in the United States was also established during the administration of Ballington Booth. The program was carried to completion under the direction of his successor, Booth-Tucker.

"Work for the workless" was one of the many mottoes of Commander Frederick de Lautour Booth-Tucker. Soon after he assumed command in the United States, men with pushcarts were sent out to collect paper and salvageable junk. At first the basement of the Dry Dock Hotel on Avenue D, in New York City, was used as a depot, but by 1897 the Salvage Corps was moved to the rear of 26 Cherry Street. By 1898 the Army had eight salvage depots and five woodyards.

This activity proved to be an immediate success. Its philosophy was simple. "The Army does not waste either precious time or precious money inquiring into character," wrote Lieutenant Colonel William Brewer in 1898. "It divides the people into two classes only, the willing and unwilling to work. Wherever it finds the willing, to the limit of its capacity, the Army gives them employment." The Salvage Brigade aimed to furnish employment in unskilled labor for a large number of men to tide them over until they secured regular employment. Men could earn their lodging and food at the salvage depot, and a small wage by collecting waste paper, lumber, furniture, rags, clothing, and other articles which were sold to make the project self-supporting. The main difficulty was in acquiring capital to provide buildings and to purchase horses and wagons.

Public cooperation was an important factor in the success of the Salvage Brigades. In Boston, baskets were placed in five hundred homes and periodically emptied. The Army contracted with the City of Chicago to keep several of the city's wards free of waste paper. The waste paper and cast-off articles collected were not the most important material salvaged by the Salvation Army, for the main object of the Salvage Brigades and their successors—the Industrial Homes and later the Men's Social Service Centers—was the salvage of *men*, who were given an opportunity to regain a position as useful members of society.

In some cities woodyards were established for the same purpose. The unemployed were put to work collecting, sawing, and delivering wood. One of the first of these was in Waterbury, Connecticut. Others were operated in Boston, Houston, San Francisco, and Seattle.

An important auxiliary of the Salvage Brigades was the Salvation Junk Shop. Situated in or near slum districts, these stores sold secondhand clothes at nominal prices, and in cases of extreme need gave away clothing. Generally, shoes were repaired, clothing mended, and furniture renewed and sold at prices within the reach of the slum families.

Another in the growing structure of agencies devoted to the service of mankind was the Labor Bureau or Employment Agency. These not only found more permanent jobs for the men working in the Salvage Brigades and woodyards but served others of the un-employed group as well.

After Commander Booth-Tucker spent a night in disguise in one of New York's flophouses, he was a strong advocate of the Salvation Army's economical hotels, which furnished clean, warm shelters at moderate prices. Dormitory beds with mattress, pillow, sheets, and blankets were available for ten cents, while fifteen cents would secure a separate room. In addition, hot and cold baths and delousing facilities were available (usually required before registration), as well as washtubs and reading rooms. While most of these shelters were for homeless men, several others were op-erated for homeless women. Inexpensive hotels for working girls were operated in many cities for the growing number of young women who left home to work in stores and offices. In connection with many of these institutions, cheap food depots provided whole-some food at prices within the reach of the patrons. In other lo-calities, "cent meals" were offered. For a penny, a person could obtain a pint of coffee with a chunk of bread or a basin of soup which he could consume there or take home to eat.

The first of the Salvation Army's homes for children was opened on February 22, 1897, in Fordham, New York, and later moved to Rutherford, New Jersey. It was called the Cherry Tree Home, a name suggested to Consul Booth-Tucker by Mrs. Grover Cleveland, who thought it appropriate because the home was opened on Washington's birthday. By the turn of the century two orphanages were operated by the Salvation Army, one near New York and the other near San Francisco—later to become the Lyt-ton Home and School, and still in operation. Unlike many other institutions, these could not be self-supporting, and limited funds prevented their extension.

A Slum Maternity Nursing system was organized in 1897, and a training home secured in the following year. At "The Pines" in Fordham, Salvation Army nurses were given a thorough theoreti-cal training which was followed by a practical course under the guidance of experienced nurses in the field. Prominent physicians gave courses and lectures at the schools.

Less formal activities were also part of the social relief program. Summer outings gave slum children and their mothers a day of relief from the oppressive heat of the city. Penny ice wagons and penny cold drinks were another popular form of summer relief. In the winter, heated Salvation Army halls were thrown open to people during prolonged spells of extreme cold.

All these Salvation Army services were offered, not as charity, but always as a means of aiding the recipient to help himself. Sensitive to the danger of pauperizing those it aided, the Army's general rule was to require payment in labor or cash for its services. Even the low prices and the small amount of labor required enabled many whose pride balked at taking charity to receive the Army's helping hand and to retain their self-respect. The major exceptions to this rule were the Christmas and Thanksgiving dinners. At these seasons large auditoriums were secured in the major cities and luxurious dinners were served to the needy. Basket dinners, distributed to carefully selected families, enabled others to enjoy the holiday in their own homes.

Thus the Salvation Army social program came to minister to the needy of all ages from the cradle to the grave—from slum maternity care to homes for indigent aged. By the turn of the century the basic outline of the vast social program of the Salvation Army was clear. As the twentieth century dawned, the Army, described by England's Cardinal Manning as the "only considerable body of Christians who had a passion for sinners as such," saw all gradations of the poor benefit from their pioneer efforts as "the Army's example of heroic self-sacrifice encouraged Protestant Christianity to redouble its efforts for the social salvation of men."

XI

The Great Schism

The prospects of the Salvation Army and its young leaders in the United States never appeared brighter than on New Year's Day, 1896. General William Booth had received wide acclaim during his visit to America; the new National Headquarters Building on west Fourteenth Street, New York, symbolized the material progress of the organization; tributes from newspapers, churchmen, and civic leaders showed that the Army had won the respect of the American public.

Yet under the surface forces of dissension were at work. Suddenly, in January, 1896, the Salvation Army in the United States was shaken to its foundations by the resignation of Maud and Ballington Booth and the controversy that accompanied it. For several months newspapers and magazines all over the country featured the story; mass meetings and protest parades were held. The question of who was to command the Salvation Army in America aroused national interest. Nothing, perhaps, could have better illustrated how the Army had grown in prestige and importance. As the Detroit *Evening News* observed, "It is less than 20 years ago that the 'Salvation Army' consisted of a small group of religious 'fanatics' here and there, whose principal business seemed to be to amuse a godless world and stir the contempt of the traditional godly ones. Today the displacement of an officer in that Army is a thing to be talked of and its significance to be debated around the world."

Like each of the national commanders who preceded them, Maud and Ballington Booth had taken out American citizenship papers when they were assigned to the United States, and after completing residents' requirements they became naturalized American citizens. That they liked and understood the country of their adoption is evident; much of their success in winning public esteem and support from Americans of all levels of society may be credited to their understanding and appreciation of the unique American temperament. To the general public Maud and Ballington Booth personified the Salvation Army. Within the Army they were loved and respected by Salvationists of all ranks.

It came as a shock to Salvationists and the general public alike when the New York *Sun* announced on January 15, 1896: "Commander Ballington Booth and his wife have been recalled from the command of the Salvation Army in the United States. In the phraseology of the Army they have been 'ordered to farewell. . . .'" This news was printed under the headlines:

RECALL OF THE BOOTHS,

The Commander and His Wife
"Ordered to Farewell."

A Story that Gen. Booth Thinks They Have Made the Salvation Army Too American and Wishes to Anglicize It Again.

This announcement in the public press was the first hint either to American Salvationists or to the general public that a change of command of the Salvation Army in the United States was contemplated. Many bewildered New Yorkers who were members or friends of the Army hurried to the National Headquarters Building for information. On the first-floor bulletin board was "A Statement from the Commander and Mrs. Booth." The news was true!

It was unfortunate that this announcement of greatest importance to Salvationists should reach them through the public press more than two weeks before the news appeared in the official *War Cry*, and that coupled with it was the charge that General Booth was attempting to "Anglicize" the American branch of the Army.

The order to farewell or to relinquish their command had been received by Ballington and Maud Booth as a complete surprise on January 6th. Four days later Ballington wrote to London questioning the wisdom of requiring him to leave the United States and asking if International Headquarters had taken into consideration all the consequences of a change of command at the time. He mentioned the tense situation between the United States and England over the Venezuela dispute; the heavy financial responsibility of the new Headquarters Building; and his own strained relations with his father, the General, from whom he had not heard in six months. According to their testimony, he and Maud wrote other letters following this, stating they were preparing to fulfill their orders and to relinquish their command.

For several days the Booths told no one of the order they had received. Then they called several high-ranking officers together and told them of the order and their decision to obey it. The officers wanted to protest the recall but were forbidden to do so by Ballington. It was decided to wait a few days before making the announcement to the Army, but before the official announcement was made the news leaked out to the press.

Official notice of the farewell order appeared in the *War Cry* of February 1st, accompanied by an editorial entitled "Our Devoted Leaders Relinquish Their Command," in which the progress of Maud and Ballington's administration was summarized. The editorial ended with the statement:

There is only one thing to do when marching orders arrive and that is to spring into readiness to obey. The Commander announces that he is already preparing to convey Army properties in this country to his successors when his name shall have been made known. Thus are our leaders getting ready to put into practice the spirit of the same rule and regulation that they have required of their subordinates. What an object lesson to the world of fidelity to principle!

In the meantime, during the interval from the time the order to move appeared in the newspapers and the announcement in the *War Cry*, the American public had rallied to protest what ap-

peared to be an act of "British tyranny." According to the daily
newspapers, the General had been angry when his son and Maud
became American citizens. On his tour of the United States the
year before, he had been displeased by the "Americanization" of
the Army and was determined that "every Country should be under English rule." American nationalism ran high, and the rela-
tively simple issue of replacing a Salvation Army commander became entangled with the irrational but powerful emotion of
patriotism.

A public protest was organized by a group of prominent and
wealthy New Yorkers who were members of the Salvation Army
Auxiliary League. They drafted a letter which said, in part, "An
effort is being made by members of the Auxiliary League of the
Salvation Army and others to bring such pressure of public opinion
to bear upon the subject of the recall of Commander Ballington
Booth and Mrs. Booth from America as will induce General Booth
to reconsider their order to farewell." Carnegie Hall was secured for a mass meeting on Monday, February 3rd, to express
public opinion on the subject. The letter was signed by many
prominent people who had aided in the construction of the Memorial Building and who were strong supporters and heavy contributors to the Army.

Carnegie Hall was crowded for the protest meeting. Chauncey
M. Depew presided with his usual store of wit and wisdom. Mayor
William L. Strong of New York canceled a meeting in Albany to
attend and to give a short speech. Among the clergymen who spoke
were Josiah Strong, Bishop E. G. Andrews, A. H. Bradford, and
R. Fulton Cutting, while William E. Dodge read letters of support
from Frances E. Willard, Lyman Abbott, Smith Agnew, John Fulton, and others. A petition to General Booth requesting that Ballington and Mrs. Booth be allowed to remain in America was unanimously adopted. In his speech, Chauncey M. Depew, noting that
Ballington Booth and his wife had become naturalized American
citizens, jokingly suggested that we assert the Monroe Doctrine on
their behalf, a suggestion that brought "cheers, laughter, and prolonged applause."

The international situation did play a part in the controversy, and the Monroe Doctrine was involved. Anti-English feeling in the United States in 1895 and 1896 was at a height over the Venezuela boundary dispute. The dispute itself was one of long standing between Venezuela and British Guiana. England refused to arbitrate the matter. When Secretary of State Richard Olney sent a strong request for arbitration of the dispute, which he said concerned the Monroe Doctrine, the British Government replied, after a delay of four months, that it could not accept this interpretation of the Monroe Doctrine. Again it refused to arbitrate. President Cleveland was "mad clear through." On December 17, 1895, he sent a message to Congress that in effect asked the United States to run the boundary line itself and if necessary fight to maintain it. Congress responded by voting the appropriation for a commission promptly and with great enthusiasm. A wave of jingoistic patriotism swept the country, and talk of war became common. With diplomatic relations between the United States and England thus strained almost to the breaking point, the news was made public that the English General of the Salvation Army proposed to remove the naturalized American Commander of the Salvation Army in the United States.

While the American press deplored their recall and public protest meetings were held, Maud and Ballington Booth prepared to relinquish their command. They felt the order to farewell was unwise and unjust, but there is no evidence to indicate that they ever contemplated disobedience. In a joint letter that appeared in the *War Cry* of February 8, 1896, the last notice written by them to be printed in that paper, they declared, "We, who have required obedience from others, are ourselves obeying. We are, therefore, carrying out the instructions we have received, and shall be ready to resign our Command at the appointed time or sooner, if necessary." Carnegie Hall was secured, and a farewell celebration was planned.

While Ballington and Maud Booth were willing and ready to relinquish their command as ordered, they were unwilling to accept another command, for a number of reasons. These reasons they stated in a letter dated January 31, 1896, addressed to Bramwell Booth, who was both Chief of Staff and Ballington's brother, sixteen months his elder. The family relationship is important. Bramwell appears to have been imperious and tactless both in his method of issuing the farewell order and during the controversy that followed. The General was in India, out of direct contact with either Bramwell or Ballington when the order was issued and for several weeks after the disagreement developed. When he did return to London the situation was beyond his control. What might have remained a family quarrel had been aired before the whole Salvation Army and the world, and bitter words had been spoken from which the sting could never be extracted.

In their letter of January 31st, Ballington and Maud plainly stated their position. They declared their intention of relinquishing their command as quickly and as quietly as possible and then retiring from the Salvation Army. The principal reason that they felt they could not conscientiously accept another command was estrangement from the General. Certain actions and incidents of his visit to the United States in 1894-1895 had caused them to lose confidence in him and had alienated their affection from him. They listed still other reasons: for four or five years they had been left out of consultation on international policy; they objected to the number of rules and "red tape" commissioners were required to enforce without being consulted about making; and they complained that social work was being pushed to the detriment of spiritual work. Their course, they declared, was "to obey your orders and resign our command, and then as quickly and as expeditiously as possible, retire."

They proposed to farewell and to say nothing of their future intentions so that their plans would not become public, and they especially urged that no member of the family be sent to try to talk them out of their decision. "It must not be said at any time that we left the Army because we were unwilling to leave America," they wrote. "This would be untrue as we have made no remonstrance, nor have we refused." Perhaps they were thinking of the Moore schism when they further wrote: "We have not taken advantage of the confidence of the troops and the public and retained this command, though, undoubtedly, many would have thought it the wisest for the country and the Army here. . . . If we can avoid it, not a man shall leave. We shall be glad if you will have your new Commissioners early on the ground, as we do not want a prolongation of this unsettlement for the troops or for ourselves."

As soon as this letter reached London, Colonel Alex M. Nicol was dispatched to the United States to attempt to persuade the Booths to reconsider. Nicol arrived in New York on February 15, 1896. He was quick to see that American feeling had been aroused by the newspaper reports of the order to recall the Booths and that the full weight of public opinion was on their side. As a person outside the family, Colonel Nicol was in a position to talk with the Booths with as little emotion as possible. He entered objectively into his job as mediator and he succeeded in getting Ballington to agree to go to London and talk with his brother Bramwell before making a final decision to leave the Army. At this point a cable arrived saying that Ballington's young sister, Evangeline Booth, was on her way to America to affect a reconciliation. This news undid all of Nicol's work. From that time on, Ballington showed no interest in further discussing the questions at issue.

The crisis was brought to a head during the week of February 19th to 24th. Herbert Booth arrived on the scene from Canada. It was an open secret in the Army that he was slated to succeed to the command of the United States. The newspapers reported that he was "eagerly desirous" of obtaining the position held by Ballington. His participation in the dispute only increased the ill feeling that had been generated and cost him whatever chance he might have had of becoming an acceptable leader to the Americans. Evangeline arrived soon after Herbert, the last of the principals of the drama to reach New York.

On Thursday afternoon, February 20th, Ballington and Maud, Herbert and Evangeline Booth and Colonel Nicol met at a fatefully critical conference. It is impossible to know what actually was said at this meeting, so greatly do the reported versions vary.

The important fact is that after a long and heated discussion, Ballington and Maud left the meeting and spent the night clearing their personal belongings out of their office in the Headquarters Building. In the early hours of the morning they placed their keys on their desks and left the building. They believed and maintained that Herbert Booth had ordered them by virtue of authority from International Headquarters to turn over their command and their keys by a certain deadline. The other participants of the meeting later publicly denied that any such ultimatum had been given. The Booths believed that they had been so ordered, however, and acted as though they had been.

Ballington Booth appeared in Salvation Army Headquarters just twice after handing over his keys. Two days later, on Sunday, he was present at a meeting held in his office on the fourth floor. Among those reported to have attended were Evans, Fielding, Stillwell, Taylor, Marshall, Damon, Eadie, and Nicol. Nicol left the meeting and posted a notice that the General had appointed Emma and Frederick St. George de Lautour Booth-Tucker to succeed Ballington Booth.

On the following day Ballington again came to Headquarters. The public press reported only that he had been urged to lead a revolt and had refused. This must have been the meeting described by Nicol and mentioned in a recent biography of Evangeline Booth, in which he relates that Ballington had promised before he left on Sunday that he would return the next day. A number of officers— Nicol puts the figure at ninety—were ready to follow Ballington if he would declare the Army in America independent of International Headquarters. Ballington would have been less than human if he had not been pleased by this appeal from his close friends and comrades. Yet there is no evidence to show that Ballington and Maud Booth ever actively planned to lead a secession movement. Had they been willing to be persuaded, the meeting on February 24th would have been the time.

The situation looked serious enough to cause Nicol to call for Evangeline Booth, who was ill and resting in her room after the nervous strain of the past few days. She rose and with Nicol proceeded to the fourth floor of the Headquarters Building where she was refused admission. Nicol knew the building, and led her up a fire escape and on to the floor where she dramatically appeared in a room where the officers were waiting for a decision from Ballington, who was then in another room with the leaders of the secession movement. Evangeline begged for a hearing and then, with her simple eloquence and personal charm, won the support of the group.

Had Ballington Booth taken a strong stand, and proclaimed his intention to reconstruct the Salvation Army in the United States as an independent, incorporated organization, Nicol declared, "There can be no doubt that the eloquence of Miss Booth would have been as water spilt on the ground." But he did not, and when he did begin a new movement he and Maud publicly declared, "We have not sought to call to our side any of the associates still standing and believing in the International Organization." [1] Evangeline was tactful enough to offer forgiveness to the officers who had contemplated secession, and nearly all of them were glad to remain with the Salvation Army.

Although the danger of a major split was past, Evangeline Booth and the Salvation Army faced many problems. The press was indignant at the treatment of Ballington, and urged him to start a new organization. The New York *Tribune* observed, "The dismissal of Commander Ballington Booth and Mrs. Booth . . . will seriously weaken the organization in its work, at least for a time, and alienate from it the sympathy and support of many outside of it, who will conclude, whether rightly or wrongly, that Ballington Booth and his devoted wife have been the victims of petty jealousy and persecution."

Adverse press reaction and alienated public support were of great importance to the Salvation Army, however, because it depended on the public for much of its financial support. Almost all of the Auxiliary League, composed of wealthy and influential friends of the Army, supported Ballington Booth. One newspaper estimated that they numbered about six thousand and contributed from $30,000 to $40,000 a year to the organization.

In this time of crisis, the Salvation Army was fortunate in having at the scene a temporary commander of the caliber of Miss Evangeline Booth. Her first public appearance in the United States was on Sunday, March 1st. Cooper Union was jammed for the event. For several weeks the Salvation Army had been featured in all of the metropolitan papers, and Evangeline had been characterized as a "minion of British despotism." Foes as well as friends crowded into Cooper Union. When the daughter of the General arose to speak, boos and hisses drowned her voice. Hostile crowds were not a novelty to this thirty-one-year-old veteran, and with the quickness of mind and of action that characterized all the Booths she seized an American flag and waved it above her head. "Hiss that, if you dare!" she said. The crowd was silenced. Evangeline spoke, and a victory was won.

What, after the smoke and heat of discord have waned, were the issues behind this controversy? Perhaps the unhappiest aspect of the controversy was the family quarrel. But the family issue was not the only one. Underlying both the Moore schism and the Ballington Booth controversy was the question of polity. The General of the Salvation Army was more powerful in his organization than was the Roman pope, for he could choose his own successor and his fiat was law to Salvationists in every country in the world. William Booth—as Founder—was strong enough to make this system work, but his successor was not so fortunate. At a High Council in 1929, in harmony with the 1904 supplementary Deed Poll, the General was elected and the principle of election established. Ballington Booth could foresee the future more accurately than his father. As he stated to Nicol at the height of the controversy:

A grave fundamental principle separates me from the International Headquarters. Long experience on this continent has taught me that England does not understand America any more than America understands England. Yet we are being governed as if America was part of England. It is true that we speak the same language, pay homage to the same literature, and profess the same religion; but there is as much difference between the American and the English nation as there is between the French and German. The one subject that separates me in spirit from my father, as General, is the system that he persists in developing to the detriment of the work in America. . . . I have no quarrel against Mr. Bramwell Booth. He is a gentleman, a competent executive officer, an able administrator, a man of vast experience in handling men, and he is a loyal son and soldier to his father and General. He is a thorough system-worker. But mark this: it is not the system-worker I object to, it is the system, and the author and upholder of that system is my father. My quarrel is with him, and *if he is not compelled to admit the despotism of his system before he passes away his successors will live to curse it.**

This astonishing prediction, made in 1896, was quoted in a book published in 1911, eighteen years before the fateful High Council finally changed the system of appointing succeeding Generals.

On the other hand, once the order to farewell had been given, the General could hardly compromise. If he were to insist on the transfer of some twenty commissioners who did not bear his name, and then permit his son to keep his post in the United States, it would be a justification of the charges of nepotism that were frequently hurled at the Army. To have recognized the demands of nationalism in the case of the United States and Ballington Booth would have seriously weakened and perhaps destroyed the General's vision of a truly international organization—independent of family influence, governed by one code of commands, no respector of person or country, and determined to be in reality world-wide in its unity—with one faith, one aim, one flag, and one General.

The controversy is a tragic chapter in the history of the Salvation Army. It was a personal tragedy for the General, who lost a son; it was unfortunate for the Salvation Army, which lost the services of two talented and able leaders. For Ballington and Maud Booth it was a bitter experience that cut them off from family and from old comrades in an organization they had faithfully served and helped to build. But unhappy as it was, the controversy served to strengthen rather than to weaken the Salvation Army. As Wil-

* Italics added.

THE PIONEER PARTY IN NEW YORK, MARCH 10, 1880

Major Thomas E. Moore

MAJOR FRANK SMITH

COMMANDER BALLINGTON BOOTH

MAUD BALLINGTON BOOTH

COMMANDER FREDERICK BOOTH-TUCKER

"The Consul," Emma Booth-Tucker

COMMANDER EVANGELINE BOOTH

liam Booth wrote in reply to a question from the *Independent*
about the controversy, "The late events have forced all our officers
and soldiers to ask themselves why they follow the flag and the result has already been a greatly deepened resolve to devote themselves to a fuller consecration than ever to the Christ-like task of
seeking the salvation of the whole world."

XII

Healing the Breach

The new commanders of the Salvation Army in the United States were courageous soldiers in the Salvation War. Emma Booth-Tucker sailed for America with two small children, leaving a third—a sick infant—behind in England in the care of a nurse. The thirty-six-year-old woman who was the fourth child and second daughter of General William Booth was known as "The Consul." Her husband, Frederick St. George de Lautour Booth-Tucker, followed her on another ship and reached New York on April 1, 1896, four days after his wife. Here he learned of the death of his six-week-old infant son who had been left behind. The administration of the Booth-Tuckers had begun as it was to end—with death and sorrow.

Frederick St. George de Lautour Tucker had been born forty-three years earlier in Bengal, India, the son of a commissioner in the Indian Civil Service. Young Tucker was educated in England at Cheltenham College and entered the Indian civil service himself, rising to the position of assistant commissioner. In 1881 he gave up his position to join the Salvation Army and to begin its missionary work in India.

In India, Tucker and a small band from England adopted native dress and moved into the native quarters to live with the Indians as equals instead of preaching to them as Europeans. The representatives of Her Majesty's Imperial Government were horrified by this action, and set about to prevent it. Fined and jailed

time and again, Tucker persisted in preaching Christ to the various castes of India in their own language. He became Fakir Singh
who lived on a native diet, walked barefoot from village to village,
and everywhere won converts for Christ and for the Salvation
Army. From the pioneer party of four officers who landed in Bombay in September, 1882, the Salvation Army in India grew to 479
officers at 250 stations and outposts; 3,666 converts were enrolled
as soldiers before Booth-Tucker left India in 1891.

This intrepid missionary became Booth-Tucker in 1888 when
he married Emma Moss Booth and, following the practice of all
the men who married into the Booth family, adopted the hy-
phenated surname.[1] When the ill health of his wife forced them
both to leave India in 1891, he was appointed Foreign Secretary
of the Salvation Army in charge of the entire work of the Army
outside the United Kingdom. This was the position he was holding when the crisis of 1896 made it necessary for the General to
send the most outstanding officer available to assume command of
the Salvation Army in the United States. He made a wise choice in
Frederick Booth-Tucker and the Consul.

Commander Booth-Tucker was not long in showing the American public that he was like his predecessor—a newsworthy personality. A man of striking appearance, he was also a successful
speaker.

Booth-Tucker had not been in New York a month before he
was the subject of a newspaper story. The new commander of the
Salvation Army set out one night in disguise to see for himself the
slums of New York. Rumor had it that the commander was recognized by his flowing gray-blond locks at a seven-cent lodginghouse
where he went to spend the night, and was thrown out. Booth-
Tucker's own story of his first tour of New York's slums was
printed as a feature story of the New York *Sunday Herald* with a
picture of the commander in disguise. It ended with a description
of the Army's plan to aid the slum inhabitants and with an appeal
for funds.

This excursion set off a regular epidemic of disguises in the
ranks of the Army. A *War Cry* reporter donned a disguise to spend

a night in the Salvation Army's new Women's Shelter at 34 Bayard Street. Commander Booth-Tucker set out again on a second excursion in disguise that ended in jail.

"Who is Steve Brodie?" the commander inquired of his staff at Headquarters. Information about the famous Brooklyn Bridge jumper and East Side saloon keeper was promptly volunteered. Brodie had apparently read of Booth-Tucker's desire to get "inside" the slums, and wrote offering his services. Not unmindful of the potentialities of a person of such fame could he be "won to the cross," the commander set off one evening for Brodie's saloon. There he donned a wig and false whiskers offered by his guide and then set off with Steve Brodie and his brother, Tom, for a tour of Chinatown and the Bowery. Before they had gone far, the sight of the striking tall thin figure in a set of "glossy brown Hester street whiskers" attracted a policeman, who stopped the party and took them to the station where Booth-Tucker was locked up for going about the streets in disguise. Brodie furnished the necessary bail, and the commander was released to face a battery of reporters. The next morning he appeared at Magistrate's Court and was discharged.

As Booth-Tucker pointed out to the newsmen, this was not his first arrest—he had been imprisoned in Bombay for leading a Salvation Army parade through the streets—nor was it to be his last. In April, 1897, he was brought into court on the complaint of several residents of west Thirteenth Street near the National Headquarters Building on the charge of keeping "an ill-governed and disorderly house." The long-suffering neighbors charged that in the course of an "All Night of Prayer" on April 13th, two thousand persons with five brass bands had "caroused" through the night. A parade of witnesses led by the chief complainant, Phineas Smith, a real-estate dealer, told of sleepless nights while bands played and the Salvationists sang hymns to the tune of "We'll Never Get Drunk Any More" and "We Won't Go Home Until Morning."

The trial lasted three days. A Salvation Army band showed up in the courtroom to demonstrate the music played but was not permitted to perform. Booth-Tucker and the Consul both testified that the band and bass drums were not used after midnight on the night in question, but that from that time until four-thirty there was only singing by the two thousand persons present.

Booth-Tucker was defended by A. Oakey Hall, former New York City mayor of Tweed Ring fame, who volunteered his services. "Twenty-five years ago," reminisced Mr. Hall, "I stood where this man, my client, stands today. I was hounded into court by hungry reformers, who sought to convict me of crime. The jury did for me what I hope you will do for Booth-Tucker—they acquitted me."

Mr. Hall was disappointed. The verdict the jury handed down was "Guilty." After five hours of deliberation they found Booth-Tucker guilty as charged—of maintaining a public nuisance. As the prosecuting attorney stated to the jury, Booth-Tucker was not on trial for his religious convictions but "for disturbing the peace of his fellow men." The commander protested the verdict in a long statement given to the press. The action of the jury "jeopardizes the religious liberties of tens of thousands of the best citizens of the United States," he declared. Furthermore, the law under which he had been convicted was "legislation of a class character, prohibiting the workingman from meeting to pray, while the rich man is allowed to meet under precisely similar circumstances to dance."

The verdict aroused little public sympathy. The newspapers were unanimous in their editorial opinion that the verdict was just, that it was not the result of prejudice against the Army, and that it would do the Army no harm. After all, one paper pointed out, the right to sleep was as positive as the right to worship. The commander was released on $25 bail until sentencing, which was postponed, apparently indefinitely.

Steve Brodie and A. Oakey Hall were not the only acquaintances Booth-Tucker made in America. Just two months after his conviction for "keeping and maintaining a common, ill-governed, disorderly house," he had an interview with President William McKinley at the White House. It was arranged by Vice President Garret A. Hobart, who introduced the Salvationist leader. From that time until his tragic death, McKinley was a good friend of Booth-

Tucker and of the Salvation Army. Eugene V. Debs endorsed the work of the Army in a letter for the Labor Day issue of the *War Cry*, as did the president of the Typographical Union and the United Mine Workers' secretary. In contrast to these labor leaders, a number of New York's most socially prominent people were also listed as patrons of the Army.

Meanwhile, the Army continued to grow in numbers. The Ballington Booth schism failed to do more than momentarily halt the rate of growth. As Evangeline Booth pointed out, "Our losses in officers do not exceed about two dozen altogether out of a total of some 2,000; and between 200 and 300 soldiers (so far as we can tell) out of about 25,000." The total number of officers and cadets dropped from a total of 1,952 in March, 1896, to a low of 1,921 in June; but by August of the same year the total stood at 1,967, and each successive month saw an increase. By January, 1897, there were over 2,100 officers, cadets, and accepted candidates serving 685 corps and outposts and operating 34 units such as slum posts, rescue homes, food and shelter depots, outrider circuits and labor bureaus. The number of corps and outposts grew at a less rapid rate than did the social institutions, as the efforts were made to put the Army's entire "social scheme" into operation.

To inspect his rapidly growing forces in the United States, General William Booth made his third visit to America in 1898. The old evangelist, tall and gaunt, with flowing white beard and black plug hat, arrived in New York on January 15, 1898, and two days later left for Canada to begin his tour of the continent. Booth-Tucker accompanied him as far as the border. After a month in Canada, his schedule called for him to begin his American tour in Washington, D.C., then to the Pacific Coast by way of Philadelphia, Harrisburg, Cincinnati, St. Louis, and Kansas City. After visiting Los Angeles, San Francisco, Portland, and Seattle, his route took him through Minneapolis, Chicago, Cleveland, Buffalo, Boston, and Philadelphia to New York. In all, the trip took three months.

While General Booth was inspecting his Army, the country was mobilizing its army for a different sort of war. President McKinley, harried by belligerent patriots, a jingoistic press, and a confused Congress, moved slowly into war with Spain over Cuba. "It wasn't much of a war," as Theodore Roosevelt ruefully remarked years later, "but it was the only war we had." The country made the most of it—and it marked the beginning of the war services of the Salvation Army.

A joint resolution that was the equivalent of a declaration of war was passed by Congress on April 19, 1898, and signed by President McKinley on April 20th. General Booth was in New York ready to conclude his tour with a gala celebration before returning to England. The war news nearly crowded him out of the newspapers; nearly, but not quite.

On April 23rd customers and clerks emptied out of stores from Broadway and Seventh Avenue along Forty-second Street and down Sixth Avenue to Union Square as the sound of martial music and the sight of mounted men started wild rumors. It was not New York's sons off to fight the Spaniards, but the Salvation Army, men, women, and children, two thousand strong, marching in review for their General. Several novel floats and mounted men added to the parade.

The sixty-nine-year-old evangelist showed the strain of his American campaign at the final meetings in New York. His voice was exceedingly husky, but when he raised it he could be heard throughout the Academy of Music. At his farewell meeting he talked for an hour and a half to a large crowd in the Metropolitan Opera House. It was natural that the General should make some reference to the war. The New York *World* quoted him as predicting victory over Spain. "This country is at war with Spain. Battleships will be lost; more Maines will be blown up, there will be defeats. Give up then? Give up? No! This war will be won if it takes the last dollar and the last drop of blood," cried General Booth to an audience that stood up to cheer and shout "Amen!"

Before General Booth sailed on the liner *Germanic* on April 27th, he wrote to President McKinley, offering to send a large corps of trained nurses from the various branches of the Army in Europe to serve in hospitals for the wounded in the war. Nearly a thousand people gathered at the dock for a final farewell.

The Spanish-American War was a good opportunity for the Salvation Army in the United States to show its Americanism. In addition to the number of Salvationists who served as soldiers in Uncle Sam's army, Salvation Army officers were sent to each of the major military camps in the country. When war broke out, Brigadier Alice Lewis and Ensign Annie S. Anderson were sent to Tampa and Key West, Florida, to work with the soldiers and if possible to join the expeditionary force to Cuba. In Florida the two lassies opened a free reading and writing room and supplied it with papers, literature, stationery, and cold water. They conducted meetings with the aid of a United States Army band, but they could not secure permission to join the troops for Cuba, and Brigadier Lewis returned to New York to head the Salvation Army's Naval and Military League.

The purpose of this League was "to visit sailors on board and hold meetings among them on shore, and visit the camps of soldiers and follow them into battle as far as possible. As the Red Cross Society is so well organized for the latter work, the Salvation Army's purpose is to keep more strictly to the moral, temperance, and spiritual lines." The Salvation Army saw a need for spiritual and moral guidance among the men and boys of the hastily recruited army and, without attempting to compete with the Red Cross or any other agency, set about to meet it.

At Camp Alger, near Washington, D.C., Major Edith F. Marshall set up a tent seating over four hundred persons, purchased with funds donated by friends of the Salvation Army. Among the contributors was Mrs. William McKinley. Salvation Army officers served at Camp Tampa and De Soto in Florida, at Camp Chickamauga, Tennessee, at Camp Thomas, and at other installations, conducting religious services, distributing literature, and listening to the thousand and one problems of homesick volunteer soldiers.

For the West Coast, the Philippines were the center of interest in the war. As troops poured into the San Francisco port of embarkation, the Salvation Army erected tents at the various camps and conducted services for the soldiers. Here, Major John Milsaps became the first Salvation Army chaplain officially recognized by the United States Army. The War Department gave the Salvation Army permission to appoint an officer to go overseas to minister to the spiritual and moral welfare of the troops that would sail to Manila. Milsaps, the first Salvation Army officer commissioned on the West Coast, and leader of the pioneer party that opened Hawaii, was a man well suited to work with soldiers. The sturdy Texan, who had grown up on the frontier, was a man among men whose sincerity and splendid Christian character won the respect of those who met him.

The first Salvation Army chaplain sailed with Major General Wesley Merritt and his staff on the *Newport*, leaving San Francisco on June 29, 1898. Only his transportation was furnished by the Army. The first night he borrowed a blanket and slept on the deck until he found a bunk. He ate in the engineers' messroom. With him he brought a phonograph, some records, and a supply of literature. He held meetings on the ship. The Spanish had not surrendered Manila when the troops arrived on July 25th. General Merritt gave Milsaps permission to visit all of the United States regiments camped around the city. He ate where he could, slept in a different place each night, and held meetings whenever the men were not drilling. For a time he roomed with three war correspondents and with Emilio Aguinaldo and General Merritt. He was with the troops when they entered Manila, and he watched the Spanish surrender.

In Manila, Major Milsaps set up the first Salvation Army service center for United States troops abroad. He hired a seven-room house in central Manila and set up a kitchen, shower bath, and recreation room supplied with phonograph, records, newspapers, and magazines from America. He furnished stationery, stamps, wrote letters, and carried messages. The major held his religious meetings at the center, and won twenty-two converts in the first month.

In full Salvation Army uniform, his only dress in the eighteen months he served in the Philippines, Major Milsaps traveled to all the outlying camps and posts. He held the only Protestant services on the ships of Admiral Dewey's fleet anchored in the bay. When battle with the Filipinos broke out, Milsaps followed the troops, worked in the hospitals, and conducted funeral services. Wounded Filipinos were assisted as well as American soldiers. He also worked with native Protestants, held a service in a leper hospital, and many services in Bilibid Prison, where he used Salvation Army songbooks and distributed the *War Cry*. Salvation Army work in wartime had been ably inaugurated by Major John Milsaps when he returned to San Francisco on the troopship *Hancock* on February 23, 1900.

Commander Booth-Tucker, in common with the great majority of the Protestant clergy, had no doubts about the righteousness of the war. It might be expected that this scion of a family of British colonial administrators would support the United States' course of imperialism after the Spanish-American War. In a poem published in the *War Cry* that anticipated by two months Kipling's famous "The White Man's Burden," he offered an answer to the question, pondered by so many Americans: "What Shall I Do With the Philippines?"

> What shall I do with them? Methinks I hear the call
> Of those who 'neath their load of sorrow staggering
>   fall!
>
> .   .   .   .
>
> I hate to cast my eyes beyond my borderland,
> And yet, I would not fail to heed a higher hand
> Which calls me, as it seems, the downcast to
>   uplift,
> And share with those dear lands each Heaven-
>   proffered gift.
>
> .   .   .   .
>
> What shall I do with them? Shall I refuse to roam
> Beyond the borders of my present sea-girt home?
>
> .   .   .   .

I did not seek the task. I would, but durst not
    shirk!
The destiny seems strange that doth these islands
    bind
To us and we to them! And yet, and yet, and yet
These heathen millions mourn! Their cheeks with
    tears are wet—
With tears I know and feel my hand in God's can dry.
I know the task is hard and thankless,—much abuse
Will make my pathway dark; but that is no excuse!

.   .   .   .

Booth-Tucker's position was a reflection of the popular "imperialism of righteousness" advocated by such men as Josiah Strong and John W. Burgess. By this premise, it was America's duty to spread the benefits of Christianity and of the Anglo-Saxon genius for political organization to the barbarous or semibarbarous regions of the world. Other individuals pointed out to the American business community that imperialism could be profitable also. That the "New Manifest Destiny" was supported by a majority of the American people was shown by the election of 1900. In vain did William Jennings Bryan and the Democrats denounce Republican imperialism and inveigh against "American aggression" in the Philippines. William McKinley was reelected with a popular majority of nearly a million votes.

Americans faced the future confidently at the turn of the century. Faith in progress was strong as succeeding innovations made drastic changes in everyday life. Electricity released factories from dependence on steam engines, lighted homes, and made possible a host of labor-saving devices. The automobile, probably more than any other invention since the Civil War, changed the daily life of the people, making Americans the most mobile people in the world. The movement from farm to city continued at an accelerated pace, but the farmer was no longer isolated. Rural free delivery put the daily newspaper in his hands. The telephone kept him in contact with his neighbors and with his relatives in the city. The mail-order catalogue brought his family the clothing styles and conveniences of city stores.

One of the new inventions which the Salvation Army was quick to utilize was the stereopticon or magic lantern. Slides were proved to be very effective in illustrating lectures, and in 1901 a stereopticon manufactured to the specifications of Brigadier Edward J. Parker, then Trade Secretary, was put on sale by the Army's Trade Department. The gramophone was adopted as a Salvation Army aid, and through its use small groups in many places all over the country heard the stirring exhortations of William Booth.

The period was one of political reform. Educational opportunities were opened to more and more people. The spirit of pragmatism demanded that education should have an easily evaluated usefulness. New fields of adult education were opened. Important media of education and entertainment were the Chautauqua lectures and lyceums that brought information and culture to multitudes of Americans.

Commander Booth-Tucker of the Salvation Army became known to thousands of Americans who attended these lectures or who read some of the numerous pamphlets and magazine articles he wrote as an authority on relief measures, especially on farm colonies. No other American Salvationist was as prolific a writer as Booth-Tucker. His Chautauqua address "The Salvation Army as a Temperance Movement" was published in pamphlet form, as was his address on "Our Future Pauper Policy in America." He wrote one of a series of monographs on American Social Economics for the United States Commission to the Paris Exposition of 1900 entitled "The Social Relief Work of the Salvation Army in the United States." His pamphlet on "Farm Colonies of the Salvation Army" was published as a Bulletin of the Bureau of Labor and a House of Representatives Document. The farm colonies were his pet project, and he wrote several other pamphlets and many articles about them.

XIII

"The Landless Man
to the Manless Land"

Booth-Tucker's knack for aphorisms was required to summarize the farm colony plan. "Place the waste labor on the waste land by means of waste capital, and thereby convert this trinity of modern waste into a trinity of production," or in more direct form, "The Landless Man to the Manless Land." It was the project foremost in his mind as commander in the United States, and the one to which both he and the Consul devoted much of their time and energy.

Farm colonies were part of General Booth's "In Darkest England" scheme. His threefold plan included a city colony to "gather up the poor destitute creatures, supply their immediate pressing necessities, furnish temporary employment, inspire them with hope for the future, and commence at once a course of regeneration by moral and religious influences." From the city colony those who could not be sent home to friends or placed in permanent jobs were to be settled on farm colonies. "As the race from the Country to the City has been the cause of so much of the distress we have to battle with, we propose to find a substantial part of our remedy by transferring these same people back to the Country." Here they could be trained for agriculture and finally sent as an immigrant to an overseas colony in some country where land was cheap and man power was needed.

Industrial homes filled the place of city colonies in the plan, and a farm colony was secured at Hadleigh, Essex, near London, in 1890. This colony operated at a substantial loss during its first few years. It is still in existence today, however, as Hadleigh Land and Industrial Colony. Other farm colonies were operated in Australia, India, and South Africa.

Fort Romie, California, was the first Salvation Army farm colony in the United States. Five hundred and twenty acres of land in the Salinas Valley, four miles from the Southern Pacific railroad station at Soledad, were purchased early in 1898. The San Francisco Chamber of Commerce, to whom Booth-Tucker explained the farm-colony plan, joined with the Salvation Army to inaugurate the colony. The land, purchased for $26,000, had been used for dry farming. It was rich, light loam that needed only water to be productive. Eighteen families of unemployed city people were chosen to begin the colony, but they proved to be inept farmers and were further discouraged by a drought that plagued the colony for three years. Of the original group only one family stuck it out, the rest returning to the haven of the more familiar city.

The Salvation Army provided for irrigation and in 1901 selected new colonists, wisely drawn from the surrounding region and all with farm backgrounds. Plots of about twenty acres were sold to each family at $100 an acre, payable in equal sums over a twenty-year period with a 5 per cent interest charge on the balance. The necessary equipment (cows, horses, and implements) was sold on a five-year installment plan. In 1905, when H. Rider Haggard visited the colony, twenty families formed the colony, and none had left since 1901. The colony, which the Salvation Army had spent $64,000 to establish and maintain, not including a loss of $27,000 suffered during the first three years of drought, was now appraised at $113,280, most of the increment belonging to the individual colonists. The initial failure cost the Salvation Army $21,000, which was charged to the account of experience.

Critics of the plan pointed out that the Fort Romie farm colony had not succeeded in returning the city's unemployed paupers to the soil, but had merely given a few families of farm laborers the opportunity to become independent proprietors. Probably money expended in other ways might have benefited a much larger number of people in the class of society with which the Salvation Army worked most closely.

Fort Amity, the Salvation Army's largest farm colony, was exhibited as the answer to these charges. After an extensive search through the West, a tract of land was purchased in 1898 on the line of the Santa Fe Railroad in Colorado a few miles from the Kansas border. Though the land was 3,500 feet above sea level, it was situated in the Arkansas River Valley, and had an adequate supply of water for irrigation. The land was purchased from the Amity Land and Irrigation Company on time, without a down payment. By 1905 the colony consisted of 1,760 acres purchased at a cost of $47,000.

In April, 1898, the first families were brought to the colony, most of them from Chicago and a few from other cities. Only a small number had farming experience. The Salvation Army had to pay the transportation costs of many of the families, and lend them money for subsistence for the first year. The land was covered with a heavy prairie sod that required considerable working. There were no crops the first year and only fair ones the second, but after the first two years crops were good. Seven years after the colony was established, there were thirty-eight families in the colony, a population of about 275 persons. Only sixteen to eighteen families had left the colony during that period.

Amity had the appearance of a prosperous Western town in 1905. In that year the Santa Fe Railroad built a stone depot at Amity with stone from Castle Rock, Colorado. The Salvation Army contributed $1,000 toward its cost. It was estimated that the town business of over $200,000 brought the railroad $50,000 in freight charges that year. The town had sixteen established businesses, including a blacksmith shop, grain store, drugstore, two meat markets, a hardware store, grocery, a bank, newspaper office, barbershop, and mail-order house.

In the burst of enthusiasm for Fort Amity, Consul Booth-Tucker determined to move the Salvation Army Cherry Tree Orphanage in Mount Vernon, New York, to the healthier climate of

Colorado. A large stone building was erected at a cost of about $20,000 (incidentally furnishing employment for the colonists to supplement their income), and in 1901 the children were moved to Fort Amity. Unfortunately, the venture was not successful; it could hardly be expected that Eastern children taken from a beautifully landscaped estate covered with trees and shrubbery of all sorts could share the enthusiasm of the Booth-Tuckers for the barren, treeless, arid region of eastern Colorado. Some eighty to one hundred children were there in 1905, but when an estate was secured in Spring Valley, New York, the Amity orphanage was given up. For a time the building was used as a sanatorium for tuberculosis patients, but by January, 1908, it stood empty.

Alkali was the chief curse of the Amity colony. Haggard on his inspection tour in 1905 criticized the land as not suitable because of its tough virgin sod, lack of trees for lumber, and poor drainage. Constant irrigation of the alkali land with no drainage resulted in a concentration of alkali at the surface so that crops could not be grown. The only solution was an expensive drainage system that added an intolerable expense to the already overburdened colony.

The colony began to decline soon after Haggard's visit in 1905. In January, 1908, the population of the colony was about two hundred, and a number of the homes, many built of stone quarried on the colony, stood empty. The colony was abandoned by the Salvation Army in 1908, when nearly all the land was sold. The Army aided the colonists in moving their families and goods to a place of their choice and helped them to secure employment. Thus ended what was described as "one of the most perfectly planned and executed of the many agricultural colonies planted in Colorado between the years 1854 and 1900."

Another product of the farm-colony plan was Fort Herrick. In July, 1899, Myron T. Herrick, later Governor of Ohio and Ambassador to France, and James Parmelee gave the Salvation Army a 280-acre tract of fine land in Mentor Township, only twenty miles from Cleveland. Booth-Tucker accepted the land to begin a farm colony in Ohio, and eight or nine families were put on the land to start the colony. It was soon evident that the amount of land was insufficient for a farm colony and that surrounding land was too expensive to purchase. The settlers were disposed of, and a small industrial colony similar to that in Hadleigh, England, was undertaken. This did not work out well, and for a time an Inebriates' Home was operated on the land. This experiment was an expensive burden to the Army, and today Fort Herrick is a Fresh Air Camp.

With all their failures, it is difficult to evaluate the benefits of the farm colonies. The plan was one that even today seems sound in theory, and it is not strange that it received the enthusiastic support of many people when explained with enthusiasm by Booth-Tucker. Why did the farm colonies fail? A number of reasons may be suggested. First, the type of person whom the plan was conceived to benefit—the city slum dweller—was not able to adjust to an agricultural life. As an experiment to remove the surplus population of the city to the country, the plan was certainly a failure. Again, the expense of the colonies was out of proportion to the number of persons benefited. The same amount of money spent in assisting emigration might have been of greater benefit. A man transported from the city and thrown on his own resources in a favorable rural environment might be more likely to succeed than a person who is part of a colony which has assumed the responsibility for his success.

Some of the blame for the failure of the two colonies may also be attributed to the poor selection of land, for both colonies were in arid regions dependent on expensive irrigation systems. The colonization plan suffered a severe blow when the leadership of Colonel Thomas C. Holland, national colonization secretary, was lost when he suffered serious injury in a train wreck. When Booth-Tucker left the United States, the farm colonies lost their greatest enthusiast. His successor was not as interested in farm colonies, and did not give them the same support.

Farm colonies were Booth-Tucker's first interest but by no means the only innovation during his administration. The Harvest Festival appeal, so familiar to Salvationists today, was conducted for the first time in the United States from September 5 to 8, 1896, when each of the Army's corps collected food, vegetables, fruit, canned goods, drygoods, or almost anything of value, and sold it at auction or to institutions of the Army. The money secured was used for the operations of the Army.

In 1899 a step long postponed, but one that had become increasingly necessary was taken: the Salvation Army was incorporated. A special act of incorporation was passed by the New York State Legislature, avoiding the necessity of incorporating under the more restricting general laws. Commander Booth-Tucker spent a week in Albany meeting members of the legislature and explaining the Army and its functions. The act provided for the incorporation of the Salvation Army as "a religious and charitable organization." The incorporated Salvation Army was to own the property then held in the name of Booth-Tucker, and was given the right to establish homes, shelters, hospitals, and other institutions. The property of the Salvation Army was to be tax-exempt in the State of New York. The passage of the act was the occasion for expressions of approval of the Salvation Army by many of the legislators. The act became law on April 28, 1899, when it was signed by Governor Theodore Roosevelt.[1] Roosevelt met Booth-Tucker in Albany, and was a good friend of the Salvation Army later when he became President and after he left the Presidency.

To inspect the three farm colonies and other phases of Salvation Army work in the United States, General William Booth made his fourth visit to America in the fall of 1902. As the Salvation Army expanded into a great international organization, the General spent more and more of his time traveling all over the world to keep in touch with the work and to offer his unique inspiration to Salvationists of all lands. The seventy-three-year-old evangelist had become a figure of international renown, an authority on aiding the poor, to whom he had dedicated his life, and a man received with honor by presidents, kings, and statesmen.

It was twentieth century America that General Booth saw on his fourth visit. From the S.S. *Philadelphia*, on which he sailed, he sent back to International Headquarters the first wireless telegram the Army had received. On a later trip he was to have Marconi as a traveling companion. When he was escorted to a waiting automobile for a farewell parade, and the auto wouldn't run—this was 1903—forty to fifty men had to push it, and the General soon transferred to a carriage. It was the twentieth century, but only the beginning of the century.

Once more the General was given a triumphant American welcome. Nearly two thousand persons sailed down the bay in a flotilla of eleven tugs and two sidewheel steamers to meet his ship at quarantine. The vessels were decorated with streamers of "Welcome General," and on each a Salvation Army band played. After a twenty-one-gun salute and seventy-three bombs—one for each year of the General's life—the flotilla escorted the *Philadelphia* to her dock. Booth-Tucker boarded the ship from a revenue cutter, and the Consul was waiting at the dock. The Salvationists from the welcoming fleet disembarked at the foot of west Twentieth Street and paraded to the Headquarters Building, where General Booth reviewed them. The General faced a battery of reporters and photographers and told of his plans for the visit. All in all, as he wrote back to London, "It was a day of days, one of the most remarkable of my life."

General Booth arrived in New York on October 4, 1902. The following day was Sunday, and the Salvation Army leader had no rest. The Academy of Music was filled three times to hear him give hour-long addresses. An estimated eight thousand persons heard him speak that day and fifteen hundred were turned away from the evening meeting.

"I belong to the poor," he told his audience. "My mission is to the poor. I am glad to see the rich and well-to-do at my meetings; but my eyes are on their pocketbooks. The poor are my people. I have given my heart to them. I shall be true to my bride."

The General was so deeply serious about his work and his mission that his sense of humor seemed incongruous at times. On many occasions when pleading for funds he would turn to the chairman and say, "Why bless your heart, Mr. Chairman, in our Prison Gate establishments we have 300 ex-gaolbirds, and if the gentlemen on the front row do not help the General, I'll give 'em their names and addresses, let 'em loose, and send them to fetch it themselves!" He was forced to explain in New York that the reporter who said he had threatened to turn loose 15,000 criminals to plunder society unless the rich men of the country loosened their purses had no sense of humor.

On Monday night Carnegie Hall was crowded, and fifty policemen were busy handling the crowd that blocked Fifty-seventh Street. Mayor Seth Low presided, and introduced the General with a story that became one of his favorites. "Do you like the Salvation Army?" inquired an English vicar of his bishop. To which the bishop replied, "Well, I cannot say that I do, but to be honest I must confess I believe God does."

The crowds at the New York meetings were duplicated at the other cities in the United States and Canada where General Booth appeared. The itinerary included Buffalo, Columbus, Toledo, Chicago, Minneapolis, St. Paul, Kansas City, Denver, Los Angeles, San Francisco, Oakland, St. Louis, Birmingham, Cincinnati, Pittsburgh, Washington, D.C., Baltimore, Philadelphia, and New York.

The high point of the trip came in Washington, D.C., when General Booth had lunch at the White House with President Theodore Roosevelt, Secretary of State John Hay, Secretary of War Elihu Root, and Secretary of the Interior Ethan A. Hitchcock. Senator Marcus Hanna was his sponsor in Washington. The General gave the opening prayer at the United States Senate and met a large number of senators, congressmen, and other members of Washington officialdom. Senator Hanna gave a dinner for the General in the parlors of the Arlington Hotel.

Four thousand persons crowded the Metropolitan Opera House for his farewell meeting in New York. The General had fallen on the stairs at headquarters and sprained his knee. Despite this injury and the fact that he had traveled sixteen thousand miles in twenty weeks, visiting fifty-two cities and holding two hundred meetings, the tall white-bearded leader spoke for nearly two hours. On March 7, 1903, General Booth sailed from New York on the *Campania*.

The year 1903, inaugurated so auspiciously by the General's

tour, bade fair to be the most successful to date for the Salvation Army in America. Commander Booth-Tucker toured the country and was one of the speakers at the National Irrigation Congress. He told fifteen hundred delegates from twenty-six states about the Salvation Army's experience with colonization. In October, the Consul began a tour, stopping at Buffalo to open a new Rescue Home and at St. Louis for some important meetings before arriving at Fort Amity, the Colorado farm colony. Here she spent a week inspecting all aspects of the colony and discussing with Colonel Thomas Holland, national colonization secretary, the problems of colonization in general.

After a busy day on Tuesday, October 27th, the Consul, Ensign Damnes, her secretary, and Colonel Holland boarded the Santa Fe train for Chicago. It made a short stop in Kansas City, and she took the occasion to pay a flying visit to a new Men's Industrial Home before continuing to Chicago, where Commander Booth-Tucker awaited her for a conference on the colonization project.

On Thursday morning Booth-Tucker arrived at the station to meet the train carrying his wife. He was met instead by the Salvation Army officers in charge of the Chicago work, taken to headquarters, and told, "Commander, your wife is dead; she was killed in a wreck."

The train was passing the depot at Dean Lake, Missouri, when it ran into an open switch. The last three cars of the train were torn off, and dashed into a steel water tower on a siding. In the first of these cars, the one that bore the brunt of the crash, were the Consul and Colonel Holland. Both were removed unconscious from the wreckage. Emma Booth-Tucker died two and a quarter hours later, without regaining consciousness, on October 28, 1903. Colonel Holland recovered and lived eight years longer, but never completely got over his injuries.

Frederick Booth-Tucker was prostrated by the tragic news. Here was a test of faith indeed. But God gave him strength to accept his loss without bitterness and to face the ordeal of the funeral services. The Salvation Army uses the phrase "promoted to Glory" for the death of one of its members. Its funeral services are supposed to be occasions for rejoicing over a Christian warrior gone home. The usual black for mourning is discarded for white, and a call to the penitent form is part of the funeral service. The body of the Consul was brought to Chicago and placed in the Princess Rink, where more than seven thousand persons viewed the body before the service was held in the evening. In New York a public funeral service on November 1st, in Carnegie Hall, attracted more than fifteen thousand persons, only a third of whom were able to gain admission to the hall. Ten thousand paid a final tribute to the Salvation Army leader as the body lay in state in Memorial Hall of the National Headquarters Building on west Fourteenth Street. Interment was in Woodlawn Cemetery.

The loss of his beloved wife was a shattering blow to Booth-Tucker. In addition to the six-week-old son who died in England while he was en route to America, the commander had lost two infant children born in the United States and his father during the seven years he had served in America. Now left alone with six children, all under thirteen years of age, Booth-Tucker tried to carry on as commander of the Salvation Army in the United States and act as both father and mother to his children. The strain was more than any person could endure. Soon after the funeral he visited England for a few weeks, but returned in time to help distribute Christmas baskets in New York at the annual Christmas dinner for the poor.

It was a heartsick commander who led the Salvation Army in the United States in 1904. Evangelical campaigns, inspection tours, and the routine office work that Booth-Tucker threw himself into could not fill the aching void within him. The Salvation Army lost a stanch supporter and its commander a personal friend when Senator Marcus A. Hanna died in April, 1904. In June the commander headed a delegation to an International Congress in London. Before leaving he spoke in Carnegie Hall on the subject "The Landless Man to the Manless Land."

In London, General Booth gave his consent to Booth-Tucker to leave the United States, and his farewell was announced, after his return, in the *War Cry* of August 27, 1904. After a three-month farewell campaign Booth-Tucker and his family left the United States in November, 1904.[2]

American Salvationists paid the man who had been their leader for eight critical years a number of tributes in which they were joined by many prominent public figures. At the last farewell meeting in Grand Central Palace, New York, messages were read from President Theodore Roosevelt, the Vice President-elect, two Cabinet members, and twenty-four governors, with Governor Albert B. Cummins, of Iowa, expressing the prevailing sentiment when he said:

Those of us who have had something to do with public affairs, and therefore, something to do with our social and industrial problems, have come to look upon The Salvation Army and its eloquent and efficient Commander as one of the most powerful allies of good government. I have long recognized the Salvation Army as one of the most potent, if not the most potent, force for the betterment of humankind now at work for the safety of mankind.

XIV

"Send Eva!"

Booth-Tucker's successor to the command of the Salvation Army forces in the United States has been described as "one of God's best gifts to America." During an administration of thirty years, Evangeline Cory Booth, known to Salvationists as the Commander, became for most Americans the personification of the Salvation Army.

Born on Christmas Day, 1865, the fourth daughter and seventh child of William and Catherine Booth, Eva was one of the most outstanding members of a remarkable family. When her older brothers and sisters, with whom she was educated at home, went into active service Eva was anxious to join them. She was only fifteen when she donned a sergeant's uniform, less than a year after Railton and the seven lassies sailed to America. From this lowest rank, Eva Booth was to reach the highest position in the Salvation Army, and America was to be her home.

If, as some have said, the stage lost a great actress when Evangeline Booth dedicated her life to the Salvation Army, it might also be said that the Salvation Army gained a consummately dramatic leader. At the age of seventeen, Eva Booth went into full-time service. The teen-age captain was striking in appearance; her bonnet covered a wealth of flowing auburn hair and framed a handsome face dominated by deep, flashing eyes; her figure was tall—five feet ten inches—and slender. The first woman Salvationist to adopt the bicycle, an excellent horsewoman and an enthusiastic swimmer and diver, Evangeline Booth was always active and kept physically fit. She had the temperament of an actress. Dramatic, impetuous, headstrong, she would drive herself for weeks of strenuous work until forced to retire completely for a period of rest. She was gifted with a magic name and she lived up to it. Her biographer has compared her voice with that of Sarah Bernhardt, and she soon proved that she had her mother's and her father's gift of stirring audiences—both small and large.

Evangeline Booth suffered mob violence and police persecution along with other Salvationists in the 1880's. She came to be used as a trouble shooter—sent wherever a critical battle was in progress. On one occasion Gipsy Smith, later an internationally famous evangelist, quit the Salvation Army when ordered to give up a gold watch presented by the people of a town he had served. The order went out: "Send Eva!" She faced a rebellious crowd and won it back to the Salvation Army. When the Army faced a severe legal test in Torquay, it was "Send Eva!" and again she won a victory. After four years directing the International Training College at Clapton, she was appointed field commissioner for the area around London.

In 1896, when Maud and Ballington Booth resigned as head of the Salvation Army in the United States, and when it appeared to London that a number of Salvationists would follow suit, still again it was "Send Eva!" and the young trouble shooter arrived in the United States for the most difficult job in her career. She was successful, and able to turn over to her sister and brother-in-law, the Booth-Tuckers, an Army of American Salvationists almost unbroken by a very trying experience.

Evangeline Booth's next assignment was in Canada, where she directed a successful eight-year administration following the rather disturbed term of her brother Herbert Booth. When the gold rush to the Klondike began, the Canadian commander ordered the extension of Salvation Army work to Alaska, and made three trips to the Yukon to inspect the forces there. The successful commander of a neighboring country seemed to be well qualified to succeed

Booth-Tucker as commander of the Salvation Army in the United States. Evangeline Booth assumed her new command just before her thirty-ninth birthday, Christmas, 1904.

The position Evangeline Booth assumed in 1904 was one whose duties and responsibilities previously had been divided between two persons—the national commander and his wife. The difficulty that Booth-Tucker experienced during the months he commanded the United States forces after the death of the Consul showed that the job was too much for one alone. Since Evangeline was not married, the General divided the United States into two departments. A Department of the West, with headquarters in Chicago, was created, and the command given to Commissioner George A. Kilbey. In addition to her duties as national commander, she directly administered the Eastern States as well.

Thousands of Americans remember Evangeline Booth for her unusual and stirring lectures. Perhaps her best known was the lecture "My Father," presented in all parts of the country after the death of General Booth. This dramatic presentation of the life and ideas of her father became almost as famous and was repeated nearly as many times as Russell H. Conwell's "Acres of Diamonds." Another specialty of the Commander was to appear in a costume of rags to deliver a presentation of the Salvation Army's social work complete with tableaux, lighting effects, and dramatic delivery. Her lectures were always crowded beyond capacity, and cities gave her a royal welcome on her tours, urging her to return again and again.

To the American public, Evangeline Booth personified the Salvation Army, and as its head she received the tributes paid to the Army. Presidents Theodore Roosevelt, Taft, Wilson, Harding, Coolidge, Hoover, and Franklin Delano Roosevelt each received her and endorsed the work of the Salvation Army. But Evangeline Booth was more than the head of a great organization; she was a personality in her own right. One of the eminent speakers of her day, she was recognized as a leader in the movement for women's suffrage and prohibition legislation. Any list of outstanding American women in the first half of the twentieth century would certainly include the name of Evangeline Cory Booth.

Less famous than the lectures of the Commander but perhaps even more important in explaining the Army's work were the lectures, illustrated by lantern slides and motion pictures, that a number of officers presented to audiences at YMCA's and churches all over the country. Five years before *The Birth of a Nation*, Edward J. Parker had taken a motion-picture film and numerous slides of the Salvation Army's social work in New York's East Side and worked out an illustrated lecture entitled "Problems of the Poor."

General William Booth, revered by Salvationists as the Founder, was actively interested in the land where he had appointed his favorite daughter, and in less than three years after she assumed command in the United States he visited the country to inspect her forces.

General William Booth paid two visits to the United States in 1907, one a stopover on his way to Japan. The General reached New York on March 5th and after three days continued across Canada to the Pacific Coast. He sailed from Seattle, Washington, on April 1st. In Canada he was the guest of Earl Grey and met Sir Wilfrid Laurier. In Japan he was accorded a welcome beyond expectations both by the government officials and by the people. The Emperor of Japan received him, and 25,000 people gathered to see him off with a "banzai" that broke all records. The seventy-eight-year-old patriarch was back in England no longer than two months, during which time he received an honorary doctorate of civil law from Oxford before he set out again for a full-scale visit to America.

His sixth—and last—visit to the United States was plagued by illness. The old man's physical body, weakened by thousands of miles of nearly continuous travel and constant meetings and speeches, could not keep the pace set by the still young mind and spirit. The ocean trip on the *Virginian* was a pleasant one, with Marconi as a fellow passenger and interested visitor to the General's shipboard lectures. The ship landed at Rimouski, Quebec, on September 20, 1907. After visiting St. John, Halifax, and Moncton, New Brunswick, the General began his tour of the United States at Boston on September 27th. The itinerary included the principal cities of the East and Midwest—Pittsburgh, St. Louis, Des Moines, Chicago, Cleveland, Columbus, Washington, Baltimore, Philadelphia, and New York.

The General reached Chicago seriously ill with dysentery, and for nearly a week submitted to the treatment of doctors and nurses before setting out again on his tour. Several of his meetings were postponed, but he made them all except Cleveland, which had to be dropped from the itinerary, much to his regret.

In Washington, President and Mrs. Theodore Roosevelt had a luncheon for the General and Evangeline. General Booth told the President about his trip to Japan and about the work of the Salvation Army with different nationalities. John Wanamaker, one of the Army's stanchest friends and supporters, was chairman of his meeting in Philadelphia. But as the General met emperors, presidents, famous statesmen, and educators, he always thought of the value of these contacts to the Salvation Army, and of how they could be translated into tangible aid for the unfortunate and downtrodden.

Throughout the trip there were reporters to face. In New York he was so weak that several times during the interview he was forced to put his head down on the table to get his strength. Though he appeared to have broken down physically, with his large frame fallen in on itself, the old air of command was still there, and in appearance he resembled the prophet Moses more than ever. One reporter wrote, "Feeble as he is, that little spark in his eye that electrifies anyone he looks at tells the secret of his endurance—he is a human live-wire perpetually charged from an inexhaustible storage battery of nervous energy."

The sense of humor was still keen also, as the old man told the story of a new convert who confessed to him between sobs, "I'm a convert, all right, General, but when I came into this place, I'm damned if I had any idea of getting saved."

On Sunday, November 3rd, the General spoke at three meet-ings before at least five thousand people. About 175 came to the penitent form. At his meeting in Salvation Army Headquarters on the preceding night, sixty-one were converted. He appeared to be in better physical shape than when he had met the reporters on Friday. His voice, although throaty, did not quaver, but was marred by a breathless sort of delivery owing to lack of lung power. One observer said:

The General's characteristic posture is with his hands clasped loosely behind his back, his feet planted a little distance apart and his body tilted backwards away from the hips. He makes no gestures at all, except to-ward the end of an address when he thumps repeatedly the Bible lying before him.

He is a very serious speaker. At one time last night he stopped in the middle of a sentence, and, pointing to a woman in the front row, said sharply: "You will kindly refrain from fanning if I am to keep on talk-ing." Hand clapping he abided as little and always checked such applause peremptorily.

The official farewell for the Founder was on November 8, 1907, on the steps of the City Hall in New York City, where Railton had been refused permission to hold outdoor meetings twenty-seven years earlier. On this occasion a police inspector and fifty police-men escorted the General and his party through the crowd of some 2,500 people while five Army brass bands played.

Because the old man's voice was too weak to be heard beyond the steps, three officers with megaphones repeated his words:

Maybe I will see you again—who can tell? I won't say good-by for good then, but only for a little while. I will see you again if I live, and if I am dead I will try to see you anyhow, if they let me. God be with you till we meet. Hallelujah!

For five minutes the crowd cheered; then the bands began to play and fireworks were set off. With a prophecy that was all too true, a reporter wrote that this farewell in all probability "will mark his last public appearance on this continent." On November 9, 1907, accompanied by his daughter Evangeline, the General sailed from New York. The band played "God Be With You Till We Meet Again" as General Booth bade farewell to America for the last time.

Soon after returning from the United States, William Booth's sight began to fail; but he refused to allow the affliction that brought total darkness to him before his death to keep him from the active life he had always led. Whenever he was able, he traveled throughout England and the Continent conducting large meetings, speaking to convicts in prisons, or addressing small groups from an automobile. He planned still another trip to America in his eighty-first year, but was forced to cancel it.

The old warrior was able to enjoy a huge celebration meeting in honor of his eighty-third birthday. His daughter Evangeline was in England in May, 1912, when he addressed 10,000 people in Albert Hall, his last public appearance before "going into dry-dock for repairs." They heard the bent and nearly blind old man declare:

While women weep as they do now, I'll fight; while little children go hungry as they do now, I'll fight; while men go to prison, in and out, in and out, I'll fight; while there is a poor lost girl upon the street, I'll fight; while there yet remains one dark soul without the light of God, I'll fight— I'll fight to the very end!

An operation to remove a cataract left him totally blind. For three months this soldier of God fought for life because he felt it was his duty to fight, but he longed for a rest. At last, at 10:13 P.M. on August 20, 1912, William Booth went home:

> The hosts were sandalled, and their wings were fire!
> (Are you washed in the blood of the Lamb?)
> But their noise played havoc with the angel-choir.
> (Are you washed in the blood of the Lamb?)
> Oh, shout Salvation! It was good to see
> Kings and Princes by the Lamb set free.
> The banjos rattled and the tambourines
> Jing-jing-jingled in the hands of Queens.

And when Booth halted by the curb for prayer
He saw his Master thro' the flag-filled air.
Christ came gently with a robe and crown
For Booth the soldier, while the throng knelt down.
He saw King Jesus. They were face to face,
And he knelt a-weeping in that holy place.
Are you washed in the blood of the Lamb? [1]

The news was flashed around the world, and the world mourned its citizen. "In the list of those who have unselfishly devoted their entire lives to the uplifting of humanity, no name stands higher than that of General William Booth. . . ." The obituary in the New York *Tribune* sounded as though it had been written several days before, yet it had the ring of true sincerity. "His field of labor was the world, and the peoples of every race and every clime had opportunity to hear the message of hope and promise he so effectively preached to the downtrodden and unfortunate. . . ." President Taft sent a message of tribute and condolence. The German Emperor, George V of England, the Prime Minister, the Archbishop of Canterbury, and other officials of church and state sent messages.

Commander Evangeline Booth in New York was prostrated by the news, but caught the earliest ship and reached England in time to attend the burial service.

On Friday and Saturday, August 23rd and 24th, 150,000 persons filed through Congress Hall, where the body lay in state. Over 30,000 crowded the Olympia for the funeral service, which was turned into a memorable revival. The funeral procession, solemn yet triumphal, was led by banners of white. Forty bands played the death march from Handel's *Saul*. The crowds that packed the line of march from London to the Abney Park Cemetery in Stoke Newington could not be estimated; streets, sidewalks, windows, even the housetops were crowded. Business houses closed and flags hung at half mast. *Punch* declared:

No Laurelled blazon rests above his bier,
    Yet a great people bows its stricken head

Where he who fought without reproach or fear
Soldier of Christ, lies dead.*

On the day after William Booth's death, August 21, 1912, an
envelope written and sealed twenty-two years earlier was opened
and the name of the General's successor read. No one was surprised
to note that William Booth had appointed his eldest son, William
Bramwell Booth, Chief of Staff for so many years, to succeed him.
Fifty-six-year-old Bramwell Booth, deeply moved, accepted the appointment and became the Salvation Army's second General.

He had stood at his father's side devoting his life to the Christian
Mission and the Salvation Army since he was sixteen. The two
were of entirely different but complementary characters. It was
William Booth, inspired and inspiring others, who set the goals
and pointed the way for the Salvation Army, and Bramwell Booth,
utterly devoted, gifted with a legal mind, was the able administrator who helped furnish the vehicle to carry forward his father's
ideals and keep them expanding. While William Booth was stirring
thousands of souls with inspiring sermons, Bramwell was seeing to
finances, sending out directives and orders, building up the organization necessary to run a world-wide Army. Bramwell Booth
could never have founded a Salvation Army, but it is also probable
that William Booth could not have built as efficient an Army
without the aid of his eldest son as Chief of Staff.

The United States soon had an opportunity to see the difference
between the two Generals. In November, 1913, General Bramwell
Booth paid his first visit to America. He arrived in New York on
Friday, October 31, 1913, on the *Lusitania*. In contrast to the headlines that his father had inspired, the new General of the Salvation Army was given no more than a paragraph in a story on
arrivals on the *Lusitania* by the New York *Tribune*. It is characteristic of Bramwell Booth that he made comparatively little impact upon the American reporters, and that he spent nearly three
of his four weeks in America in Canada.

The Salvation Army in the United States tendered its General

* Reproduced by permission of the proprietors of *Punch*.

a loyal welcome, but the public was generally apathetic. Notices advertising his meetings in New York were run in the papers, and Carnegie Hall was filled for a Sunday-afternoon service. The brief newspaper accounts described his talk as some eulogistic remarks about his father and mentioned that American Salvationists were disturbed by a rumor that their Commander, Evangeline Booth, was soon to be transferred to head an international bureau in London.

When General Bramwell Booth sailed from New York on November 26, 1913, many Americans would have agreed with the description given by the London *Times*. Bramwell Booth "lacks the personal magnetism, the apostolic fire of his father. His mind is eminently cautious, conservative, lawyer-like. He is . . . by nature no lover of crowds and strange faces."

The contrast between the new General and his dashing, dramatic sister who commanded the forces in the United States was evident. The fact that Bramwell Booth's entire experience was in Britain while Evangeline was an adopted American served only to accentuate the basic differences of personality that future events were to magnify into a complete rupture.

XV

Approaching Maturity

The period from 1904 to 1917 in the history of the Salvation Army in the United States is generally one of consolidation and advance along lines already laid down. There were few innovations, and these were not of enduring significance. Social institutions increased in numbers and extended their service. Evangelical campaigns went hand in hand with increasingly emphasized attacks on liquor and tobacco. That the attitude of the Salvation Army toward intoxicants coincided with that of a large portion of the American public is shown by the fact that by 1916 three-quarters of the area of the United States—with half the population—was legally dry and the Eighteenth Amendment, passed by Congress in 1917, was ratified by all but two states by January, 1919.

Soon after Evangeline Booth assumed command of the Salvation Army in the United States, she borrowed from Canada a campaign known as the "Siege." The first Siege in the United States, announced by a Proclamation of War that took up the whole cover of the *War Cry*, was scheduled from February 5 to March 14, 1905, and was outlined as a special campaign "to destroy every kind of evil work resulting from sin, such as drink, blasphemy, hatred, half-heartedness, shame, hypocrisy, cant, lukewarmness, jealousy, cowardice, fashion, pride, conceit, lies, and other enemies of God and man."

The month-long campaign was divided into Backsliders' Week, Juniors' Week, Notorious Sinners' and Drunkards' Week, and Hospitals and Prisons Week. In 1918 it included a Week of Prayer and Preparation, Reconciliation Week, Prisoners' and Notorious Sinners' Week, Young People's Week, and Soldiers' and Candidates' Week, a program that lasted from January 7th to February 12th. The Siege was a purely evangelical effort, and its effectiveness is difficult to assess. It was held annually until 1919, when it was replaced by the Flaming Revival, another month-long revival effort held in that year.

Another, more spectacular, innovation was the Boozers' Convention or Boozers' Day, an event featured in newspapers all over the country, and one whose fame spread abroad. Colonel (later Commissioner) William McIntyre conceived the idea of collecting as many drunkards as possible and making a special effort to aid them.

The first Boozers' Day was on Thanksgiving Day, 1909. "Down and out" alcoholics were attracted by the offer of a free meal and by a novel parade that included a walking whisky bottle ten feet high to which a man was chained, floats depicting scenes of a drunkard's life, Men's Industrial Home wagons, Salvationists in uniform, mounted officers, and several Army bands. Another feature of the parade was a city water wagon with a number of "bums" aboard and with uniformed Salvationists alongside to keep them "on the wagon." These tactics helped to fill Memorial Hall with twelve hundred inebriates combed from the dives of the Bowery and brought to the meeting in hired buses. Colonel McIntyre directed the meeting, but most of the speaking was done by reformed drunkards, whose testimony had the most effective appeal. The men and women on the platform had once been what the poor creatures in the audience were now, and clearly there was hope for everyone.

One unhappy man at the Boozers' Convention in 1910 was a former newspaper editor who had slipped down to the level of a Bowery bum; doctors at Bellevue Hospital had pronounced him an incurable alcoholic. He was Henry Milans, who was converted at a Salvation Army meeting and who never again touched liquor nor had any desire to do so. Until his death he conducted a lively ministry by writing and correspondence. Milans' case is probably the most miraculous result of this program, but there were other, less spectacular cases. Converts were carefully followed up, and if they had no homes they were brought to Salvation Army Men's Hotels and Industrial Homes until they could get on their feet and be placed in jobs.

The Boozers' Convention became an annual event until the passage of the Eighteenth Amendment. It was given up, it was claimed, because the advent of Prohibition cut off the supply of drunks.[1]

An Anti-Suicide Bureau was opened at Salvation Army Headquarters under the direction of Colonel Thomas Holland on March 1, 1907. A new feature in the United States, this followed the example of a similar movement in England that had proved to be successful. Persons who contemplated suicide as the only solution for their problems could tell their troubles to a trained Salvation Army officer and receive understanding help.

America's greatest disaster since the Chicago Fire occurred in the early morning of April 18, 1906, when an earthquake began in the region of San Francisco, California. The quake destroyed water mains and began a fire that raged for two days unchecked, destroying most of the City of San Francisco. An area of 2,593 acres, or more than four square miles of the city, was burned out. Included in the 28,188 buildings destroyed was the Salvation Army provincial headquarters building, with all its equipment and records and all of the social institutions, corps halls, and property in San Francisco—thirteen institutions in all, worth from $130,000 to $150,000.

In Oakland, across the bay, the Salvation Army was the first to open a relief camp for some of the thousands of refugees that swarmed out of San Francisco. The Oakland Citadel was thrown open and meals were served. A camp ground at Beulah Park, three miles from Oakland, was secured, tents were erected, and a relief camp was set up. Clothing was distributed, and the homeless were fed and housed. Chinese Salvationists served as cooks and dining-room and kitchen help. A depot for lost and strayed children was set up. As Colonel George French told a reporter from the San

Francisco *Examiner,* "We are always ready for an emergency," and the work of the Army backed up his statement.

While relief work was carried out in the San Francisco area, Commander Evangeline Booth held a mass meeting in New York's Union Square to raise funds for the stricken city. Some $12,000 was collected as the gifts came in, including $1,000 from General Booth in England, and pennies, nickles, and dimes collected in unseasonal Christmas kettles. At the end of May, Miss Booth made an inspection tour of the devastated region, traveling eight thousand miles in twelve days.

The Salvation Army has not publicized its disaster work because it has never felt that it has the financial resources to operate as a Disaster Relief Agency. It emphasizes that its services are emergency disaster services which it is particularly well qualified to provide. As *The Salvation Army Disaster Emergency Service Manual* points out, "Salvation Army personnel is a well-disciplined, cohesive, mobile force. It is motivated by a love for God which expresses itself in service to man, even to the point of sacrifice. It is this spirit that makes our service so acceptable." The important thing to outside observers about Salvation Army disaster work is that it is prompt on the scene of disaster, efficient without red tape or formality, and is not ostentatious.

Wherever a major flood, hurricane, explosion, fire, or other disaster has hit any section of the country in the past forty years, the blue-uniformed Salvation Army men and bonneted Salvation Army lassies have been seen serving sandwiches, coffee, and doughnuts, and offering reassuring spiritual counsel. With a quiet cheerfulness that helps to restore calm, they act in the first hectic hours of the tragedy before more extensive relief work is organized and operating. The Salvation Army was first on the scene after the Texas City, Texas, explosion on April 16, 1947, had wrecked most of the community and taken nearly five hundred lives. When six hundred tons of ammunition blew up in South Amboy, New Jersey, at 7:26 P.M. on May 19, 1950, damaging the entire city, Salvation Army units were on hand with coffee by 8:00 P.M. These are only two dramatic examples; but the Salvation Army is also present to serve at less publicized emergencies—forest fires, tenement fires, localized tornadoes, or floods.

Another innovation that developed into an important Salvation Army service was the summer outing, added to the social welfare program during this period. For a glorious day the Salvation Army enabled thousands of children and their weary mothers to escape from the oppressive heat of the slums into the country or to the seashore. Not all the summer outings were on as grand a scale as the one conducted by Major and Mrs. Wallace Winchell, of Jersey City, but in all the larger cities—New York, Chicago, San Francisco, and others—the children had their day. The Winchells conducted their eighth annual outing in August, 1911, when 4,200 children and mothers from Jersey City filled a steamer and two barges for a cruise and visit to the seashore. Over four thousand quarts of milk were provided for the children, and a doctor, ten Salvation Army nurses, fifty Salvation Army guards, and three local policemen were on hand to assure their health and safety. Local businessmen contributed to pay the expenses of the trip.

A memorable Salvation Army highlight for 1914 was the grand International Congress held during the summer in London, marking the beginning of the Salvation Army's fiftieth year. It was a real Congress of Nations. Every country in which the Salvation Army operated sent delegates—each in special costume typical of the country. The gala event was marred by a tragedy before it began and ended in the shadow of an even greater tragedy. On a foggy night in May, the *Empress of Ireland*, with 165 members of the Canadian delegation to the Congress on board, was cut in two by a freighter. One thousand and twenty-four persons, including Commissioner and Mrs. Rees of Canada, lost their lives. Only twenty Salvationists, including young Ernest Pugmire, later to be national commander of the United States, were saved.

Though the *Empress of Ireland* tragedy threw a shadow over the Congress, it did not spoil its magnificence. The United States delegation—seven hundred strong—crossed the ocean on the *Olympic* with former President Theodore Roosevelt, long a Salvation Army supporter, as a fellow passenger. In all, some forty thousand Salvationists participated in the greatest Salvation Army international gathering to date. About half of them were from the United Kingdom, but over fifty different countries and colonies were represented.

For two weeks in June, 1914, London was treated to an exhibition of Salvation Army strength and unity. An estimated fifty thousand people filled the Crystal Palace building and grounds for one ceremony when the flags of each participating nation were raised: France, Germany, Sweden, Russia, Italy, Norway, Switzerland, Denmark, Canada, New Zealand, Australia, South Africa, Argentina, China, Japan, Belgium, Finland, and the United States were all represented. The costumes attracted much attention. The American delegation with red cowboy hats were singled out for praise by the London *Times*, but there were Swiss guides, Koreans, Indians in turbans, Zulus, and Kaffirs with red blankets. Plumed and helmeted Germans marched beside French and British soldiers of Salvation. Salvationists of all races and colors, white, brown, yellow, and black, marched side by side; every continent was represented. A babel of tongues ensued as the delegates marched with fifty-seven bands to Hyde Park to preach in their different languages from the twelve platforms erected there.

Evangeline Booth, riding on a fine horse, led the American delegation. The London *Times* declared that she was the outstanding woman of the Congress, and quoted some of the English Salvationists as saying, "She's the old General come to life." Her oratory, fire, and magnetic personality were a great feature of the gatherings.

But, like a nearing shadow, while Salvationists of all nations marched side by side, singing praises to one King—the King of Kings—other troops, devoted to other monarchs, marched in Austria, in Serbia, in Russia, in Germany, in France.

The stage was set. Archduke Francis Ferdinand of Austria was assassinated in the little town of Sarajevo on June 28, 1914, while the International Congress was still in session in London. After the Congress the American delegates scattered all over Europe to spend furloughs visiting friends in Germany or France or to see the sights

of the Old World. World War I began in August, and a number
of American Salvationists were caught within the borders of the
belligerent nations on the Continent. Still others were in England,
and watched British mobilization. Colonel McIntyre, Colonel Holz,
Lieutenant Colonel Parker, and Brigadier Barker all came home
with eyewitness accounts of the outbreak of the war.

The World War caught the Salvation Army in the dilemma of
all international religious organizations. Salvationists fought in
German uniforms as well as in French and British. With International Headquarters in London, the English Salvation Army offered
its humanitarian services to the British Government. In the United
States, where President Wilson in proclaiming neutrality urged
Americans to be "impartial in thought as well as in action," the
Salvation Army followed his injunction, at least in the columns of
its official publication, the *War Cry*. Each issue contained war news
with such articles as "With the Troops in France" and "Salvation
in the German Army," although more space was devoted to activities with the Allied forces.

In America, Commander Evangeline Booth went into action
soon after war broke out in 1914, and organized the "Old Linen
Campaign." Old linen was collected, rolled into bandages, sterilized,
and baled to be shipped to Europe for the use of wounded soldiers
and civilians. The drive was such a success that on December 19,
1914, sixteen cases of bandages weighing nearly six thousand
pounds were shipped abroad, and the material poured into collection depots so fast that it became necessary to appeal for funds to
hire some of the unemployed to supplement volunteer workers. As
badly needed material piled up waiting to be processed, the Commander became more forceful, heading one appeal for funds, "Pity
All You Like, but for God's Sake Give!'"

As 1915 gave way to 1916 and 1916 passed into 1917, event
after event brought the United States closer to involvement in the
conflict raging in Europe. President Wilson's head called for the
neutrality he had proclaimed, but his heart was with England, then
fighting "to make the world safe for democracy." Like Woodrow

Wilson, Evangeline Booth's heart and sympathy lay with England and the Allies, but she, too, maintained a position of neutrality.

An interesting episode illustrative of American neutrality was the visit of Major Wallace Winchell, of Jersey City, to Belgium in 1915-1916. International Headquarters had a fund contributed for the purpose of feeding and clothing needy Belgians under Salvation Army direction. Since Belgium had been occupied by the Germans, the Salvation Army units of that little country had been cut off from communication with International Headquarters in England. A neutral was needed to direct the relief work, and an outstanding neutral was secured in the person of Major Winchell.

This outstanding and original officer was a truly representative American Salvationist. In fact, his ancestors had been Americans for two centuries. He had begun Salvation Army work in 1886 as a youth of twenty, and his career was outstanding. Blessed by a very capable wife, he held positions in Fort Romie, California; Chicago and Springfield, Illinois; Milwaukee, Peoria, Boston, St. Louis, and in Waterbury, Connecticut. His last and most successful position was in Jersey City. It was Winchell who had subpoenaed Colonel Robert G. Ingersoll to appear at a mock trial of the Devil, who had organized relief wagons for the strikers' families during the Pullman strike, and who had operated one of the Army's first salvage depots in Waterbury, Connecticut.

In Jersey City he had attended a Holy Name breakfast of the Police Department and with a well worded speech won the sympathy and support of influential Catholic politicians. When he left for Belgium in October, 1915, Major Winchell carried letters of introduction from many important political officials, including the governor of New Jersey, the mayor of Jersey City, and political boss Frank Hague. He knew the value of publicity, and proved to be colorful copy for the newspapermen. His methods, often sensational, were usually surprisingly effective. He broke up a brawl between Irish and Poles in his district by distributing flowers, and his work with the slum children of all nationalities in Jersey City was especially outstanding.

Winchell's assignment to Belgium came unbidden, and involved considerable sacrifice; but once undertaken it was pursued wholeheartedly. Mrs. Winchell filled the major's position in Jersey City alone while he was gone. The story of Major Winchell's mission to Belgium, written by a journalist and published in 1916 when he returned, received considerable criticism from those who were working to involve the United States in the war because it exposed the falsity of the Belgian atrocity stories then coming from the British propaganda service, and called on America to hold fast to her cause of neutrality.

There was no Pearl Harbor in 1917 to shock the nation into solidarity. America, the melting pot of all nationalities, with the advice of Washington backed by the tradition of generations, found it difficult to contemplate the prospect of American boys on the battlefields of Europe. Many German-Americans could not believe that the Kaiser was determined to rule the world. Many Irish-Americans, whose homeland had suffered for centuries from British exploitation and suppression, found it difficult to picture England as liberty's sole defender. Although prominent statesmen and clergymen, most newspapers, and many organizations were highly articulate in their demands that the United States join England and France in the "War to end Wars," many Americans actively opposed this policy and still others hoped against hope that we could keep out of the war. Consequently, many Americans were caught psychologically unprepared when war was declared against Germany on April 7, 1917.

The Salvation Army in the United States and the Commander were not unprepared, however, and with characteristic promptness moved to meet this new opportunity for service. The tradition of service to American soldiers, established so firmly in the Spanish-American War, was upheld and enlarged upon. World War I was to open a new era in Salvation Army history.

XVI

Doughnuts for Doughboys

"The die is cast! The tocsin has sounded, and our beloved land has plunged into the unprecedented war that for the last two and a half years has been rocking the world." The United States at last had entered the battle at the side of England, but Commander Evangeline Booth, in a *War Cry* editorial "The Salvation Army and the War," showed no elation. She warned: "The Salvation Army is ready for the emergency but the Salvation Army is an international organization; our flag is interlaced with flags of all peoples. As our great Founder was, and bade us to be, we know no man after the flesh, and yet recognize our brothers in all the families of the earth; hence there is only one war in which we can glory—that supreme struggle in which we are ceaselessly and desperately engaged—the struggle to triumph over sin and strife and death, with purity, peace and life everlasting—all other war we deplore. But the Salvationist stands ready, trained in all necessary qualifications in every phase of humanitarian work, and, to the last man, will stand by the President for the execution of his orders."

World War I probably marks the climax of Salvation Army history in the United States. The Army had quite generally won the confidence of the city slum dwellers and the respect and support of many wealthy persons in the thirty-seven years before 1917. But the great majority of Americans knew little and cared less about the uniformed figures they saw in small groups on the street corners playing musical instruments or exhorting a lethargic group of bystanders. World War I gave the Salvation Army the unique opportunity to demonstrate more fully to Americans the qualities that were always part of the Army's tradition.

The popularity that came to the Salvation Army as a result of its overseas work during the war was greatly out of proportion to the quantity—though not to the quality—of its service. In France the Salvation Army won the affection of the doughboy and the gratitude and respect of the whole nation, yet the spirit of those Salvationists who went to France was no different from those who stayed in America and ran slum nurseries, homes for destitute men and women, or other similar programs. But the eyes of the nation were turned on France; the thoughts of the nation were with its men on the battlefields; and there millions of Americans learned of the spirit of the Salvation Army for the first time.

Before America entered the war, Evangeline Booth had pledged to President Wilson the loyalty and service of the Salvation Army in the United States, at the same time pointing out the part played by Salvationists of other lands in support of the armed forces of their countries. When war broke out, a Salvation Army National War Council was called and a National War Board created to direct Salvation Army war work. Edward J. Parker, then colonel, was appointed national war secretary in addition to his position as head of the Social Service Department. Lieutenant Colonel Arthur T. Brewer was secretary for war work for the Department of the West. Commander Evangeline Booth, as national commander, and Commissioner Thomas Estill, Department of the West, were codirectors of the National War Board.

In the United States the Salvation Army set up service centers outside but adjacent to the various camps. Known as "huts" or "huts and hostels," these buildings contained canteens to furnish a change from United States Army "chow," recreation rooms, writing facilities, meeting rooms, and libraries. In some instances hotel facilities were provided for soldiers and their friends and relatives. On Sundays religious services were conducted. In all, 19 huts, 6 huts and hostels, 16 hostels, 17 naval and military clubs, 33 rest and recreation rooms were established. Railway Canteen Service was carried out at three stations in Chicago, and in Tacoma and Seattle, Washington.

The Salvation Army led a campaign against camp followers and the diseases they spread, not only in the interests of the young soldiers but to save and to help reform the girls themselves. In addition to the officers assigned to huts and special service centers, the regular corps officers were ready to assist members of the armed forces and their families.

However, it is not for its work in the States that the Salvation Army won its recognition during World War I, but for its work overseas. A happy choice for director of war work in France was Lieutenant Colonel William S. Barker, who left New York with Adjutant Bertram Rodda on June 30, 1917, to survey the situation in France. Armed with a letter of recommendation from Joseph P. Tumulty, President Wilson's secretary, Barker was received by the American Ambassador to France, who arranged for him to see General Pershing.

Meanwhile, in the United States, preparations were underway to follow the boys overseas. Evangeline Booth borrowed $25,000 to finance the beginning of the work, and later another $100,000 was borrowed from International Headquarters. Financial support for Salvation Army war work was slow at the beginning; but, as the Commander said, "It is only a question of our getting to work in France, and the American public will see that we have all the money we want."

Colonel Barker cabled from France to send over some lassies. Commander Evangeline Booth was greatly surprised but, having confidence in Barker, she included some carefully selected women officers in the first group sent to France. The work of the "Sallies" justified Barker's wisdom in making the request.

The first group of Salvation Army officers to join the AEF left New York on the *Espagne* on August 12, 1917. Six men, three women, and a married couple formed the party of eleven, all from the Eastern Department. A second party of eleven, that sailed on

September 13th, was composed mainly of officers from the Western Department. Each Salvation Army officer accepted for war service in France was carefully screened. It was determined at the beginning to restrict the number to be sent overseas and to keep the quality of the highest. Not one hint of scandal was ever associated with a Salvation Army lassie in France, although in nearly all cases the girls were subject to a constant adoration from thousands of homesick boys that might have turned their heads.

The Salvation Army in France first went to work in the area of the 1st Division. The first party landed in France on August 22, 1917, and work on the first hut began on September 1st. The first "hutment," as it was called, was a long sectional building, 40 x 150 feet, with ten windows on each side. It had a staff of five men and six lassies, all of whom were musicians, who gave concerts and conducted song services in addition to operating the canteen. The Salvationists conducted Bible classes, but their building was available to other denominations or fraternal orders. In it Jewish services were held, and on one occasion the Loyal Order of Moose conducted an initiation. A clothes-mending service was provided by the girl officers.

Like the other organizations that operated canteens in France during World War I, the Salvation Army sold candy, toilet articles, and writing material to the soldiers at a nominal charge. It is hard for veterans of the Second World War to imagine paying for articles that were furnished to American soldiers overseas so freely in the form of Post Exchange rations, but in 1917 the United States Army had not assumed this obligation and the task was given to private agencies, who were forced to operate on a budget and whose canteen managers had to account for the material that passed over their counters.

The Salvation Army might be criticized for its lack of business-like methods, but it won the lasting affection and gratitude of the doughboy. A soldier need not have the cash in hand to purchase an article from a Salvation Army canteen; he could get "jawbone," or credit. No records were kept. The soldier was asked to remember what he owed and to settle his account at payday. This trust in the doughboy not only paid incalculable dividends in good will, but proved to be sound business judgment as well. Although there was no check on them, the soldiers paid what they owed and very little was lost from bad debts.

One Salvation Army officer on occasion loaned money without identification or receipt, asking only that it be returned to any Salvation Army hut marked for his attention when the recipient could pay. He claimed never to have lost by this policy.

It was the doughnut, however, that caught the doughboy's fancy. The rations of the AEF were limited indeed. Four Salvation Army "lassies" with the American First Division wondered what they could do to supplement the chocolate bars in their canteen. "Why not make doughnuts?" suggested Ensign Margaret Sheldon. Flour and lard were secured, but because the girls had no rolling pin the dough was patted into shape. The top of a baking powder can served to cut out the doughnuts, and a camphor ice tube to cut out the holes. The first doughnut was fried by Adjutant Helen Purviance, and the first batch was an immediate success with the soldiers.

Although the doughnut became the symbol of the Salvation Army in France, pies and cakes were also baked by the girls in crude ovens, and lemonade was served to hot and thirsty troops as well. It was not only the delicious home cooking but also the spirit with which it was served that captivated the men. The simple secret was that the Salvationists were serving not only the soldiers but God, and they brought to mind thoughts of home and of the people there. At the Salvation Army hut the men could not only bring their uniforms to be mended; they could also bring their problems to share. As buttons were sewed on, a brief message of help was offered.

Soldiers in France frequently had more money than opportunities to spend it. To discourage gambling and the purchase of wines and liquors, and to aid families in the United States, the Salvation Army officers encouraged the soldiers to take advantage of the

Salvation Army's money-transfer system. In those preallotment days soldiers would give their money to a Salvation Army officer, who would enter the sum on a money-order blank and send it to National Headquarters in New York. From there it went to the corps officer nearest the soldier's home, who would then deliver the money in person to the soldier's family or relatives. Often cases of need were discovered through these visits, and other Salvation Army services might be made available to help those in distress. The money-transfer plan also worked in reverse on occasions when friends sent money to soldiers overseas.

One of the things that the American soldiers marveled at was the fact that the Salvation Army followed them right to the front. The women as well as the men went where the troops happened to be, and often were in danger from shells and gas.

Enthusiasm for the Salvation Army spread like wildfire through the AEF in France, from the lowliest doughboy to General Pershing himself. The stories of the work of the Salvation Army in France first reached America through the letters of the men "over there," and then through the stories of war correspondents.

A special correspondent of the New York *Times* wrote, under the heading "With the American Army in France": "When I landed in France I didn't think so much of the Salvation Army; after two weeks with the Americans at the front I take off my hat to the Salvation Army. The American soldiers take off their hats to the Salvation Army, and when the memoirs of this war come to be written the doughnuts and apple pies of the Salvation Army are going to take their place in history."

Received with an attitude of skepticism in the fall of 1917, the Salvation Army soon became the most popular organization in France. There were other agencies at work, and with these the Salvation Army cooperated; there was no open competition and much cooperation. On one occasion when a Salvation Army canteen ran out of supplies with a long line of soldiers still unserved, a YMCA truck drove up and pulled in beside the Salvation Army vehicle, and continued serving where the Salvation Army had left off. Many newspaper articles attest to the Army's popularity. While the

Salvation Army never made comparisons with other agencies, the newspapers were bound to do so. As one paper editorialized:

Few war organizations have escaped criticism of some sort, but there is, so far, one shining exception, and that is the Salvation Army. Every soldier and civilian who have been brought into contact with its workers sing their praises with enthusiasm. Wherever they have been they have "delivered the goods"—they have proved 100 per cent efficient as moral and material helpers.

Some Americans were ashamed of their sneers at the Salvation Army in the past and were quick to make amends. Under a cartoon showing two soldiers at a Salvation Army canteen was the caption: "Mmm. Some pie, Phil! 'Member how we used to guy the Salvation Army?" "Yep. Never again."

Financial support for the Salvation Army's war program came with a rush. A plea for a million dollars, endorsed by President Wilson and Secretary of War Newton D. Baker in December, 1917, was soon answered. In 1918 the Salvation Army joined the YMCA, YWCA, War Camp Community Service, National Catholic War Council, Jewish Welfare Board, and the American Library Association in a United War Work Campaign to raise $170,000,000 of which the Salvation Army was to receive $3,500,000. This drive was under way when the armistice was signed on November 11, 1918.

Salvation Army war work in France did not end with the armistice. Hospital visitation and nursing aid continued after the war, as did other services for the troops in France and later in occupied Germany. The Salvationists were frequently given a commission to get a watch repaired or to buy a Christmas or birthday gift for some loved one. They furnished paper and pens and urged soldiers to write home.

A grim but tender Salvation Army activity was carried on from headquarters in Paris in the form of grave-identification service. Thousands of letters from the States with all available information about lost ones were received. The service was to find missing men, but it generally ended in the identification of their graves. By working from slim clues, Salvationists would often find a mound of earth and cross with identification tags nailed on it. A photograph of the grave, with a record of its exact location and all other available data, would then be made and sent to the inquirer.

Lieutenant Colonel Barker returned from France in the summer of 1919 after a job well done. He had been the first American Salvationist to go overseas, and he was almost the last to return. In addition to directing the work of Salvation Army activities with the AEF, Barker had been the purchasing agent for all the material used or sold through Salvation Army huts and canteens; some he secured from New York, but most of it he had to purchase in Paris or other large European cities. Transportation was always a difficulty, and some of the supplies were carried a distance of fifty-five miles.

The Salvationists in France were not many in number. The War Service Report declared that there were never more than 500 officers and other workers under its control in France with the AEF. Official figures vary, but the number of regular Salvation Army officers and Salvationists commissioned as envoys sent from the United States was close to 250. In addition, about 400 men and 150 women workers were secured on the other side.

When the doughboys began to return to the States, they found the Salvation Army waiting for them at the docks with coffee and doughnuts. Transports were met at the debarkation ports of New York, Boston, Philadelphia, and Newport News, Virginia. Telegrams were sent free of charge to the families of returning men, announcing their safe arrival.

A convalescent home for soldiers was established in Atlantic City, New Jersey, and hospital treatment for servicemen's families was provided in New York. Wounded and disabled soldiers were visited regularly by Salvation Army women. In Chicago a Clothing Bureau was organized, and several hundred needy men were assisted in securing civilian clothes after their discharge.

For a quarter-century the Salvation Army had operated free employment agencies throughout the United States. After the war, preference in securing jobs was given to veterans.

Active domestically during the war was the Home Service League, similar to the old Auxiliary League. A half-dollar membership fee was charged, and members were asked to contribute money and to work on such projects as knitting and sewing.

To the next of kin of war dead went a specially prepared card of condolence signed by Commander Evangeline Booth, who was active in directing and financing the war work of the Salvation Army from the United States. Her picture in the uniform authorized by General Pershing and worn by Salvation Army workers overseas was given wide circulation. Her official biographer states that a planned trip to the battlefields of France in June, 1918, was vetoed by International Headquarters.

A few months after the United States entered the war, an interesting decision affecting the Salvation Army was handed down. William Booth denied vigorously during his lifetime that the Salvation Army was a denomination, and resisted incorporation for this reason. In September, 1917, a declaration by the Judge Advocate General of the War Department, that the Salvation Army was indeed a religious denomination, was welcomed by its leaders. The Salvation Army offered the services of its officers as chaplains. Among the qualifications of chaplains was the requirement that they must be "a regularly ordained minister of some religious denomination." The decision stated in part:

It seems that the Salvation Army is a world-wide religious organization, with followers in great numbers, property in generous measure, and doing great good. It has distinct legal existence; a recognized creed and form of worship; a definite and distinct ecclesiastical government; a formal code of doctrine and discipline; a distinct religious history; a membership not associated with any other church or denomination; a complete organization, with officers ministering to their congregations, ordained by a system of selection after completing prescribed courses of study. In common with other churches, it has literature of its own; established places of religious worship; regular congregations; regular religious services; a Sunday-school for the religious instruction of the young, and schools for the preparation of its ministers. The functions of its ministers seem to be similar to those of the clergy of any other church. In addition to conducting religious services upon stated occasions, they perform marriage ceremonies, bury the dead, christen children, console the bereaved and advise and instruct the members of their congregations.

In addition to making Salvation Army officers eligible for service as chaplains, this decision permitted draft exemption for officers on the same basis as that for ordained ministers of other denominations.

Five Salvation Army officers wore the uniform of United States Army chaplains during World War I. The first to be accepted was Adjutant Harry Kline of the Omaha Men's Industrial Home. He was commissioned as First Lieutenant Chaplain of the 6th Nebraska Infantry. Kline was a veteran of the Spanish-American War and had seen service in the Philippines, where he had worked with Major John Milsaps, the Salvation Army chaplain of the Spanish-American War. Born at Fort Leavenworth, Kansas, during an Indian War when his father was in the 12th Kansas Cavalry, Harry Kline had been a cowboy and professional gambler throughout the West before his conversion in 1891. After the Spanish-American War, he entered the Salvation Army as an officer, devoting most of his time to Men's Social work. It would be hard to imagine a man better suited to work with soldiers than the first Salvation Army chaplain of World War I.

Another chaplain, John J. Allan, reached the rank of major and served at General Pershing's headquarters with the chaplain-general of the AEF. Allan had been very successful in command of the Bowery Corps in New York before his appointment. Other Salvation Army officers who served as chaplain first lieutenants were J. A. Ryan, Ernest R. Holz, and Norman Marshall.

In October, 1919, Commander Evangeline Booth received the Distinguished Service Medal with the approval of the nation. Though the honor went to the Commander, it was awarded to America's own Salvation Army in appreciation for the self-sacrifice and loving labor of Salvationists in France. It was a sign that the United States had at last fully recognized its Salvation Army and appreciated it.

As one writer confessed, "It took the great World War to open our eyes to the fact that the Salvation Army is a vital force in the community; it needed the testimony of our returning heroes to convince us that its activities were by no means confined to standing on street corners and singing hymns."

During World War I America saw, as if for the first time, what the Salvation Army had become in the United States. "The Salvation Army has had no new success. We have only done an old thing in an old way," declared Commander Evangeline Booth. The spirit of the Salvationists in France was the same spirit that had been seen in the slums of New York and Chicago, at the San Francisco Fire, in countless smaller cities and towns, and at minor tragedies without number. For decades men in crimson and blue uniforms and women in poke bonnets had served wherever mankind suffered, with quiet self-sacrifice. Always as they worked to alleviate the physical sufferings they encountered, they presented the message of salvation—the cure for spiritual maladies. It was this consecration that made a difference in the service of the Salvation Army in France, and brought out the similarity between this war service and other services of the Army since its founding. The Salvation Army was an American institution long before doughnuts were made in France, but for the first time the American public as a whole came to recognize and support its endeavors.

XVII

Prosperity and Prohibition

American Salvationists found themselves in a new position in the postwar decade of the "roaring twenties." Their work in France had won from a grateful public universal acclaim and liberal financial support. The principle of equality of women, so long practiced by the Army, was recognized at the polls when women received the vote, and in the business world as women continued to hold the positions they had assumed during the war.

The Salvation Army found its greatest satisfaction, perhaps, when the saloons were closed with the adoption of the Eighteenth Amendment. The outlook was not entirely favorable, however. Although prohibition ended the saloon, it brought the speakeasy and the hip flask. It was the age of the flapper, bobbed hair, and skirts above the knee. The ascending hem line caught the eye of Commissioner William Peart. "Lassies' dresses must be seven inches from the ground," he ordered from Chicago in 1922. Salvationists' skirt hems would remain close to the ground and their feet firmly upon the earth.

Commander Evangeline Booth was quick to recognize the Salvation Army's new position in America and, deciding that this was the psychological moment to put the organization on a sounder financial footing, she sought to do away with tambourine collections of nickels and dimes and to free corps officers from hectic days of fund begging. In May, 1919, a Home Service Fund Campaign was launched to raise $13,000,000. It was estimated that this sum would meet all of the expenses of the evangelical and social branches of the organization.

The campaign was well planned by professional publicity men; leading citizens served on the campaign committees; there were no large-salaried officials. Most of the work was contributed, and the campaign was run with strict economy. President Wilson, General Pershing, Marshal Joffre, and David Lloyd George were among the statesmen who endorsed the Army's work in the war. Colored posters by prominent artists advertised the campaign, as did a booklet telling of the work of the Army. Publicity men furnished newspapers with local copy, and the press responded with favorable editorials and cartoons.

Salvation Army Sunday was observed in churches of many denominations. A Doughnut Day was a great success, as doughnuts were cooked and sold for various contributions. The first was cooked by Commander Evangeline, and sold for $5,000. A total of $16,000,000 was achieved, most of it in small contributions—the nickels, dimes, quarters, and dollars of people from all walks of life and all social classes.

This successful campaign marked the first time Salvation Army fund-raising activities were conducted on an organized basis. Under the old system, where each unit financed itself as best it could, some units suffered because they were inadequately financed. With the introduction of budgetary procedure and organized fund raising, it was possible for the Army as a whole to ensure that all of its operations were maintained at a more uniform standard.

The national campaign plan that proved so successful in 1919 was used again in 1920. When three territories were created in that year, finances were no longer conducted on a national level but by each of the territories. The Salvation Army today, unlike many nonprofit organizations, does not have a national fund-raising drive each year. Each community determines the type of fund-raising activity to be conducted. In some cities the Salvation Army is a member of the Community Chest; in others, such as New York, an annual fund-raising campaign is conducted. Other funds are obtained through bequests and endowments.

In 1920 Commander Evangeline Booth visited Europe while General Bramwell Booth was on a tour of Australia. She returned to New York in July in time to confer with the General on his way back to London. On August 7, 1920, following the conference, an important territorial reorganization was announced. The United States was to be divided into three territories, each with a commissioner in command. Commander Evangeline Booth remained as national commander supervising all three of the territories but with no direct responsibility for any one.

Commissioner Thomas Estill left the old Department of the West to assume command of the new Eastern Territory, which included twenty-two Eastern and Southern states.[1] Commissioner William Peart was the first commander of the newly created Central Territory, consisting of fifteen Midwestern states with headquarters in Chicago.[2] To head the Western Territory with headquarters in San Francisco, Lieutenant Commissioner Adam Gifford was selected. This territory recognized the distinct status of the Western states for the first time since 1887, and included the eleven Western states and the Hawaiian Islands.[3] The formal creation of the new commands took place in October, 1920.

The administrative division of the United States was completed in the form of its present status with the creation of a fourth territory—the new Southern Territory—in 1926, including fifteen states south of Mason and Dixon's line, and the District of Columbia.[4] It began to function officially on January 1, 1927. William McIntyre was promoted to lieutenant commissioner and appointed as the Southern Territory's first commander.

The Salvation Army had made less progress in the South than in any other section of the country in the years before 1926. There were few large cities in the South; the evangelical Protestant churches were active in the South and nearly all the population were devout churchgoers. Perhaps the Salvation Army tradition of racial equality before God also acted as a handicap in the early period. Commander Evangeline Booth, in announcing the formation of the Southern Territory in 1926, explained that the Salvation Army would "carefully regard Southern sentiment and its work among the negroes would be in the nature of missionary work" in the new territory.

William McIntyre was especially well qualified to command the new territory. A Canadian-born Scotsman, McIntyre had served in the United States, pioneering in the Far West, since 1891. He was a veritable dynamo who wore out his staff officers. The stories of the originality and practicality of his ideas are today part of Salvation Army folklore.

After a survey of the South, Atlanta, Georgia, was chosen as the site of territorial headquarters. A training college was established, and the publication of a Southern *War Cry* was begun. Under the leadership of Commissioners McIntyre, Alexander Damon, Ernest Pugmire, William Arnold, Albert Chesham, and William Dray, the newest territory has become an important part of the Salvation Army in the United States.

Through these few decisive years of change and policy formation, the Salvation Army was keenly aware of social developments. There was no stancher supporter of prohibition in the United States than Commander Evangeline Booth of the Salvation Army. A campaign in favor of the adoption of prohibition was conducted in the *War Cry* throughout 1919. A column entitled "Strengthen America" attacked the "liquor men" for wasting "food, labor, and life." The adoption of the Eighteenth Amendment and the passage of the Volstead Act was hailed by the Army as an example to the world, and England was encouraged to follow Uncle Sam.

Throughout the fourteen years the Eighteenth Amendment was in effect, the Salvation Army, and especially its dynamic Commander, carried on an aggressive defense; not only was absolute prohibition praised but all attempts to modify or repeal it were strongly attacked. The Salvation Army, declared Evangeline Booth on many occasions, through its close contacts with the poorer people was better able to judge the effects of prohibition than most organizations. "Since the enactment of the Volstead Act drunkenness among the poor has almost entirely disappeared," she stated in 1922. After the adoption of prohibition, the Army found it difficult to find men to do the work in their industrial homes where

19,000 men, 75 per cent of whom were alcoholics, had worked before the war.

Commander Evangeline Booth was called upon to testify before the Senate Judiciary Committee in 1926 and the House Judiciary Committee in 1930 on the effects of prohibition. While unable to attend in person on either occasion, she went on record in each case with a strongly worded statement in defense of the Eighteenth Amendment.

The core of the Commander's argument was that prohibition had made liquor more difficult to obtain and more expensive, and therefore largely removed it from the reach of the poor and the average workingman. Boozers' Day in New York City was given up because not enough alcoholics could be found where literally thousands had been found before. Since prohibition there were fewer women in Salvation Army homes for unmarried mothers, fewer men in the industrial homes for destitute men, fewer cases of drunkenness in the Army's cheap hotels. "Prohibition is here to stay," declared Evangeline Booth time and again to audiences in all parts of the country. Drinking in speakeasies by the "idle rich" was merely a fad which would pass away, she maintained.

Attempts to modify the law to permit the sale of light wines and beer were subject to a strong attack by the Commander; 90 per cent of the drunkenness before prohibition was caused by beer, she declared. Modification means the return of the saloon, she asserted in Providence, Rhode Island, at the same time declaring that those who advocated modification were frequently in partnership with the bootleggers.

It was recognized that this position cost the Salvation Army some financial support. On at least two occasions Evangeline Booth declared she had refused contributions from wealthy men offered with the condition that she modify her stand in public. When it was discovered that James Speyer, a prominent banker who had been chosen chairman of the Salvation Army fund-raising drive in 1922, was also an officer of an organization that staged a meeting to protest the prohibition amendment, Commander Evangeline Booth declared that he must recant his views or resign.

When prohibition became a political issue, the Salvation Army was placed in a difficult position. In the 1928 campaign, with Alfred E. Smith, a well known "wet," as the Democratic candidate, the Salvation Army's sympathy was with Herbert Hoover, supporter of prohibition. In September, 1928, Lieutenant Colonel Thomas Cowan was reported as declaring in a sermon in New York that the Salvation Army preferred the election of Hoover. In October, when Wallace Winchell went too far in advertising an illustrated lecture on "Six Months with Herbert Hoover in Belgium Relief," followed by a talk on "Hoover the Man," at the Bowery Corps, Commander Evangeline Booth ordered it canceled and issued the statement: "The Salvation Army is not in politics and neither our places of worship nor our officers are employed to take part in the election."

Evangeline Booth became subject to much criticism on the ground that her stand on prohibition constituted interference in politics. Mayor James Curley, of Boston, not only refused to appear at the opening of a fund-raising campaign, but declared he would not contribute until there was "a return to the policy of non-participation in matters political by the Salvation Army." Prohibition is not a political issue but a moral one, replied the Commander to her critics. "We must fight every enemy of the body and soul of man," she told a Chicago audience in June, 1932.

On the following day she gave the opening prayer at the Democratic National Convention. By a strange irony it was this convention that endorsed a repeal plank in its platform and nominated Franklin D. Roosevelt, whose election ensured the end of the "noble experiment." After the repeal of the Eighteenth Amendment was assured, Evangeline Booth made clear the position of the Salvation Army. At a luncheon launching the 1933 fund appeal, she declared, "Long before prohibition the Salvation Army was the greatest temperance organization in this country and will continue its unalterable opposition to intoxicating liquors." The battle against alcoholic beverages was to go on.

For many years it became increasingly evident that the Salvation Army had outgrown its National and Eastern Territorial Headquarters in New York. From 1895, when the building was so proudly dedicated, to 1928, the Army had increased from 1,768 to 4,814 officers, staffing 1,735 corps. In the latter year plans were proposed for a group of buildings that would serve the Salvation Army for many decades to come. The old Headquarters Building was to be torn down to make way for the new buildings. The plans included an eleven-story office building for National and Territorial Headquarters, a large auditorium to seat 2,000, and a young women's residence hotel with a capacity for housing 350 business women, a gymnasium, and swimming pool.

Temporary headquarters were established for a year in a new office building at Broadway and Fourteenth Street while the old structure was razed and the new one erected. On October 5, 1929, the new cornerstone was laid by Commander Evangeline Booth. The original copper box from the cornerstone of the old building was placed in the new cornerstone with its contents intact beside another with up-to-date photographs and data. About five hundred Salvationists and their friends were present at the modest ceremony.

The buildings were completed in 1930, the fiftieth anniversary of Railton's arrival in the United States, which was celebrated as the golden jubilee year. A Golden Jubilee Congress was held in New York from May 16 to 23, 1930, the high light of which was the dedication of the new Headquarters Building and auditorium. In some ways reminiscent of the anniversary celebrations held annually during the first few years of the Salvation Army in the United States, the Golden Jubilee Congress summarized the progress made in fifty years.

President Herbert Hoover sent a message to the Jubilee Congress at its opening meeting, on May 16, 1930, at the Seventy-first Regiment Armory at Park Avenue and Thirty-fourth Street. A pageant with a cast of three thousand depicted the history of the Army during the past fifty years. The following day, after a service at the Battery where Railton and the seven lassies had landed, a parade of three thousand marched up Broadway in a shower of ticker tape. Twenty Army bands and three floats were spaced between the sixteen divisions headed by Commander Evangeline Booth riding in an open automobile.

In the evening more than seven thousand people crowded into the Seventy-first Regiment Armory to hear John Philip Sousa lead the massed bands of the Salvation Army in "The Salvation Army March," composed by him and dedicated to Evangeline Booth.

Another feature of the Congress was a women's meeting on May 20th, with Mrs. Eleanor Roosevelt, wife of the governor of New York, as chairman. Messages were received from Mrs. Herbert Hoover, Mrs. Calvin Coolidge, and Lady Astor; 3,500 women filled Carnegie Hall for the program, as Evangeline Booth gave the main address, "Women Who Have Made History."

The climax of the Congress was the dedication of the new National and Territorial Headquarters and the Centennial Memorial Temple on May 18, 1930. Fifteen commissioners were present, including the Chief of Staff, who came from England for the Congress. Commander Evangeline Booth was decorated with the Order of the Founder at the dedication ceremony. Only eleven others had been elected to the order founded by General Bramwell Booth in 1915. The John and Mary R. Markle Memorial Residence, better known as the Evangeline Residence, was dedicated on June 14, 1930. It was made possible by a $500,000 gift from John Markle.

The attractive buildings of yellow brick and modern design, erected at a cost of $2,500,000, still dominate West Fourteenth Street today, a quarter of a century later. They are a fitting monument to the far-sighted planning of Commander Evangeline Booth. Their construction coincided with the end of a decade of prosperity in the United States. In this same decade other foundations were laid. Reforms in the international government of the Salvation Army were accomplished, and these too were the result of the leadership of Commander Evangeline Booth.

XVIII

High Council

A High Council, called in 1929 to adjudicate General Bramwell Booth's fitness to continue in office, was the climax of a long period of agitation to reform the basic government of the Salvation Army. The success of this reform movement made possible the continued progress of the Salvation Army under democratic leadership. Much of the impetus behind the movement came from American Salvationists, particularly Commander Evangeline Booth, and the High Council and its results must be considered one of the decisive events in Salvation Army history.

The government of the Salvation Army in 1928 had not been changed since it was set up by the Army's Founder, General William Booth. According to the original Foundation Deed of 1875, the organization was to be "under the over-sight, direction and control of some one person." An advisory committee set up in the same deed was abolished by another Deed Poll in 1878, at which time William Booth was secured in office for life and given the power to appoint his successor.

In addition to having absolute authority over all activities of the Salvation Army, the General was the sole trustee of all the property and monies of the Army, holding them in his own name. This system proved unworkable when the Salvation Army spread overseas. In the United States the Salvation Army was incorporated in 1899, and corporations were set up to hold the property of the Salvation Army in other countries, although in England and the colonies property continued to be held in the name of the General until 1930.

This autocratic system of government did not go uncriticized. Many able officers, including three of William Booth's own children, resigned because of disagreements over arbitrary orders. But no organized opposition to the autocracy of the General developed during the command of the Founder, William Booth. Instead, Salvationists developed a certain pride in stories of the old General's irascible temper and eccentricities. In his absolutism William Booth resembled a prophet—a man with a noble vision, divinely inspired, and so utterly devoted to carrying out his mission that few associates questioned his methods.

The selection of Bramwell Booth to succeed his father as General was expected and virtually unanimously approved by the Salvationist world, since it was conceded that no other individual was so well qualified for the position. Though Bramwell Booth assumed the same absolute powers of his father, he was unable to exercise them as the Founder had done without breeding resentment. Bramwell was an administrator who lacked the mystic commanding power of the prophet. Whereas William Booth had drawn his contemporaries to him and dominated them by his personality, Bramwell Booth in controlling his contemporaries alienated their affection. Yet he might have continued in office until his death had not the leader of the opposition against him been another Booth— his younger sister Evangeline.

The first important clash of wills between the two concerned the subject of a change of command. It was customary to change territorial commanders every five years, and in 1920 Commander Evangeline was completing her sixteenth year in the United States. In November and December of that year, General Bramwell Booth visited Canada and the United States, appearing in Chicago, Boston, Philadelphia, and then in New York, where he talked to Evangeline about a transfer. "You cannot expect to remain at the head of the organization [in the United States] all the rest of your life," the General warned his sister. Evangeline Booth had no desire to leave the United States, and protested vigorously. Before

Bramwell sailed for England, he and his sister talked it out for twelve hours in the Algonquin Hotel in New York—inner circles knew the day as the Army's "Black Friday." The result was a respite of two years.

The two years were up in 1922, and on Saturday, September 9th, the New York *World*, in an exclusive front-page story, said it had learned of an impending announcement of the "promotion" of Commander Evangeline Booth to some other station. The story was sent to Commander Booth before publication, but she refused to see a reporter. In London, General Booth could not be reached, and Commissioner Higgins, Chief of Staff, refused to comment. Two days later Commander Evangeline received a *World* reporter in her office at National Headquarters and declared, in answer to his question about a change of assignment, "I can only say I have had no official orders as yet from the General."

She admitted that the question of her term as commander in the United States had been discussed in 1920. "I was reappointed by the General at that time," she said. "Before I received that definite appointment something was said about my remaining on for another two years or thereabout, but I do not think I have had anything of a definite nature. . . . Whatever orders reach me will find me a true soldier of the Salvation Army flag. I can obey orders as well as give them. But I want to say there are no words to express how deeply I would feel leaving America. You know I am an American citizen. I have given the best years, the best energy and the best gifts of my life to its betterment and its people."

The *World* scooped the New York press again on September 14th when it published an exclusive interview with General Bramwell Booth, cabled from London the day before, confirming that plans were being made to recall Evangeline Booth from her command in the United States and to eliminate the office of national commander. "Commander Evangeline Booth's farewell to the United States has been under consideration a number of years," the General declared, "but the war made the change impossible. It is not my intention to re-district the United States. The present three commands will remain, each of the three Commissioners being responsible directly to me, as Commander Evangeline Booth hitherto has been."

Commander Evangeline Booth admitted to reporters that she had received a radiogram from her brother with orders to farewell. "I shall obey the order when the date is set for me to go. I have cabled . . . for further information," she said. One reporter wrote, "No reason for deposing her was given and she said she knew of none." It was unfortunate that a routine order to farewell should be interpreted by the press as a deposition, although the Commander did not try to conceal her reluctance to leave the United States. To a group of local officers and soldiers she declared, "If I must go, ending my work here and leaving so many friends behind in America, I will depart with a broken heart."

The announcement that Commander Evangeline Booth was ordered to farewell produced a situation that was almost identical with that in 1896. The newspapers were quick to make the comparison, and again American supporters of the Army organized to protest the farewell order. The same dire threats of loss of financial support that characterized the earlier protest movement were voiced, and several important Americans wrote to record their objections to the order. One cable of protest was signed by twenty prominent Americans, including Herbert Hoover, Thomas R. Marshall, William G. McAdoo, Bishop William T. Manning, and Rabbi Joseph Silverman.

"I am taking no part in any statement or protests that may be sent to General Booth. I am simply a soldier in the Salvation Army and feel that it is my duty to obey any order that is given to me, or to go when he decides that I must relinquish my work here," declared Commander Booth. The protest movement spread among the officers and soldiers of the Salvation Army as well as among its friends. American Salvationists were almost solid in support of the Commander.

For the nearly three months that the newspapers reported the controversy, the Army in the United States was kept in a state of uncertainty. Protest after protest was dispatched to London, until on December 3rd General Bramwell Booth receded from his position. In a cable that was an attempt to back down and at the same time to save face, the General declared:

I have been informed by my representatives in the United States of America that the statement in the New York *World* on September 15 [*sic*] has been interpreted by a number of people as being an official intimation for my sister, Commander Evangeline Booth to farewell from her present command. Those, however, who carefully read that statement will remember that it did not contain such intimation, but referred to the programme for future developments in the United States upon which I had fully conferred with the Commander two years ago.

Certainly such information as deciding definitely upon the Commander's removal would not have been conveyed to her through the medium of the public press. As, however, I am given to understand some uncertainty still exists upon this matter, I deem it advisable to say that I have had no thought of an immediate farewell.

The failure to carry out the decision to change the command of the Salvation Army in the United States represented a disintegration of the absolute power wielded by William Booth as General and claimed by his son and successor. As Evangeline Booth's official biographer commented, "The prestige of General Bramwell Booth was shaken." More than this, the power of Evangeline Booth was shown and the long-smoldering disagreement between brother and sister was brought to a head.

General Bramwell Booth's final visit to the United States in 1926 was marred by fears of his sister's actions. She was reported to be sick during most of his visit, and yet he had great difficulty in obtaining specific information about her health. In other respects his visit was a success: his meetings were crowded, his talks with the various officers encouraging, and he left the United States on May 5, 1926, with spirits improved.

Then in September, 1927, Commander Evangeline Booth went to France to participate in an American Legion convention in Paris, and on her return visited London. In an interview with her brother, the last time the two were to meet face to face, she presented him with a statement of demands known as the Fifteen Points. Although there were indeed fifteen paragraphs, the actual statement contained only two major points: Bramwell Booth was asked to refrain from exercising his right to designate his successor and to provide a method for electing future generals of the Salvation Army. Bramwell rejected emphatically any idea of a change in the Salvation Army government as it had been handed down to him from his father.

The reform movement led by Evangeline Booth aimed at two major changes in the government of the Salvation Army. The first of these was the practice of each General choosing his successor. No one had objected to the choice of Bramwell Booth, but it became evident that he intended to select his successor from his family. It was commonly agreed that none of his sons or daughters had the qualifications for the office and that the attempt to create a dynasty would be harmful to the Army. Many felt that Bramwell's sons and daughters already had too much influence and authority.

Then, too, the absolute power of the General was criticized. The position of the General as sole trustee of all the temporalities of the Army, and his authority to make all appointments, came under attack; cases were cited where General Bramwell Booth consigned to the "cooler" (transferred to less favorable positions) those who disagreed with him or who offered criticisms.

It soon became evident that the highest Salvation Army officers, in England as well as in other countries, were in favor of these organizational changes. Even Commissioner Edward J. Higgins, Chief of Staff and General Bramwell Booth's closest confidant, believed these reforms necessary if the Army was to continue its mission of service most effectively.

In May, 1928, General Bramwell Booth, then seventy-two years old, took his first vacation on the advice of his physicians. Chief of Staff Edward J. Higgins was in charge during his absence. In November the General's illness became serious.

Under a supplementary deed poll drawn up by William Booth in 1904, provision was made for a High Council with the power to remove from office a General judged "unfit" and to elect a successor. The High Council was to consist of the Chief of Staff, the Secretary for Foreign Affairs, all commissioners not on the retired list, and all officers holding territorial commands regardless of rank. A request to call a High Council "for the purpose of adjudicating whether the General for the time being is unfit for office" was presented to the Chief of Staff on November 14, 1928. It was signed by seven commissioners, most of whom were associated with International Headquarters. On November 15th the call for a High Council to meet on January 8, 1929, at Sunbury on Thames, twenty-three miles from London, was cabled throughout the world.

General Bramwell Booth's serious illness, from which he had nearly recovered by the time the High Council met, served as the excuse for its formation, but the real reason was the almost universal desire on the part of the high-ranking officers of the Army to elect the next General rather than to permit the selection by the reigning General through a sealed envelope. They feared Bramwell Booth might die and that his chosen successor would take office before they could act. The New York *Times* described the situation:

> What is described as the most serious crisis in the history of the Salvation Army now exists as the result of the failure of eight years' effort by a "reform" movement within the Army, headed by Commander Booth, to persuade her brother to give up the autocratic and dynastic powers now vested in him by the constitution.

The call for a High Council and its subsequent actions created indeed the most serious crisis in the history of the Salvation Army. For nearly six months scarcely a day went by without a reference to the affair in the newspapers. On five consecutive days stories of the High Council were carried on the front page of the New York *Times*.

The High Council met as scheduled. Leading the fight to prevent the deposition of General Bramwell Booth was his oldest daughter, Commissioner Catherine Bramwell Booth, although her position as defender of her father was weakened by the fact that it was commonly believed that she was Bramwell Booth's selection as his successor.

On January 17th, just after midnight, a vote of the sixty-three delegates was completed. By a margin of 55 to 8, General Bramwell

Booth was voted unfit to continue in command of the Salvation Army. Four of the eight who voted to support the General were his wife, his sister Lucy, and his two daughters. This first action of the High Council was declared invalid by the courts because General Booth's request to explain his position before the council had been refused. After the General's case had been presented by his attorney, the Council voted again in February 13, 1929, to depose the General by vote of 52 to 5. Four abstained from voting.

Immediately after deposing General Bramwell Booth for the second time, the High Council proceeded to elect his successor. Edward J. Higgins, Chief of Staff, was elected by 42 votes, with Commander Evangeline Booth, who received 17 votes, second, and the first High Council dissolved. It is interesting to note that General Higgins was elected with all the authority and powers formerly held by Bramwell Booth.

After Bramwell Booth was deposed, it was said that he lost his desire to live, and on June 16, 1929, he was promoted to Glory, four months after his final deposition. Bramwell Booth had been popular among the rank-and-file of British Salvationists, and a continuous line filed past his body as it lay in state in the Salvation Army Congress Hall at Clapton. Vast crowds paid tribute as the mile-long funeral procession, rivaling that of his father, wound its way through London to Abney Park Cemetery.

Even the death of the old General failed to settle the controversy over his deposition. Months of wrangling and litigation in the courts followed before the property of the Salvation Army in England and Northern Ireland was turned over to Edward J. Higgins as General.

The reforms anticipated by those who led the High Council were the subject of a Commissioner's Conference called by General Higgins in November, 1930. Forty-two commissioners from all over the world met in London to revise the Salvation Army's constitution, and after considerable discussion four major proposals were approved: the General was no longer to choose his successor, and future Generals were to be elected by the High Council; the General was no longer to be the sole trustee of the Army's property, and a board was created to serve as trustees of the property in England and Northern Ireland, similar to boards already operating in the United States and in other countries of the world; retirement at the age of seventy was to be compulsory for a General; and a board was recommended to arbitrate between the General and the high officers, with the power to make decisions binding on each.

These last two provisions were stricken out by the British Parliament, and the remainder was passed as the Salvation Army Act in July, 1931. Opposition to the bill was active, and came from two very different sources. The family of Bramwell Booth, led by Commissioner Catherine Bramwell Booth, opposed the bill because it proposed to change the autocratic system of government founded by William Booth, while Commander Evangeline Booth opposed the bill because it was not democratic enough.

Following the High Council of 1929, American-born officers began to be appointed to top administrative positions. The first American-born commissioner was Samuel Logan Brengle, an evangelist, who as National Spiritual Special had no administrative duties. He had become a lieutenant commissioner in 1926. The first administrative officer born in the United States to reach commissioner's rank was Edward J. Parker, national secretary, who was appointed lieutenant commissioner by General Higgins in 1930. A territorial commander, Massachusetts-born Alexander M. Damon, received the same rank in the same year.

General Edward J. Higgins was well known to American Salvationists. For nine years he had served in the United States as chief secretary to Commanders Booth-Tucker and Evangeline Booth. He left the United States in 1905 for a position at International Headquarters that led eventually to the highest office in the Salvation Army. As General he visited the United States, and after his retirement he made America his home until his death on December 14, 1947.

The significance of the High Council of 1929 can hardly be over-emphasized. Personalities undoubtedly played a role in the controversy. It is unfortunate that an aged and ailing man who had devoted his whole life to the development of the Army had to be put aside in order that the Army might continue to grow. Unfortunate, too, that a question of personal ambition should becloud Evangeline Booth's leadership of the reform movement. But the principles involved were more important than the personalities. From the foundations laid at the first High Council, the Salvation Army built a more democratic international organization. The principle of the election of the General prevented the establishment of a Booth dynasty, and enabled the Army to utilize its finest available talent as leaders. Events have proved that the future success of the Salvation Army was not dependent upon any one family or any one individual. Since 1930 the ministry of the Salvation Army throughout the world has become increasingly effective under a series of able international leaders.

XIX

Depression

"No man need steal, starve, or commit suicide; come to the Salvation Army," a slogan that has become part of the Army's tradition, was sorely tested in the depression that gripped the United States in the 1930's. In October, 1929, a few weeks after the cornerstone of the new Salvation Army Headquarters in New York was laid, the stock market crashed and the great depression fixed its grip on the nation. The Salvation Army was faced with the dilemma of increased demands for social service coinciding with a diminished income from contributions and endowments.

No other organization was better situated to feel the first effects of the depression than the Salvation Army. In June, 1930, the Army commented on the serious unemployment in the country, but added that indications pointed to better business conditions. While anxious to support President Hoover, the Army soon realized that the policy adopted by the Hoover Administration of radiating optimism while waiting for the specter to go away was not working. The Army saw its free employment service swamped with applicants for whom no positions could be found; Men's Social Service centers filled up and could take no more; the cheap hotels and food depots reported capacity crowds. A record number of 9,665 people passed through the Salvation Army's thirteen food depots in New York City in one twenty-four-hour period late in 1930. Similar conditions were reported in the other large cities.

The winter of 1930 posed new problems for the millions of unemployed in the nation. As cold weather approached, public commissions were set up to shelter and feed the homeless unemployed. In New York City the Salvation Army played an important part in the over-all plans. In October, 1930, eight free food stations were established as the beginning of the Salvation Army Emergency Relief Program. "It is the aim of the Salvation Army," declared Commissioner John McMillan, "that no human being in the city shall be without food and shelter this winter."

In New York City the Salvation Army cooperated to integrate its services with the municipality's effort to solve its problems. As a supplement to the Municipal Lodging House, crowded to overflowing each night, the Salvation Army operated Gold Dust Lodge. This was a six-story structure furnished by the Gold Dust Corporation, with a sleeping capacity for 2,000 to 3,500 homeless men and facilities for feeding about 10,000 a day. It was opened on December 1, 1931, and in less than five months had sheltered 4,587 unemployed men and served 429,318 meals. In one week 34,000 meals were served at a cost of only $857.50. This average of two full meals for a nickel was made possible by contributions of food from individuals and corporations. The Salvation Army Emergency Relief Program was expanded as far as available funds would permit. By February, 1933, in New York City, 26,161 lodgings and 106,771 meals were provided in one week by emergency institutions in addition to the regular agencies.

The importance of the Salvation Army program is made evident by the editorial statement from the New York *Times*, endorsed by the Commissioner of Public Welfare and the Police Commissioner of New York City: "Any break in the program of the Salvation Army would throw the city's welfare machinery seriously out of gear and would entail an immediate menace of social disturbances by the destitute unemployed." The service to New York City was repeated in the other cities of the country.

The expanded services in times of curtailed income from endowments and contributions created a serious problem for the Salvation Army. Emergency relief work in New York City increased 700 per cent in two years, declared Commissioner John McMillan at

Founder's Day exercises in April, 1932. In June, 1932, with emergency relief funds exhausted, the Army was forced to turn away thousands of deserving applicants for relief. Brigadier Thomas Seaver, of the Family Welfare Department, decried the situation as "the first time in Army history that it could not provide immediate relief to the needy."

To meet the crisis the Salvation Army took drastic steps. Officers' already low salaries were cut 10 per cent. As a further economy measure, the four officers' training colleges, in New York, Chicago, Atlanta, and San Francisco, were closed for one year. Field and social services were extended, especially in the larger cities.

The philosophy of Salvation Army Emergency Relief work was enunciated in the *War Cry* thus:

The Salvation Army does not concern itself with politics or economics. Causes and remedies of the present depression have little interest except in so far as they materially affect the people who require aid. We cannot manufacture employment on a larger scale. Our sole province, therefore, is to minister to those who have been wounded in the struggle for existence.

Throughout the great depression in the United States, the Salvation Army demonstrated the same desire to serve and willingness to self-sacrifice that was so evident on the battlefields of France in 1917–1918. As the federal government came to take over the burden that had been borne largely in the early years of the depression by local governments and private agencies, the Salvation Army sought other ways to serve.

In December, 1933, and January, 1934, the Salvation Army served sandwiches, doughnuts, and coffee to men who stood in line, sometimes all night long, to register for CWA and PWA jobs. As a factor in building morale, Cheer Lodge was established in New York. It was a five-story building furnished with washtubs and ironing boards, shower baths, game rooms, writing rooms, barbershop, library, and gymnasium. Open from 10:00 A.M. to 5:00 P.M., the only requirement for admission was to be unemployed. These are typical of some of the simple but original services of the Salvation Army during the depression.

Meanwhile, on the international scene, in May, 1934, General Edward J. Higgins announced his intention to retire on November 10, 1934. There was no compulsion for a General to retire at the age of seventy, but that age had been agreed upon at the Commissioners' Council in 1930. The call went out for a High Council to meet at the end of August to elect his successor.

Commander Evangeline Booth was a leading candidate despite the fact that she was but a year younger than the retiring General. "I should be prepared to take office if I was so honored," she replied to reporters when asked if she would be willing to accept the Generalship.

The second High Council met on August 28, 1934, in Clapton Congress Hall. Preliminary business occupied several days, and not until September 3rd were the ballots cast. Five ballots were necessary before a candidate received the required two-thirds vote. The successful candidate was Commander Evangeline Booth, who now added the title of General to her long list of honors earned in the service of the Salvation Army.

America rejoiced with General Evangeline Booth. President Franklin D. Roosevelt cabled his congratulations, and a New York *Times* editorial expressed a popular sentiment: "She herself declares that it gives her a 'pang' to think that she must leave America for a time. But whenever she returns she may be assured of a welcome which her new honors may enhance but cannot make more cordial or sincere." On her return to the city, Mayor La Guardia and 250 leading citizens formed a reception committee, as New York gave her a hero's welcome complete with brass bands and ticker tape.

Her public farewell was spectacular, with matching celebrations in various parts of the country. In New York, twenty thousand persons gathered in Madison Square Garden to honor her. United States Attorney General Homer S. Cummings presided, as Helen Keller, Bishop Manning, and Mayor La Guardia paid their tributes.

General Evangeline Booth had completed thirty years of service in the United States when she sailed for London on November 23, 1934, to assume the arduous duties of the highest office in the Salvation Army. With her went the prayers and best wishes of American Salvationists and the American public.

XX

The Era of Respectability

When General Evangeline Booth sailed from New York in 1934, the Salvation Army in the United States was left without the direct leadership of a member of the Booth family for the first time in nearly fifty years. No national commander was chosen to succeed her. Instead, the system proposed by Bramwell Booth in 1922 was adopted, with each of the American territories governed directly from International Headquarters. Commissioner Edward J. Parker, as national secretary, was in charge of National Headquarters and helped to coordinate the four American territories. As commander in the United States, Evangeline Booth had pursued a policy of subordinating the territories to the National Headquarters even to the extent of attempting to secure the right to appoint the territorial commanders. But as General she reversed this policy and adopted one of decentralization—weakening the National Headquarters to the point where the territories became nearly autonomous.

For nine years there was no national commander. It became evident that the organization was handicapped in a legal sense and in its relations with the public by the lack of a recognized national leader, and in January, 1943, Commissioner Edward J. Parker was appointed national commander, serving in that capacity until his retirement in December of the same year.

In line with the policy of decentralization, a plan to rotate the office of national commander among the four territorial commanders —each holding the office for a year—was then proposed. Commissioner Ernest I. Pugmire, Eastern territorial commander, was the first to assume the position under this system. He continued to hold the two offices with the assistance of a national secretary, Commissioner Donald McMillan, and an assistant territorial commander, Commissioner Norman Marshall, until 1947, when he was relieved as Eastern territorial commander and appointed full-time national commander. Commissioner Pugmire's sudden death on June 24, 1953, at the age of sixty-five, cut short an outstanding career. He was succeeded as national commander by Commissioner Donald McMillan, member of a prominent family of Salvation Army pioneers.

After 1934 it is no longer possible to describe the growth and development of the Salvation Army in terms of picturesque personalities. For thirty years Evangeline Booth *was* the Salvation Army to millions of Americans. As national commander, she made and interpreted her own rules. Today the range for personal rule or arbitrary judgment is very narrow indeed. Policy, not personality, has become the basis for the operation of the Salvation Army in the United States today.

William Booth frequently echoed the message expressed in the prayer of Bishop Francis Asbury, "O Lord, save Thy now despised Methodist children from the praises of this world." To some extent his fears were realized. As the Salvation Army outgrew the persecutions, scorn, and indifference of its early years, it lost some of the vitality that caused its phenomenal growth. Its ideals and aims and the spirit of consecrated service did not change. What was lost was the daring and audacity of the early period.

It was not uncommon for a teen-age captain and a young cadet with a few dollars in their pockets to "bombard" a town in the 1880's and 1890's and in a few months have a flourishing new corps. Others have borrowed Army methods with degrees of success. Today, in the poorer sections of American cities, new churches for spreading the old gospel have been organized in rented store buildings. In their simplicity and their spirit they are similar to the Salvation Army of sixty and seventy years ago—but they are not Salvation Army corps.

William Booth feared the danger of acquiring property, and Railton was ever apprehensive of "property and forms." One Salvationist remarked jokingly, but with more than a grain of seriousness, that organization and property were devices of the Devil to render a religious group impotent. It cannot be denied that property has cut down the mobility of the Salvation Army. Although officers could leave a rented hall to move to any section of a city where the need was indicated, once they owned the corps hall they were in a static position similar to that of a church and must make the congregation come to them. When the character of a neighborhood changes, as it is bound to do in a period of fifty years or more, a Salvation Army corps hall may find itself totally out of reach of the people that need it most, and often the corps can overtake them only at great cost in current property markets. But the acquisition of property was inevitable, and the Army has had to face the dilemma of every crusading religious order and church, a dilemma that none has yet successfully solved—the problem of acquiring property without loss of mobility.

In its attempt to meet the problem the Salvation Army has become three organizations in one—a trinity of mission, church, and social-service agency. On occasion this triune existence produces the complex difficulties of split personality, but generally the three parts complement and support one another.

The Salvation Army began as a mission devoted to the salvation of the social and economic outcast. It is true that while many and perhaps most of those who joined the Army in the United States were from respectable, churchgoing families, others were unfortunates whose inability to compete in a swift-moving industrial society brought them to the bottom of the social scale, and still others were victims of alcohol. Once they had been saved and had become members of the Salvation Army, they found that the new habits they adopted led to an improved economic condition. With little education themselves, they were able to help their children through high school and perhaps college. Some who had worked as laborers or at unskilled or semiskilled jobs saw their children become skilled workers, craftsmen, tradesmen, or white-collar and professional people. Although these children were higher in social scale than their parents with whom the Salvation Army had begun its work, they grew up to regard the Salvation Army as their church, attending its Sunday school, joining its youth clubs, Girl Guards, and Sunbeams, playing in the band, and many of them finding Christ at the Army's penitent form. Thus the character of a Salvation Army corps changed from a mission for the salvation of the outcast to a broader program, including the mission, but often with congregations of well dressed, sometimes well-to-do people.

Today many Salvation Army corps are indeed corps-churches whose members are almost entirely drawn from middle-class Salvationist families whose economic status is secure, and who contribute to corps support as members do in other churches. The Army still maintains its original function as a mission, and in the slum areas of the larger cities corps are operated at a financial loss to serve the more unfortunate members of society.

The evangelical and church work of the Army is known as field work, and the officers who direct the program of the corps are field officers, each a clergyman engaged in an active evangelical ministry. The Salvation Army corps commander is likely to be more frequently called upon for social service than is the ordinary pastor, however.

The social work of the Salvation Army is an outgrowth—or rather an expression—of its religious work. The officers engaged in social work have the same theological training and religious experience as the field officers. This spiritual motivation, the Salvation Army feels, makes its social services unique and often more valuable than those of purely secular agencies. As Colonel Holland French explained: "The work of the Army, through the growth and development of the organization, is carried on through various departments, but all the services are expressions or practical applications of the dominating motives of the organization as one spiritual unit. . . . The use of our social-service program in connection with the religious program is in reality 'Christianity-in-action,' i.e., the social forces of practical religion applied to the problems of day to day living. . . . The greatest contribution we can make (in fact our only reason for doing social work) is to demonstrate the dynamics of a vital religious experience in strengthening the inner resources of the individual, changing behavior-patterns, breaking down attitudes and in the development of personality. The Salvation Army officer, along with all Christian social workers, has in his possession resources not in the possession of the individual who does social work from a *purely secular point of view*."

Although any officer is in theory capable of directing a corps, doing mission work or working in some social branch of the organization; temperament, aptitude, training, and preference are considered in making assignments. Generally, successful social officers are not transferred to the field nor are outstanding corps officers assigned to social institutions.

Among Salvation Army officers an unusual spirit of comradeship and brotherhood exists. A number of factors contribute to this *esprit de corps*, which is international in its scope. In addition to a common religious experience and dedication to the same goal, the mobility of officers brings them closer to their fellow pilgrim travelers. Although officers are not moved from station to station as frequently as they were in the early period when six months was the average length of a corps command, the policy of change remains. An officer who has served at one corps for one or two years knows that he will soon be moved. In many cases the bond between Salvation Army officers is also one of family relationship. It is not uncommon to find Salvationists of the third and fourth generations. The regulation that officers may only marry other officers has united the principal Army families so that officers are likely to find cousins of some degree wherever they go.

Perhaps the greatest factor in building the unique Salvation Army morale is the training program that every officer in any part of the world must undergo. In the earliest days outstanding converts who were willing to devote their full time to Army work were commissioned with more or less informality and went to work.

Some of the early officers were recruited from the slums; many of them were reclaimed drunkards; and these converts, although reborn in spirit, did not change their table manners nor their rough language. The women who joined the Army, generally better bred and of a gentler nature than the men, were naturally sensitive to table manners and to other of the ordinary social amenities. Since regulations required that they find their husbands among the men officers, William Booth was forced to "tame" his men officers and to teach them table manners.

A Training Home for Women Officers was established in England in May, 1880, the year of the Army's establishment in the United States, and in October of the same year a Training Home for Men Officers was set up. The first training home in the United States was for men in the Brooklyn Lyceum. In September, 1882, an announcement in the *War Cry* stated, "We now have room for 6 young men (who love God and souls so much that they are willing to sacrifice everything to please the one in saving the other) to train as officers in the Salvation Army. They must be able to give the best of references and must be able to lead singing."

The training program in the 1890's was a strenuous one. The study day was from 6:00 A.M. to 10:30 P.M. Included in the course of study were "scrubology, sweepology, bootology, bed-makingology and other household work." The quality of the meals depended on the Training Garrison officer's ability as a money raiser. "Saloon bombarding," *War Cry* selling, and door-to-door visitation were also part of the training course, and each night, rain or shine, hot or cold, the cadets conducted an open-air meeting.

Today Salvation Army cadets undergo a concentrated nine-month course designed to fit them to meet present-day problems. There are four training colleges in the United States, one for each territory, in New York, Chicago, San Francisco, and Atlanta. The courses, prescribed by International Headquarters, are uniform in each of the colleges.

Cadets are carefully selected. After six months' active service as a soldier in a Salvation Army corps, a person may apply for officership, although in almost all cases a prospective candidate will have had much longer than this required minimum. Many applicants are from Salvation Army families and are already steeped in the tradition of the Army. In many cases a candidate has completed a six-year corps cadet course in Bible study and Salvation Army doctrine, history, and discipline.

A detailed file is compiled for each prospective candidate. In addition to his application he must write a narrative account of his personal religious experience and sense of calling to officership. Six endorsements are required. Medical forms, health history and dental chart, educational transcript and summary of work experience, citizenship questionnaire, birth certificate, and entrance fee complete the file. The candidate's case is presented to the territorial candidate's secretary, who brings it before the Candidates' Board with his recommendations. If accepted, the prospective candidate becomes a candidate until he enters a training college as a cadet at the beginning of a session.

Each session is given a name such as *Peacemakers, Standard Bearers, Ambassadors,* which is the same at every training college in the world. Into one academic year is crowded the basic training for a lifetime of service. The basic course of the curriculum is Bible study, to which the most time is devoted. Sermon preparation and delivery, pastoral work and evangelism, and music are next in order of importance. Courses on Salvation Army doctrine, corps accounts (bookkeeping), and social work are given. Practical experience is acquired by conducting open-air meetings, and through door-to-door visitation. On week ends brigades of cadets visit nearby corps and conduct the day's meetings from Sunday school through the evening open-air and Salvation service.

The regular training college staff is headed by a principal who directs the program, in which his wife also participates. The college is divided into two "sides," each headed by a side officer. The women's side officer is comparable to the dean of women of an academic institution, while the men's side officer supervises the men cadets. An educational officer, general secretary (business manager), and other officers bring the staff to about sixteen. In addition, other officers from headquarters, social institutions, and the field give lectures on missionary work, public relations, social work, and other special phases of an officer's work.

Each cadet is rated at three different times during the year by each of the training officers. He is evaluated according to a scale of characteristics under three major headings: spirituality, leadership, and personality. At these intervals cadets who are not satisfactory are eliminated. The emphasis in the training program and in the rating procedure is on the whole person, and deficiencies in scholastic ability may be offset by religious zeal or by some special aptitude. The potential of an individual is weighted heavily; thus, usually less than 1 per cent are "released" or "flunk out" in a session.

The commissioning, as Salvation Army commencement or graduation exercises are called, is the most colorful Army ceremony of the year. The public services are preceded by private covenant services at the training college at which each cadet makes a covenant for life service in the Salvation Army. Later, at public dedication ceremonies, the cadets make a more formal pledge.

The commissioning ceremony is full of color and suspense. A brass band, flags, and uniforms contribute to the color. The suspense derives from the fact that none of the cadets about to be commissioned knows his destination. The speeches are very much like other college commencement addresses. Commissioning is truly a commencement—the commencement of a career of service.

An officer's training does not end with his commissioning. Each officer is pledged to a post-training college program of five years' duration. Those few officers who may be deficient in their studies must complete high school by correspondence course. Other correspondence courses, on a wide variety of subjects and interests, are administered by the territorial educational officer.

In addition, many officers continue with specialist training at colleges or universities. Earlier, professional training was distrusted by conservative officers who feared that it would lead to a reliance on education rather than on faith; but the value of training in acquiring knowledge and techniques that will supplement and increase the Army's unique service is now generally recognized. Many Salvation Army officers hold bachelors' and masters' degrees; some are trained social workers, registered nurses, accountants, educators.

Young people contemplating officership are often encouraged to attend college before entering training college. In each of the four territories, scholarships are available for young Salvationists entering college. If these later enter officership, only one-half the scholarship loan need be repaid. A growing realization is evident that modern education is an aid in meeting the changed condition of the world.

The problems of the modern officer have been summed up in a Salvation Army publication entitled: *Pilgrim's Progress: 20th Century, The Story of Salvation Army Officership*. "He will find the people he proposes to evangelize quite different from those among whom the Officer of the first Army years began his warfare. If not a more wicked world, certainly he may come up sharp against a more perplexing one, more difficult to reach and influence. He will sometimes find the acceptance—of the Officer and his Army— just as hard to bear as the imprisonments and riots of the first adventurous years, because acceptance often implies complacency and indifference, and these are not the stuff of drama and adventure. Economically, he will face new complexities of the eternal problem—how to adequately finance his program. . . . The problems of an ultra-scientific age; of reaching unchurched masses, particularly youth; of new demands by the community to integrate his program more closely, to conform it to the needs and rights of people—all these and more await tomorrow's Officer."

Time magazine called the present the "Era of Respectability," and observed, "The Army, taking on respectability in spite of itself, has acquired property, a standing in the community, a connection with community chests, advisory committees of distinguished citizens. It has lost some of its old hoarse, street-corner fervor. . . . But the Army had to change with the time as the Devil himself changed, or lose the fight."

XXI

World War II and USO

When Japanese bombs on Pearl Harbor brought the United States into World War II, the Salvation Army was ready to repeat its record of service in World War I. Under the leadership of Brigadier Arthur Brewer, divisional commander for the Hawaiian Islands, all Salvation Army institutions on the island of Oahu were put into use to feed and shelter the evacuees from the attack on December 7, 1941. Emergency squads operated by the Salvation Army were on duty in the bombed city; ". . . the first exploding bomb on United States soil found the Salvation Army ready and on the job."

Much of the story of the American Salvation Army in World War II can be told in the three letters USO. The idea of bringing together the agencies who were prepared to do welfare work for servicemen so that they could work out a unified plan of cooperation is claimed by Commissioner Edward J. Parker. Parker, who had been the Salvation Army's national war secretary in the First World War, remembered the experience in cooperation that had been gained then. The first steps to form such an organization were taken in the fall of 1940, after Congress had passed the first peacetime draft in American history.

United Service Organizations for National Defense, Inc.—better known as the USO—was actually incorporated on February 4, 1941, and included the Young Men's and Young Women's Christian Associations, Catholic Community Service, Jewish Welfare Board,

Travelers Aid Association, and the Salvation Army. Bringing together as it did the three largest religious groups in the United States—Protestant, Catholic, and Jewish—for a common program of humanitarian service, the USO was a daring experiment in religious cooperation. "As a component part of USO," an Army publication announced with some justifiable pride, "the Salvation Army is sharing in a noble inter-faith effort."

The purpose of the organization, as stated in the rather stilted language of its constitution and by-laws, was "to aid in the war and defense program of the United States and its Allies by serving the religious, spiritual, welfare, and educational needs of the men and women in the armed forces and defense industries of the United States and its Allies in the United States and throughout the world, and in general, to contribute to the maintenance of morale in American communities and elsewhere. . . ."

A board of directors composed of five representatives from each of the six component groups supervised the activities of USO. Walter Hoving, prominent New York businessman and president of the Salvation Army Association, was elected the first chairman of the board. In addition, there were a president and three vice presidents —one representing each of three religious groups.

Plans for the USO were presented to President Franklin D. Roosevelt through Paul V. McNutt of the Federal Security Agency. The President endorsed the organization and agreed that the government would furnish the necessary buildings. The organization's first public appeal for funds in 1941 raised $14,000,000 to begin operations. At first, operations were at training camps in the United States with the new army of draftees, but by the time the United States was thrust into the war the Salvation Army itself was operating forty-three units in the USO, from Maine to Hawaii.

Much careful consideration was given in appointing Salvation Army officers to duty with the USO. The officers chosen to direct a USO club had an average of twelve years' experience in religious and social work. They were carefully screened to assure that they had the maturity, personality, and experience to work effectively with the young men and women of the armed forces and their families. A deep, motivating religious faith was required, because, as a manual for Salvation Army officers in the USO stated, "THE FUNDAMENTAL purpose of The Salvation Army in the programs of the United Service Organizations for National Defense is to assist the enlisted men of the United States war services to develop and adhere to a true standard of Christian living and life purpose."

USO buildings were usually located outside, but in close proximity to, Army posts, Naval bases, and Marine barracks. They were also found in the large cities where servicemen came on passes or traveled through on furlough or leave. "A home away from home" was the slogan used to describe these centers. "Meet me at the USO," was a common expression among G.I.'s to whom the USO was a place to meet comrades, civilian friends, or members of the family.

It was a place for relaxation and recreation planned to satisfy many different tastes. There was always ping-pong or shuffleboard or darts, and on certain nights there were dances and planned entertainment with local hostesses. A record player, albums of classical and popular music, and a small library and easy chairs were standard equipment. For those who were interested, classes in languages or handicrafts gave an opportunity to learn new skills. Desks and plenty of stationery encouraged writing home.

These were the ordinary services of the USO. Many individual servicemen, their wives, and members of their families can testify to other functions performed by USO club directors: wedding details arranged, special medicine obtained, or money lent for train fare for a wife. These and many other types of problems were worked out for men in uniform and their families.

An integral part of every USO club operated by the Salvation Army was the period devoted to religious services. The meetings were voluntary, of course, and very simple. A familiar hymn, a Bible passage, and a short testimony by the director was the usual procedure. Of course, no effort like that at regular Salvation Army meetings was made to obtain conversions, but an opportunity to find the way to a new Christian life was offered in these USO meetings.

The USO continued for two years after the war, its operations officially ceasing on December 31, 1947.[1] In the seven years it operated, it received $236,000,000 in voluntary contributions and expended this sum for the benefit of American servicemen. The work of the USO was done largely by volunteer personnel. In July, 1944, when the number of workers reached a peak of 675,000 individuals, only 16,000 were paid employees.

Although the bulk of Salvation Army war service in the United States was routed through USO, the Army also operated about 250 war service centers in the country on its own. Aside from the Red Shield clubs in the larger cities, most of these centers were in local headquarters buildings.

The regular Salvation Army services continued to benefit the nation in war as they had in peace. The Men's Social Service centers, in particular, made valuable contributions to the war effort. Their primary function—to rehabilitate men who are temporarily down—was to furnish man power for the armed forces and for defense work. Still others worked in the centers to carry on the salvage work so necessary to the nation in time of war. Waste paper, scrap metal, old rubber—all were salvaged for direct use in war industries. The conservation of other products allowed new materials to be used for defense purposes, relieving the burden on manufacturing plants.

The Family Welfare Department of the Salvation Army served the families of servicemen, as well as other families in need. Servicemen could find a welcome at any one of more than a thousand corps halls in every part of the country. In the United States alone, at that time, more than four thousand Salvation Army officers were ready to offer spiritual guidance to American men and women in uniform.

In addition, Salvation Army officers served as chaplains in the Armed Forces. Five Salvation Army chaplains had served in World War I. Six times that number saw service in World War II. Highest ranking of the thirty Salvation Army chaplains was John J. Allan, veteran of the First World War. Called to Washington in 1940, he served two years in the Office of the Chief of Chaplains in Washington, D.C. Chaplain Colonel Allan left the service in 1942 to assume the command of the Salvation Army's Central Territory. In 1946 he was appointed Chief of Staff at International Headquarters, an office second only to the General in importance. This recognition of his administrative ability made him the first American-born officer to hold the position.

The Salvation Army was willing and ready to follow the American G.I. overseas in World War II as they had served the doughboy in France twenty years earlier. The USO offered its service for work overseas as well as in the United States. Despite the excellent record of the other volunteer organizations in World War I, the government gave to the American Red Cross a monopoly of the service to American Armed Forces overseas.

Some American G.I.'s, however, had an opportunity to meet the Salvation Army their fathers had talked about. More than three thousand Salvation Army War Service units (including one thousand mobile canteens) were strategically placed throughout the world. Salvation Army canteens that had served the British Army from the beginning of the war—in fact, two of these canteens were evacuated at Dunkirk—and Salvation Army War Service units attached to Australian and Canadian troops offered a welcome to all Allied personnel. American troops in the South Pacific area might have used any of the 845 Salvation Army War Service centers there, and in the British Isles 669 centers were available to Allied men in uniform. Not only did Commissioner Donald McMillan receive the Medal of Merit from President Truman for Salvation Army work during the war but also awards from the British and French governments.

The war services of the Salvation Army furnish an excellent illustration of the international aspects of the Salvation Army. Americans found out that the Salvation Army was an international Army whose spirit was the same wherever it was found.

XXII

"Service to Man"

The Salvation Army today has achieved a position as a recognized and respected social welfare agency. The needs of the American people have made its diversified program of social services necessary in spite of the increased extension of governmental agencies in the field of social welfare work. The variety of services offered by the Salvation Army today is amazing.

Not all parts of the Army's humanitarian program are as colorful as the emergency disaster service. Much of it is done quietly; for example, the Homes and Hospitals for Unmarried Mothers that carry on an unpublicized work to help solve a vital social problem. One aspect of the work of the Men's Social Service centers is familiar to any person who has called the Salvation Army to take away the accumulation cleaned out of a cellar or an attic.

Many social classes are served: business and professional girls away from home may find wholesome, home-like, inexpensive lodgings at an Army Evangeline Residence; Emergency Lodges in many cities offer a haven for homeless transients; day nurseries benefit not only the youngsters but their working mothers; and orphanages, youth programs, and summer camps meet other varying needs of children. Other Salvation Army agencies include the Family Service bureaus that help needy families in a variety of ways; Vocational Guidance and Placement bureaus for the unemployed; and Missing Persons bureaus to trace lost relatives and friends. Special assistance is given to immigrants, alcoholics, and men and women in prison.

The wide range of Salvation Army social services makes the subject difficult to describe, a difficulty further complicated by the complexity of the administrative organization of the Army. Although the four nearly autonomous territories operate under the same basic principles and perform substantially the same services, local conditions and local personalities result in a variety of practices. The central administration of social work within the various territories varies. In all four territories there is a Women's Social Service Department and a Men's Social Service Department. In two territories (Central and Western) there are separate prison departments, while in the Eastern Territory bureaus for the inmates of men's and women's prisons operate under the Social Welfare Department. In addition to the activities directed from territorial headquarters, some social services are under the supervision of divisional headquarters, and the duties of every corps officer include some social work.

Although the Salvation Army divides its work into departments for administrative purposes, it would be misleading to think of the Army as carrying on a religious work and a social work in separate compartments. As Colonel Holland French pointed out in a paper on "The Spiritual Nature of Salvation Army Social Work": "Do we not, when speaking of the branches of Salvation Army operations, erroneously and harmfully make reference to our 'spiritual' or 'social' work? There must not be, if we are to retain our original purpose, any division of the two. . . . All of our program should be social and all should be spiritual—one acting as a complement to the other."

A characteristic of the Salvation Army in the United States is the ability to appraise itself and its services objectively and, whenever necessary, change to meet new conditions. As Brigadier Jane Wrieden has pointed out:

The Salvation Army has had the courage, often a slow cautious courage and sometimes an impetuous courage, to change some things that need changing. In varying degrees in different departments, The Salvation

Army is recognizing that education and training are indispensable factors in working effectively with people; that staff must have a voice in the program of the agency; that programs are "built up," "not handed down" . . . that the insights which psychology has discovered are invaluable; that citizen participation in agency program is essential; that no agency can be isolated from the community. . . . True, in its changing pattern of social work, The Salvation Army has met, and still meets, some resistance from within the organization—differences of opinion, conflicting philosophies, immature and distorted concepts of God and religion, blind clinging to traditions, unwillingness to consider new methods, fearfulness about change, insecurities about scientific discoveries regarding human behavior, and misconceptions regarding social case work.

Scientific social work has proven especially valuable in the Salvation Army's thirty-four homes and hospitals where unmarried mothers of all religions and races are given a "home" at a time when sympathetic understanding and help is most important, and a "hospital" to ensure the finest medical care at the time of delivery. The necessity for professional training has been generally recognized, and several directors of homes and hospitals are officers with master's degrees in social work. The Army's achievements in this field were recognized when one authority, writing for a national magazine, declared, "The Salvation Army, one of the first organizations to give asylum to unmarried mothers, is one of the most active in departing from the rescue type of institution and adopting the newer and sounder methods of hospital and home care."

The Salvation Army's Men's Social Service centers, in all of the nation's major cities, are also good illustrations of that blend of old-fashioned consecrated zeal and modern social-work techniques that characterizes the Army's social-welfare program today. The clients are men without homes, jobs, or resources, and frequently with some deep-seated problem such as alcoholism. They may have applied for admission in person or have been referred to a Social Service Center by some other agency. While at the center they live in a dormitory with facilities for sleeping, bathing and washing, eating, and recreation.

Every client is given something to do, such as driving a truck, sorting clothes or rags, baling newspapers, refinishing furniture, or any one of the many other jobs connected with the salvage of the materials donated by people in the surrounding area. The proceeds from this material finance the rehabilitation work of the center. Each case is studied, and all available means are used to help him find a place as a useful, independent member of society. Some of the centers have chapters of Alcoholics Anonymous, for alcoholism is a major problem among destitute men today. Other techniques include counseling by professional caseworkers, and religious services. A Social Service officer, supervising such a program, must not only have the usual consecration but an understanding of the problems of the clients, a knowledge of how best to solve these problems, and considerable business acumen.

The Family Welfare Bureau of the Salvation Army is one of its most recent major social-work departments. Described as "the effort to minister to the needs of individuals *in families,* considering the family as a unit and striving to maintain its solidarity and well-being," Family Welfare service is not a separate enterprise comparable to Men's and Women's Social services. It is carried on at all levels, from territorial down to the corps, but varies considerably in importance from city to city. In the most progressive Family Welfare bureaus extensive use has been made of professional social workers, psychologists, and psychiatrists. The trend is for the Salvation Army to maintain the highest standards of scientific social work but to add the unique spirit of consecration that comes from a dynamic religious experience.

One of the oldest services of the Salvation Army is its work in prisons and with former convicts. It began in the United States in the early years of persecution when Salvationists were jailed for "disturbances of the peace." Their time in jail was spent in singing, talking, and praying with their fellow prisoners. The Army came soon to realize that persons released from prison needed special aid to prevent them from returning to a life of crime. Prison Gate Brigades met prisoners on the day of their release and brought them to Prison Gate Homes through which they were helped to find employment. If they had families, the Army saw that these dependents were provided with food and clothing until the head of the family was rehabilitated. From the first Prison Gate Brigade at Hartford, Connecticut, in 1885, the Army's prison work has expanded to the point where the Salvation Army conducts its religious and welfare program inside some 1,200 penal and correctional institutions in the United States.

The Army's prison program today is extensive and varied, including prayer meetings, Bible classes, and clubs inside prison. When called upon to do so, the Army supplies parole supervision, gives vocational guidance and training, finds jobs, and provides living quarters, food, and financial aid for released prisoners. The families of men who are in prison are also given assistance in many ways.

Another recent trend in Salvation Army social work, in addition to the utilization of professional training, is cooperation with other agencies—private and public. In 1936 the Army was reporting to the Federal Child Welfare Bureau, Crime Commission of the Attorney General's Department, and other government departments and agencies. Officers have joined, and are encouraged to join, the American Prison Association, the National Chaplains' Association, the National Prisoners' Aid Association, as well as the American Association of Social Workers. Since 1936 the Salvation Army has been an active, integrated Associate Group of the National Conference of Social Work, and serves effectively as a member agency of the National Social Welfare Assembly. Delegates from each of the four American territories have held Salvation Army sessions at the annual meetings of the National Conference of Social Work since 1936.

The Salvation Army, accepting the challenge of its role as a social agency, has acquired prestige as its professional standards have risen, but the spiritual motivation of its social program remains. General Wilfred Kitching emphasized this point on the occasion of the seventy-fifth anniversary of the Salvation Army in the United States. Paying tribute to the Salvationists whose service over the years had won the admiration of Americans in all walks of life, he explained their motivation with the words, "The heart of the Salvationist has been touched by the hand of the compassionate Christ, and for His sake we do it." For every Salvation Army officer, "Service to Man" means service to God.

XXIII

The World for Christ

The story of the Salvation Army in the United States would be incomplete without reemphasizing the international character of the organization. In a day when internationalism has come into its own and "isolationist" is a term of reproach even the most hardened conservative would hasten to disavow, the Salvation Army is in step with the times. Just as it pioneered in concern for the impoverished slum dweller and blazed the trail for women's rights, so, as a worldwide Army, it has stood from its earliest days for the principle of the universal brotherhood of man. The average corps officer today is likely to be more interested in and to know more about the Army's work in foreign lands than about the Army's early history in the United States.

"We are making *our* history now," exclaimed a young American field officer recently. The main concern of the average officer is with the present and with the future, as it was with his predecessors. The urgency of the present and the dream of the future drove the Army forward, and in the heat of battle the relics of its history were scattered and lost. Railton remarked, when the first move was made: "We turn with no small regret from the dear old birthplace of The Army in America. Only the necessity of enlarging our accommodation and securing a place capable of endurable use during the hot months could reconcile us to change, and even then we should certainly try to retain the old spot as well if we thought the expenditure profitable. But we cannot afford to pay for veneration at present." Even today there is no department or office in national or in territorial headquarters to collect and preserve papers, documents, and Army publications. A museum of Salvation Army relics in Eastern territorial headquarters was put into storage for lack of space, and much valuable material was scattered and lost. A National Research Bureau that put out several excellent publications was abandoned because of a lack of financial support as recently as 1950. Some of its functions were delegated to a Commission on Research, composed of top echelon officers appointed by Commissioner McMillan in 1954.

Although the history of the Salvation Army in America has been neglected, the major exploits of the Army in other countries are well known and often repeated. The successful campaign by Lieutenant Colonel Charles Pean to liquidate the French penal colony on Devil's Island is better known to Salvationists than many crucial American campaigns.

In its missionary efforts, the Salvation Army is second to no branch of the Christian Church. Its most extensive operations are in India, the Army's earliest missionary field. In the eastern, northern, southern Madras and Telugu regions of India, the Army has 5,193 centers. There are 734 additional centers in Pakistan, Burma, and Ceylon. Native as well as white officers minister to the people, preaching the Gospel in many languages and dialects. In addition to evangelical work, the great need for social services to combat famine, floods, epidemics, superstition and ignorance has made necessary an amazing variety of services. For more than half a century the Army has conducted medical missionary work—operating hospitals, dispensaries, and even leper colonies. In its schools all grades are taught from primary through industrial training.

Since 1894, when the Army began work in Java, a network of Salvation Army social institutions has been established to supplement the evangelical missionary work in the islands of Sumatra, the Celebes, Borneo, and the Moluccas of Indonesia. Salvation Army missionary work has been maintained in Japan since 1895, in Korea since 1908, and in China since 1916.

The Army invaded South Africa in 1883, only three years after it began operations in the United States, and is now active in South Africa, the Belgian Congo, Nigeria, and the Gold Coast. In South America the Army has centers in seven countries. It also functions in most of the countries and colonies of the West Indies and Central America.

The Salvation Army in the United States contributes its share to the support of these world-wide missionary activities, both in money and in personnel. The Self-Denial Fund, collected each year from Salvationists, is devoted to missionary work and is the only money collected in the United States that is sent to International Headquarters for use outside the country.[1] Each year officers who volunteer for missionary duty are sent abroad from the four American territories, and each class of the training colleges usually includes volunteers for missionary service.

Several missionary areas are directly under the administration of the United States. Salvation Army work in Mexico is administered by the Southern Territory, U.S.A., and work in Hawaii and Alaska is supervised by the Western Territory, U.S.A.

American Salvationists, from their membership in a great international organization, have tended to be international-minded. On his visit to America in 1926, General Bramwell Booth urged the United States to enter the League of Nations. Salvation Army officers were associated with the United Nations Organization since its founding in 1945, first as accredited news correspondents for the Salvation Army press and more recently as consultants in the Nongovernmental Organizations Division. In 1949 an official of the UN declared that the Salvation Army had been doing for generations the kind of constructive work on behalf of unfortunate people to which the UN is dedicating itself today.

The Salvation Army recognizes that it is part of the world-wide Christian Church, and has shown its intention to cooperate with the other branches of the Christian Church. Since 1916 the Salvation Army has been associated with interchurch movements. The Salvation Army was represented successively on the Council of the Christian Crusade, the World Alliance for International Friendship Through the Churches, the Religious Organizations Committee of the League of Nations Union, the Public Morality Council, the Council of Christians and Jews; and in 1948 five Salvation Army commissioners were official delegates to the first assembly of the World Council of Churches in Amsterdam. Six Salvation Army delegates attended the second assembly of the World Council of Churches in Evanston, Illinois, in 1954, including Mrs. Commissioner Donald McMillan and Commissioner Claude E. Bates, of the United States.

The Salvation Army's representation as observers at the World Council of Churches was spoken of by Commissioner Marcel Allemand at the 1949 International Commissioners' Conference in London. "Our presence was a gesture of Christian friendliness and brotherly and spiritual fraternization," he declared. "While we in The Army do not pretend in the general sense attributed to the word, to be 'a church,' yet we maintain that we are an integral part of the great church of the living God and there is no doubt that we have been accepted as such by the ecumenical movement."

The Salvation Army also cooperates with other agencies and denominations on a local scale. Officers may be members of local interdenominational ministers' councils. The Salvation Army social branches frequently receive references from, and make references to, Travelers Aid, municipal welfare bureaus, or similar agencies. In some cities the Salvation Amy is financed through the Community Chest.

In the United States, as in the rest of the world, the Salvation Army faces the future with anticipation. Popular acclaim and support have not led to complacency. Salvation Army officers are constantly subjecting themselves and their organization to a critical evaluation and scrutiny, and adopting changes whenever they appear to be beneficial. In 1924 two investigators who studied the Salvation Army in the United States observed: "We have been impressed also by the fact that there is within the Army an honest, eager disposition to learn. We find a good deal of evidence that whenever in the past the Army has detected in the criticism and ridicule which has come its way, any constructive ideas, it has tried to put them into effect." This disposition is still evident in the Army today.

With this attitude, it would seem that the problems of the twentieth century, so different from those of the past, could be met and conquered. Opportunities for the unique service of the Salvation Army are not lacking, as Commissioner Norman Marshall noted in a recent address. "People are the principal business of The Army," he declared, "not properties, finance, institutions or social services as such. God called William Booth to the unchurched. If then our principal business is people—unchurched people—we cannot complain of lack of raw material."

To its assistance, the Salvation Army has called all of the modern inventions available. Recently a fund appeal in New York City was opened over a television network. In April, 1948, General Albert Orsborn gave the first world-wide radio broadcast made by an international leader of the Salvation Army. Speaking from New York, the sixth General of the Army addressed an army in ninety-two different countries and colonies led by 26,799 full-time officers.

In June, 1950, the seventieth anniversary year of the Salvation Army in the United States, a person was "promoted to Glory" whose life span covered the entire eighty-five years of Salvation Army history. With the death of General Evangeline Booth, a link with the past was broken and the last great representative of the "era of personalities" in the United States passed into Army history.

Eighteen hundred persons filed past her bier in the Centennial Temple in New York. The Army's past, to which Evangeline Booth had contributed so much, was the theme of most of the tributes in the funeral service. But there were also symbols of the future. Among the flags that lined the rear of the platform was the blue and white emblem of the United Nations, symbol of the hope for a future "one world" of peace and brotherhood. From General Orsborn came a tribute that was also a command to march on. The past was dead—the future lay ahead. "In personality unique, in public gifts outstanding, in song excelling, she leaves an imperishable contribution to the world-wide Army. We must press forward. The world for God!"

The same note was struck in 1955 by the Army's seventh Gen-

eral, Wilfred Kitching, in his charge to the Salvation Army in the
United States as it observed its seventy-fifth anniversary with a nation-wide celebration. "Of that which has been done in your land
. . . others can tell better than I, but I feel it my bounden duty
to say at this time that it is not sufficient that we should live in the
past. The challenge of the present is that the spirit of the past should
live in us. . . . I pray that in the coming years the flag of The
Salvation Army shall find more and more legions . . . striving for
victories. . . . I believe that the contributions you are going to
make to those victories will be such that the pages of Salvation
Army history will be proud to bear them."

APPENDIX I

The Doctrines of the Salvation Army

1. We believe that the Scriptures of the Old and New Testaments were given by inspiration of God and that they only constitute the Divine rule of Christian faith and practise.
2. We believe that there is only one God who is infinitely perfect, the Creator, Preserver, and Governor of all things, and who is the only proper object of religious worship.
3. We believe that there are three persons in the Godhead, the Father, the Son, and the Holy Ghost, undivided in essence and coequal in power and glory.
4. We believe that in the person of Jesus Christ the Divine and human natures are united so that He is truly and properly God and truly and properly man.
5. We believe that our first parents were created in a state of innocency but by their disobedience they lost their purity and happiness and that in consequence of their fall all men have become sinners totally depraved and as such are justly exposed to the wrath of God.
6. We believe that the Lord Jesus Christ has by His suffering and death made an atonement for the whole world so that whosoever will may be saved.
7. We believe that repentance toward God, faith in our Lord Jesus Christ, and regeneration by the Holy Spirit are necessary to salvation.
8. We believe that we are justified by grace through faith in our Lord Jesus Christ and that he that believeth hath the witness in himself.
9. We believe that continuance in a state of salvation depends upon continued obedient faith in Christ.
10. We believe that it is the privilege of all believers to be "wholly sanc-

tified" and that "their whole spirit and soul and body" may "be preserved blameless unto the coming of our Lord Jesus Christ."

11. We believe in the immortality of the soul, in the resurrection of the body, in the general judgment at the end of the world, in the eternal happiness of the righteous, and in the endless punishment of the wicked.

APPENDIX II

Roster of Salvation Army Commanders

GENERALS OF THE SALVATION ARMY

William Booth	1865–1912
William Bramwell Booth	1912–1929
Edward John Higgins	1929–1934
Evangeline Cory Booth	1934–1939
George Lyndon Carpenter	1939–1946
Albert W. T. Orsborn	1946–1954
Wilfred Kitching	1954–

NATIONAL COMMANDERS OF THE SALVATION ARMY IN THE UNITED STATES

George Scott Railton	1880–1881
Thomas E. Moore[1]	1881–1884
Frank Smith	1884–1887
Ballington Booth	1887–1896
Maud Charlesworth Booth	1887–1896
Frederick St. George de Lautour Booth-Tucker	1896–1904
Emma Moss Booth-Tucker	1896–1903
Evangeline Cory Booth	1904–1934
Edward Justis Parker[2]	1934–1943
Ernest I. Pugmire[3]	1944–1953
Donald McMillan[4]	1953–

[1] Also Commander of the Salvation Army in Canada, 1882–1884.
[2] National Secretary, 1934–1943; National Commander, 1943.
[3] Also Eastern Territorial Commander, 1942–1947.
[4] Served as National Secretary, 1944–1947.

DEPARTMENT OF THE WEST

George Kilbey	1904–1908
Thomas Estill	1908–1920

EASTERN TERRITORY

Thomas Estill	1920–1926
Richard E. Holz	1926–1930
John McMillan	1930–1935
Alexander M. Damon	1935–1942
Ernest I. Pugmire	1942–1947
Donald McMillan	1947–1953
Norman S. Marshall	1953–

CENTRAL TERRITORY

William Peart	1920–1926
John McMillan	1926–1930
William McIntyre	1930–1939
Ernest I. Pugmire	1939–1942
John J. Allan	1942–1946
Norman S. Marshall	1946–1953
Claude E. Bates	1953–

WESTERN TERRITORY

Adam Gifford	1920–1931
Benjamin Orames	1931–1938
Donald McMillan	1938–1943
William H. Barrett	1943–1947
Claude E. Bates	1947–1953
Holland French	1953–

SOUTHERN TERRITORY

William McIntyre	1927–1930
Alexander M. Damon	1930–1935
Ernest I. Pugmire	1935–1939
William C. Arnold	1939–1948
Albert E. Chesham	1948–1952
William J. Dray	1952–

Notes

CHAPTER I

THE INVASION OF AMERICA

[1] Such as

> "He who loves not women, wine, and song
> Remains a fool his whole life long."

[2] James Kemp served as a soldier until Oct. 14, 1882, when he was commissioned Lieutenant and sent to Jersey City. From there he was promoted to Captain and sent to Boston, where he served until his death, on March 10, 1895.

CHAPTER II

PAVING THE WAY

[1] The account of the work of the Shirleys is based on articles written by Eliza Shirley at different times, and published in the *War Cry*. The first was on July 9, 1881. The second, entitled "Pioneering the Work in the United States," was printed in serial form in the issues of Nov. 28, and Dec. 5, 1908. The third was entitled "Born in American Stable," and appeared in serial form in the issues of Sept. 12, 19, and 26, and Oct. 3, 1925. Eliza Shirley, as Mrs. Commandant Symmonds, lived to be seventy, and died on Sept. 18, 1932, in Racine, Wisconsin.

[2] A complete account of the episode by the author of this book, entitled "A Salvation Army Prelude: The Christian Mission in Cleveland, Ohio," was published in the *Ohio Historical Quarterly*, January, 1955.

CHAPTER III

LAYING THE FOUNDATION

[1] Interview with Emma Morris Lambert. The officers who returned to England were Morris, Pearson, and Shaw. Morris and Shaw came back to the United States. Of the four women officers of the original pioneer party that can be accounted for, three spent their lives and died in the United States.

[2] There is little available material on Railton's travels because he traveled alone. The letters by which he sent his reports were used by his biographers and are quoted by them in part. Unfortunately, these letters

were lost when International Headquarters, London, was destroyed by bombs and fire during the Blitz on May 10–11, 1941.

CHAPTER IV

THE BRICKBAT ERA

[1] Such a procedure would no longer be possible today, for husband and wife are both expected to serve actively, and if one resigns the Army careers of both are terminated. Amos Shirley was drowned at Asbury Park, N.J., on Aug. 11, 1884. Major Moore conducted the funeral service, which was attended by large numbers of Salvationists. About two years later, Annie Shirley was remarried, to Staff Captain John T. Dale. Grandchildren and great-grandchildren of Amos and Annie Shirley are active Salvation Army officers today.

[2] The Hartelius sisters returned to the United States and helped begin the Swedish work in this country in 1887. An account of their experiences in Sweden, told by Annie Hartelius after returning to the United States, is in Frank Smith's *The Salvation War in America for 1885* (New York, 1886), pp. 152-159.

CHAPTER V

SECESSION—THE MOORE SPLIT

[1] General Moore's Salvation Army of America was under the management of five trustees. Its doctrine included the observation of baptism and the Lord's Supper. In January, 1889, "the gradual decline of the work and general dissatisfaction and loss of confidence in the Army among the officers and public at large" was blamed on "the mismanagement of General Thomas E. Moore," and the board of trustees voted his deposition. Colonel Richard E. Holz was elected his successor. Moore resisted his deposition and continued to publish the *War Cry* until March, 1890. For a time three Salvation Armies, each publishing a different *War Cry*, were in operation. Moore left Brooklyn in 1890 and entered the Baptist ministry. He died on Jan. 7 or 8, 1898 at Harper, Kansas, where he was pastor of the Baptist Church. Holz led the branch of the American Salvation Army under his command to a reconciliation with the international Salvation Army in October, 1889.

CHAPTER VI

REBUILDING FROM THE FOUNDATIONS

[1] When Commissioner Edward J. Parker joined the Army in 1885, he found no hymn books or flags. "Major Moore took them," he was told.

[2] See the articles on "Experiences in Lessening Race Tensions," by

Major M. S. Kimball, Ensign B. McIntyre, and Adjutant L. Robb, in *Addresses Delivered at Salvation Army Sessions National Council of Social Work, 1945,* pp. 56-66.

³ William T. Stead, *If Christ Came to Chicago* (Chicago, 1894). In contrast to the established churches, Stead noted, "The Salvation Army lives among the poorest people, works with them, gathers them together every night and contributes a valuable element to the building up of saner and sounder citizens."

⁴ After returning to England, Smith worked with General Booth on the "In Darkest England" scheme until he disagreed with the General and left the Army. He entered politics as a pioneer in the British Labor party and worked as a parliamentary journalist. For eighteen years he was a member of the London City Council, resigning that position in 1901 to re-enter the Salvation Army at the request of Bramwell Booth. After a few years he left the Army again for the field of politics. After ten unsuccessful campaigns, which earned him some fame as the most frequently defeated candidate for Parliament, Smith was elected as a Labor party member to the House of Commons in 1929 and served until defeated for reelection in 1931. He was the author of a book, *The Betrayal of Bramwell Booth,* published in 1929. He died in London on Dec. 26, 1940, at the age of eighty-six.

CHAPTER VIII

PERSONALITIES AND PROGRESS

¹ William Bramwell Booth (1856–1929) was Chief of Staff and second General of the Salvation Army; Ballington Booth (1857–1940) was founder and General of the Volunteers of America; Catherine Booth-Clibborn, "La Maréchale" (1858–1955), established the Salvation Army in France and in Switzerland; Emma Moss Booth-Tucker (1860–1903) served as a leader of the Salvation Army in India and the United States; Herbert Howard Booth (1862–1926) led the Salvation Army in Canada and Australia, composed many outstanding hymns, and was an independent evangelist; Marian Billups Booth (born 1864) died at an early age without distinction; Evangeline Cory Booth (1865–1950) led the Salvation Army in the United States and served as its fourth General; and Lucy Milward Booth-Hellberg (1868–1953) was a Salvation Army leader in Scandinavia.

CHAPTER IX

WINNING NATIONAL RECOGNITION

¹ The following pathetic appeal appeared in the *War Cry* for Oct. 13, 1889: "CANCER CURE! The General invites communication, describing

any real cure of the above-mentioned disease, by any readers of the *War Cry.* . . ."

[2] The building was torn down to make room for the present National Headquarters Building erected by Commander Evangeline Booth on the same site in 1929.

CHAPTER XI

THE GREAT SCHISM

[1] Maud and Ballington Booth founded the Volunteers of America in March, 1896, and Ballington served as its General until his death on October 5, 1940. Maud Ballington Booth devoted her life to prison work and gained fame as the "Little Mother of the Prisons," succeeding her husband as General of the Volunteers of America from 1940 until her death on August 26, 1948. Their son, Charles Brandon Booth, elected to command the organization after the death of his mother, is the present General.

CHAPTER XII

HEALING THE BREACH

[1] The husband of daughter Catherine became Booth-Clibborn, and the husband of daughter Lucy became Booth-Hellberg.

CHAPTER XIII

"THE LANDLESS MAN TO THE MANLESS LAND"

[1] The Salvation Army has since been incorporated under the laws of several other states.

[2] After a period of rest, Frederick Booth-Tucker was appointed foreign secretary at International Headquarters. In 1906 he married for the third time and with his wife returned to India, where he had begun Salvation Army work in 1882. From 1906 to 1919 he commanded the Salvation Army in a very successful administration in the land he loved best. A critical illness forced him to return to England; but until his death on July 17, 1929, he continued to be an active Salvation Army officer.

CHAPTER XIV

"SEND EVA!"

[1] From "General William Booth Enters Into Heaven" by Nicholas Vachel Lindsay. Used by permission of The Macmillan Company.

CHAPTER XV

APPROACHING MATURITY

[1] A network of "Harbor Light" Corps now serves an increasing number of alcoholics.

CHAPTER XVII

PROSPERITY AND PROHIBITION

[1] Maine, New Hampshire, Vermont, Massachusetts, Rhode Island, Connecticut, New York, New Jersey, Pennsylvania, Delaware, Maryland, Virginia, North Carolina, South Carolina, Georgia, Florida, Alabama, Mississippi, Tennessee, Kentucky, West Virginia, and Ohio.

[2] Indiana, Illinois, Wisconsin, Michigan, Minnesota, Iowa, Missouri, Arkansas, Louisiana, Texas, Oklahoma, Kansas, Nebraska, South Dakota, and North Dakota.

[3] California, Oregon, Washington, Idaho, Montana, Wyoming, Utah, Colorado, New Mexico, Arizona, Nevada.

[4] Texas, Oklahoma, Arkansas, Louisiana, Mississippi, Alabama, Georgia, Florida, Tennessee, North Carolina, South Carolina, Kentucky, Virginia, West Virginia, and Maryland.

CHAPTER XXI

WORLD WAR II AND USO

[1] The six member agencies were given funds to operate on their own during the year 1948, and the Salvation Army continued its services under the name Salvation Army Services to the Armed Forces (SASAF). The USO was reactivated in Aug., 1948, and operated until Jan. 31, 1950. Its services were continued after that date by Associated Services for the Armed Forces (ASAF), in which the Salvation Army and two other of the original six member agencies did not participate. In Feb., 1951, it was announced that ASAF and the old USO had surrendered their charters and united to form a new USO consisting of the original six member agencies and a seventh—USO Camp Shows. Thus, the Salvation Army continued to provide the American fighting men of the Korean War the services it had begun in the Spanish-American War.

CHAPTER XXIII

THE WORLD FOR CHRIST

[1] The first Self-Denial Week in the United States was held during Oct. 6–13, 1888, two years after it had been inaugurated in England. In contrast with most Salvation Army fund-raising campaigns, it is almost entirely an internal appeal to the members of the Army—the money that is collected coming from officers and soldiers who make some sacrifice to save the money contributed.

Sources*

GENERAL

The most important single source for Salvation Army history is the file of the organization's official publication the *War Cry*. The Salvation Army Eastern Territory Headquarters in New York has a complete file of the *War Cry* published in New York since 1887. Many of the earlier issues, published in Philadelphia, Brooklyn, and New York City from 1881 to 1887, may be found in the Rose Memorial Library of Drew University, which has other Salvation Army material not available elsewhere. Perhaps the largest single collection of Salvation Army material in the United States is the Circle M Collection donated to the Houston, Texas, Public Library by Major John Milsaps. Under the terms of Major Milsaps' will, much of this material was made available for the first time in November, 1952.

The History of the Salvation Army by Robert Sandall is an official multivolume history of the international organization. Two volumes have been published, Volume I (1937) and Volume II (1950). The Salvation Army in the United States is treated very briefly. *The Salvation Army Year Book*, published annually from London since 1906, contains some articles about the work in the United States.

There are numerous biographies of General William Booth. The best, both from the point of view of scholarship and literary style, is *God's Soldier: General William Booth* (2 vols., 1935), by St. John Ervine. The official biography, *The Life of General William Booth* (2 vols., 1920), by Harold Begbie, contains much valuable information. *General Booth and the Salvation Army* (1911) by Alex M. Nicol is a somewhat critical biography by a former Salvation Army Commissioner. *William Booth, The General of the Salvation Army* (1898), by the General's son-in-law Frederick Booth-Tucker; *Authoritative Life of General William Booth* (1912), by George Scott Railton; and *William Booth, Founder of The Salvation Army* (no date), by Minnie L. Carpenter, are useful short

* A completely documented copy of the manuscript of this book, indicating the source for every important statement of fact, is catalogued at the Columbia University Library under the title *Religion in Action: A History of the Salvation Army in the United States.*

229

sketches. Two other biographies, *The Prophet of the Poor* (1906), by Thomas F. G. Coates, and *Blood and Fire* (1925), by William H. Nelson, have little merit. *I Was a Stranger* (1954), by Harold C. Steele, is a recent sociological study.

Nearly all of the other members of the Booth family have had their biographers. Frederick Booth-Tucker wrote *The Life of Catherine Booth, Mother of the Salvation Army* (2 vols., 1892), and a brief biography of his wife, *The Consul, A Sketch of Emma Booth-Tucker* (1903). The story of his life is told in *Booth-Tucker, Sadhu and Saint* (1930), by F. A. Mackenzie. *Bramwell Booth* (1933), by Catherine Bramwell Booth, and *Herbert Booth: A Biography* (1928), by Ford C. Ottman, are sympathetic accounts of the lives of two of General William Booth's sons. *The Maréchale* (1921), by James Strahan, tells the story of the General's eldest daughter, Catherine Booth-Clibborn. *General Evangeline Booth* (1935) and *General Evangeline Booth of the Salvation Army* (1948), both by Philip W. Wilson, emphasize the early years of her life in England but are of little help for the thirty-year period of her command in the United States. Of the Booth children who were active in the Salvation Army, only Ballington and Lucy have not been subjects of biographies.

Biographies of other Salvationists who contributed to the development of the Salvation Army in the United States include *Commissioner Railton* (1920), by Eileen Douglas and Mildred Duff; *Samuel Logan Brengle: Portrait of a Prophet* (1933), and *Out of the Depths, The Life-Story of Henry F. Milans* (1930), by Clarence W. Hall; *William McIntyre, God's Harvester* (1948), by Catherine Baird. Some interesting sidelights on Salvation Army history in the United States from 1885 to 1943 are contained in the autobiography of Commissioner Edward J. Parker, *My Fifty-eight Years* (1943).

THE EARLY YEARS, 1879–1904

Background material on the early development of the Salvation Army in England may be found in the biographies of General Booth by Ervine and Begbie and in Sandall's history. Two pamphlets, *Outlines of Salvation Army History* (1927) and *The Salvation Army, Its Origins and Development* (1945), are useful. *The Salvation Army Handbook Doctrine* (1947) describes the theology of the Salvation Army. *The Romance of 'The War Cry'* (1929), by William Nicholson, is the standard work on the Army's official publication.

The general social and religious history of the United States during the period of the formative years of the Salvation Army in this country is described in *The Story of Religion in America* (1939), by William W. Sweet; *The Rise of the City, 1878–1898* (1933), by Arthur M. Schlesinger;

and *The Urban Impact on American Protestantism, 1865-1900* (1943), by Aaron I. Abell. The chapter "The Salvation Army in America, 1880-1900," in the latter book, contains a few minor errors but is the only recent scholarly writing on the history of the Army in the United States.

Contemporary newspapers are the major source for the first few years of Salvation Army history in America. The story of the Shirleys is told in a series of articles in the *War Cry* by Eliza Shirley. *Twenty-One Years' Salvation Army* (1889), by George S. Railton, contains information on his activities in the United States. The best published account of the Moore schism is told by Clifford Brindley, "Commissioner Richard E. Holz . . . ," the *War Cry*, April 13, 20, and 27, 1928. Considerable other material on this episode is preserved in the Nels Erikson papers. *The Salvation War, 1884*, by William Booth, and *The Salvation War in America for 1885* and *The Salvation War in America for 1886-87*, both by Frank Smith, are important sources for these early years.

In addition to the *War Cry*, the major sources for the administration of Maud and Ballington Booth as national commanders of the Salvation Army in the United States are *From Ocean to Ocean* (*ca.* 1891), by Ballington Booth, and *Beneath Two Flags* (1889), by Maud Ballington Booth. The controversy over Maud and Ballington Booth's resignation attracted considerable attention from the New York press. Information on the event is included in Nicol's biography of General William Booth and Wilson's biography of Evangeline Booth. Among the pamphlet literature are *The Resignation of Commander and Mrs. Booth* (1896), by Emma and Frederick Booth-Tucker; *The Unpublished Letter* (1896), published by the Volunteers of America; *Commander and Mrs. Ballington Booth's Statement of Explanation Regarding the Causes Which Led to Their Expressing Inability to Take Another Command* (1896). Very useful in evaluating press opinion was a scrapbook of clippings about the controversy from newspapers all over the United States, owned by Miss Theodora Booth.

The Barbary Coast (1933), by Herbert Asbury, describes the conditions that the Salvation Army faced in San Francisco. *Land of Liberty* (1947), by Fred Hamlin, contains a chapter on "Joe the Turk," a colorful personality from the West. A series of articles about "Joe the Turk" by Adjutant William G. Harris appear in the *War Cry*, December 23, 30, 1933; January 6, 13, 20, 27, and February 3, 1934.

Frederick Booth-Tucker, who was national commander of the Salvation Army in the United States from 1896 to 1904, was the most prolific writer to hold that position. In addition to his biographies of General William Booth, Catherine Booth, and Emma Booth-Tucker already cited, he wrote the following short sketches and pamphlets: *The Salvation Army in the United States* (1899 and 1904 editions); *The Salvation Army as a Temperance Movement* (no date); *Our Future Pauper Policy in America* (no date); *The Relief of the Poor by the Salvation Army* (no date); *Friends of the Poor, or, The Winter Work of the Salvation Army* (1902); *The Social Relief Work of the Salvation Army in the United States* (1900); *Prairie Homes for City Poor* (*ca.* 1901); "Farm Colonies of the Salvation Army," *Bulletin of the Department of Labor*, No. 48 (1903). Other sources for the farm colonies include H. Rider Haggard's *Report on the Salvation Army Colonies in the United States and at Hadleigh, England, with Scheme of National Land Settlements*, published by the British Government in 1905; and the articles: "A Successful Farm Colony in the Irrigation Country," by Albert Shaw in the *American Monthly Review of Reviews*, XXVI (November, 1902); and "Fort Amity, The Salvation Army Colony in Colorado," by Dorothy Roberts in the *Colorado Magazine*, XVIII (September, 1940). A summary of Booth-Tucker's achievements is made in "Commander Booth Tucker and His Work in America," the *American Monthly Review of Reviews*, XXX (November, 1904).

THE MIDDLE PERIOD, 1904–1934

Some of the events of the administration of Commander Evangeline Booth are described in *The Times Between 1904–1926* (1926), by Agnes L. Palmer. An undated pamphlet, with no author listed, entitled *Where Shadows Lengthen* (1907) described Salvation Army work in that year. A study by Edward G. Lamb, *The Social Work of The Salvation Army* (1909), is useful.

The Salvation Army's role in World War I is told in *The War Romance of the Salvation Army* (1919), by Evangeline Booth and Grace Livingston Hill. It is written in a style that was popular for moral stories for girls about thirty or forty years ago and cannot be accepted as completely accurate. A valuable summary is the *War Service Report of The Salvation Army, 1917–1919*, a fifteen-page pamphlet published by the Army Headquarters in New York. The *War Service Herald*, published monthly from 1917 to 1919, is an important source. An interesting account of one American Salvation Army officer's work in Belgium during the years of American neutrality is told in *A Yankee Major Invades Belgium* (1916), by George Taggart and Wallace Winchell.

An important study sponsored by the Rockefeller Foundation resulted in *Social Salvage: A Study of the Central Organization and Administration of the Salvation Army* (1924), by Porter R. Lee and Walter W. Pettit.

The controversy over the High Council that deposed General Bramwell Booth has resulted in several published accounts. Two books published in 1929, when the controversy was at its height, present the two extreme positions. *The Betrayal of Bramwell Booth*, by Frank Smith, is a defense of the deposed General; *The Clash of the Cymbals*, by Frederick A. Mackenzie, is an apologia for the High Council. St. John Ervine, in a 212-page epilogue to his biography of General Booth, carefully examines the facts and reaches a conclusion favorable to Bramwell Booth. Catherine Bramwell Booth's biography of her father presents the story from his point of view. P. W. Wilson, in his biography of Evangeline Booth, brings out the case against Bramwell. A chapter in Clarence W. Hall's biography of Samuel Logan Brengle describes the part played by the first American-born commissioner in the High Council. The newspapers, particularly the New York *Times*, carried detailed stories of the High Council.

THE RECENT PERIOD, 1934–1955

Every year since 1936, the national secretary of the Salvation Army has published a volume of *Addresses Delivered at Salvation Army Sessions* at the National Conference of Social Work. These are invaluable for the recent history of the organization. They are indexed in a pamphlet entitled *The Salvation Army at the National Conference of Social Work* (1948), published by the Salvation Army National Research Bureau. Other publications of the bureau include: *The Salvation Army and the Alcoholic* (1948) (no author given); *Pilgrim's Progress: 20th Century, The Story of Salvation Army Officership* (1950), by Don Pitt; and *The Prison Work of the Salvation Army* (1948), by J. Stanley Sheppard.

For the work of the Salvation Army in World War II, the monthly publication of National Headquarters is essential. It was entitled the *Red Shield* from January, 1942, through December, 1943; *War Service Bulletin* from January, 1944, to December, 1944; *War Service Bulletin of The Salvation Army* from January, 1945, to February, 1946; and *Service of The Salvation Army* from March, 1946, to February, 1947. Pamphlets that are useful are *Always Ready! The Salvation Army in War-Time Review* (1942), and *The Salvation Army in the United Service Organizations for National Defense* (1942).

A pamphlet by Jane Wrieden, *The Pattern of Social Work in the Salvation Army* (1946), illustrates the recent developments in Salvation Army social work. *The "Service-to-Man" Program* (1944), a report of institutes held by the Men's Social Service Department of the Eastern Territory, by A. E. Agnew, is an important source. There are a number

of unpublished manuscripts relating to the recent social work of the
Salvation Army such as: The Unique Contributions of the Salvation
Army to the Religious Life of America (Andover-Newton Theological
Seminary, 1944), by John Baggs; A Study of Salvation Army Principles
and Practices Seen in Relation to Casework (New York School of Social
Work, 1946), by Grace Mehling; Growth of a Case Work Agency To-
ward Full Participation in the Life of the Community (University of
Buffalo, 1945), by Jane E. Wrieden; A Study of Professional Social Case
Work Practice in the Salvation Army—Professional Social Case Work in
a Religious Setting (New York School of Social Work, 1946), by Zora
Thompson.

Index